ENGLISH LANDED SOCIETY
IN THE TWENTIETH CENTURY

ENGLISH LANDED SOCIETY IN THE TWENTIETH CENTURY

MADELEINE BEARD

ROUTLEDGE
LONDON

First published in 1989
by Routledge
11 New Fetter Lane, London EC4P 4EE
Published in the USA under the title
Acres and Heirlooms: The Survival of Britain's Historical Estates
in 1989 by Routledge
29 West 35th Street, New York, NY 10001

Printed in Great Britain
by Biddles Ltd, Guildford and Kings Lynn

British Library Cataloguing in Publication Data

Beard, Madeleine
    English landed society in the twentieth century
    1. Great Britain. Landowners. Social conditions, history
    I. Title
    305.5'232'0941

ISBN 0–415–03264–4

To my parents, with love

CONTENTS

LIST OF PLATES

24 Mentmore in Buckinghamshire, home of the De Rothschilds and the Earls of Rosebery before its sale in 1977 in order to pay death duties.

25 The 1987 Annual General Meeting of the Historic Houses Association, founded in 1973.

26 The Hon. Simon Howard, owner of Castle Howard, 1985.

27 John Clotworthy Talbot Foster Whyte-Melville Skeffington, thirteenth Viscount Massereene and Ferrard, 1986.

ACKNOWLEDGEMENTS

I am greatly indebted to Professor Donald Denman for his technical advice on all the chapters, his introductions to former students, and his unfailing good humour. His support has greatly enhanced the writing of this book.

For their very generous help and hospitality I would like to thank Mr and Mrs Vesey Holt at Orleton Hall in Shropshire, Mrs Imogen Skirving at Langar Hall in Nottinghamshire, and Dr Adrian Mathias at Peterhouse, Cambridge.

Those who have kindly agreed to meet me to answer my questions, and to whom I extend my thanks, include Margaret, Duchess of Argyll; the Earl of Bradford at Weston Park in Shropshire; Mr James Douglas, Director-General of the Country Landowners Association; Mr J. N. C. James at the Grosvenor Estate Office; Lord Middleton of Birdsall House in Yorkshire; the late Sir Jasper More at Linley Hall in Shropshire; the Earl of Shelburne at Bowood in Wiltshire; and Mr Giles Worsley of *Country Life*.

For reading and commenting on several of the chapters my thanks go to Miss Elizabeth Burr, Dr Richard Grove, Dr T. A. Jenkins, Canon W. H. Loveless, Dr Richard Rex, Mr Robert G. Ryan, Mr Alexander Shand, Miss E. H. Whetham, and Dr J. M. Winter. Any errors that remain are my own.

For guiding me to useful references, I thank Miss Marcia Nation, Dr Janet Seeley, Mr Steven Thompson, Dr Richard Trainor, and Mr David Weigall.

For typing the text I thank Mrs Sheena Baptie and Miss Ann Barber, and particularly Mrs Bobbie Coe, and Mrs Tricia Wilson. I would like to thank Miss Charlotte Britton for her work on the index.

My thanks go to the staff at Cambridge University Library for all their help. Plates 1, 4, 5, 8, 9, 10, 11, 13, 14, 15, 16, 22, 23, 26, and 27 are reproduced by permission of the Syndics of Cambridge University Library.

The author and publisher have made every effort to obtain permission to reproduce copyright material throughout this book. If any proper acknowledgement has not been made, or permission not received, we would invite the copyright holder to inform us of the oversight.

Madeleine Beard
Cambridge

1

'The diminishing vistas of that other England'

At Lord's cricket ground in London the cricketers walked out from the pavilion on to the field of play through two separate gates, one for Gentlemen, one for Players. For society, the greatest cricket match of all was played here every year between Eton and Harrow. Practically all the landowners in England sent their sons to one of these two schools; the owners and heirs of more than half the land in England had at one time watched this famous game. Compared with those in Russia, Spain, Prussia, or France, the English landed elite owned a very large part of its nation's territory. On this warm and languid day at Lord's, spent talking and idly applauding, it was the clothes of the ladies as they walked through the 'glowing, spangled air of summer' which held the attention during the intervals; 'the waisted gowns, the high lace collars, the frills, the richness and weight and yet lightness of these full July clothes, the feather boas, ethereal as dusting brushes'.[1]

Education at public schools such as Eton or Harrow, which were both private and exclusive, united landowners from all over England. Lifelong associations formed in childhood could sometimes be carried through to the upper reaches of government. If a prime minister and his colleagues or a lieutenant of a county and his magistrates remembered the same headmaster, if they had played on the same cricket field and taken their earliest meals in the same hall, such common experiences proved impenetrable to any outsider. Were a businessman to buy up land, attendance at Eton or Harrow by his son was the necessary path by which his son would be

1

accepted by society. His son would then adopt their habits of vocabulary and speech. The numerous quirks and subtle inconsistencies of upper-class speech in England are heavygoing for any aspirant to society, and can only be mastered by constant exposure to them from a very early age.

At Eton, a boy put on the distinctive uniform of long trousers and a black tailcoat, a white tie, a waistcoat, and a top hat. The school was close to Windsor Castle, whose grey walls towered above the trees. On the river below, a regatta was held every summer on 4 June, when garlands of flowers were thrown onto the water. During the rest of the day a cricket match was held.

The headmaster at Eton at the beginning of the twentieth century was the Hon. Edward Lyttleton, son of the fourth Baron Lyttleton of Hagley Hall in Worcestershire. The Lyttleton family, with eight brothers, a father, and two uncles, could between them make up a cricket team. During Lyttleton's time as headmaster, when a boy threw a firework into the aisle in the chapel during a sermon he was admonished from the pulpit by a master who said, '*You* have disgraced yourself, as a Christian, a Gentleman and an Etonian!'[2] Yet while he was headmaster, Lyttleton himself admitted that he 'never walked up the aisle of a church or a cathedral without bowling an imaginary ball down it and wondering whether it would take a spin'.[3]

As a boy at Eton, the Hon. Edward Lyttleton had once been bowled out at the Eton v. Harrow cricket match by Willie Grenfell, later created first Lord Desborough. Sport being the preoccupation of most landowners, Grenfell's career outdid them all. At Oxford he had rowed in the boat race against Cambridge, he had 'climbed the Matterhorn three times by different routes, killed a hundred stags in a single season in Scotland and won punting championships on the Thames'.[4] His sons Julian and Billy Grenfell went to Harrow and Oxford.

Colleges at Oxford and at Cambridge had been founded on a monastic pattern. Now in the cloisters and in the courtyards young men spent three years of rowdy freedom after years of confinement at their public schools. At Oxford, titled names were found above many of the rooms at Christ Church and days could be spent hunting with the Bicester Hunt in the country close by. The Grenfell brothers, 'handsome as Greek gods and blessed with splendid physiques', rode to hounds and were crack shots. They collected prizes for sport as easily as prizes for poetry and mathematics. 'Their table-talk was dazzling', but they too could be found blowing 'coach horns in the Quad long after midnight'.[5]

After their public school, a commission into a regiment in the Guards, the Cavalry, or the Rifle Brigade was the lot of many sons of landowners. Before joining their regiment some attended the Royal Military Academy at Sandhurst in Berkshire. In their regiments they were not taught leadership; it was assumed that, having been to a public school, they had already acquired 'the necessary social and moral qualities' of officers and gentlemen and thus military leaders.[6] In cavalry regiments, the first months were spent learning the gymnastics of staying on a horse while jumping over hurdles without saddle or stirrups, arms held wide, or picking up a handkerchief from the ground at the gallop. Such feats, so the son of Sir George Sitwell of Renishaw Hall in Derbyshire was told, 'would be of inestimable value, both to the country and to myself in the next war, when it came'. Then after a day of manoeuvres and drill, there were lectures on 'The Care of the Horse Through the Ages', 'The Place of the Horse in the Twentieth Century', or 'Cavalry Charges in the Coming War'.[7]

For Osbert Sitwell, a commission into the yeomanry and his attachment to the Hussars was arranged by a cousin, and so began a winter's training at Aldershot, a camp not far from Sandhurst in Surrey.

> When the snows melted and the fogs dissipated, it was only then that the whole horror of Aldershot, and the arid fantasy of the life round me, grew visible. For the first time I could see clearly the full uniform of the Regiment. . .a pseudo-Hungarian caprice of frogs and flaps and feathers designed by the Prince Consort in exotic mood.[8]

Winston Churchill, cousin of and for five years the heir to the ninth Duke of Marlborough, remembered his time in the army with affection.

> There is a thrill and charm of its own in the glittering jingle of a cavalry squadron manoeuvring at the trot; and this deepens into joyous excitement when the same evolutions are performed at a gallop. The stir of the horses, the clank of their equipment, the thrill of motion, the tossing plumes, the sense of incorporation in a

living machine, the suave dignity of the uniform; all combine to make cavalry drill a thing in itself.[9]

In the mess room in the evenings, dressed in uniforms with gold embellishments, officers sat at dinner among the silver and the crystal, while a small band played in the background. If a battalion was stationed in India, drill and manoeuvres took place soon after dawn. In the early evening there might be a game of polo. Then 'as the shadows lengthened over the polo ground, we ambled back perspiring and exhausted to hot baths, rest and at 8.30 dinner, to the strains of the regimental band and the clinking of ice in well-filled glasses'.[10]

When the Viceroy of India, Lord Curzon, moved into Government House in Calcutta in 1899, it so happened that its design had been modelled on his family's home of Kedleston in Derbyshire a century before. Curzon enjoyed pointing out to his guests the architectural differences between the two houses.[11] And at Simla, the Viceroy's summer palace in the hills was a 'great mock-Tudor English country house encouched in exotic trees and set against the background of the Tibetan Himalaya'.[12]

When in 1902 the Maharaja of Jaipur came to England for the coronation of Edward VII, he wondered why English sahibs ever bothered to go to India.[13] But wherever future lords of the manor went throughout the empire, they 'scratched together a pack of hounds, reinforced it with the odd terrier and set off in pursuit of fox, jackal, elk, pig, hare, red deer, hyena or whatever else was available to be chased'.[14] In India, hunting wild boar, tiger, or buffalo with a spear was called pigsticking. On the day of the competition for the prestigious Kadir Cup, 'men and their horses settled in gay tented camps upon the Punjab plains, practising their runs with stampeding hoofs and dust-clouds in sunshine, like knights before jousting'.[15]

In England, summer camps held every year with yeomanry regiments were far away from such exotic excitement. During these camps in Nottinghamshire there was 'Church Parade in the park of the squire, troops clattering, or rather thudding on the drives that run through the great domains of Thoresby, Clumber and Welbeck'.[16] In the yeomanry, the relationship between landowners and their tenant farmers could sometimes overlap with military rank. The sixth Earl Winterton of Shillinglee Park in Sussex recalled closing the canteen one evening during a summer camp of the

4

Sussex Yeomanry. Such a task 'required some tact', since among the drunken soldiers were not only some of the earl's parliamentary constituents but also farmers over whose land he hunted. For Lord Winterton, on such occasions they were 'more willing to give me three cheers or stand me a drink than to remember that I was an officer, and that they were private soldiers'.[17]

As an Irish peer, Lord Winterton continued as a Member of Parliament after succeeding his father in 1907. He had contested the Horsham constituency in Sussex in 1904 while still an undergraduate at Christ Church. This was on the suggestion of the third Baron Leconfield of Petworth House in Sussex, whose land bordered the Wintertons' Shillinglee estate, who said, 'If an untried young man barely twenty-one years of age could win the seat it would be a good augury indeed' for the Conservative party.[18] When Lord Winterton first took his seat in the House of Commons, it was during its last years of domination by landed Members of Parliament.

Their numbers had steadily diminished since 1885, when the Conservative party, 'with all its immense territorial influence and candidates of county families, was shattered, never to be restored, except as a shadow of its old strength'.[19] By 1906 just four in ten of all Members of Parliament were from the landed classes.[20] In 1885, of the many sons of the first Duke of Abercorn, three had been selected for constituencies. For Lord Frederic Hamilton, 'once the daily correspondence of a Member of Parliament had been completed the long hours in the House of Commons hung very heavily on our hands'.[21] He and his younger brother, both in their 20s, used to 'hire tricycles from the dining-room attendants, and have races up and down the long river terrace, much to the interest of passers-by on Westminster Bridge'.[22] If a Member of Parliament succeeded to a title he then took his seat in the House of Lords, where beneath its vaulted ceilings he might choose to enter into debate.

The parliamentary session had originally coincided with the London Season, when landowners had gathered in the capital to carry out their parliamentary duties. By the beginning of the twentieth century the London Season was centred around the daughters of landowners who made their début in society. Their presentation at court at Buckingham Palace followed by parties and dinners and balls were a whirl of entertainment lasting for some three months. Situated in the most exclusive parts of London, in Mayfair and in Belgravia, the houses which were owned or rented by landowners provided sumptuous settings for such gatherings. At 16 Grosvenor Street in Mayfair, with its rooms of 'grey walls, red lacquer cabinets, English eighteenth century portraits of people in red coats, huge porcelain pagodas, and thick, magnificent carpets', the hostess, the Hon. Mrs George Keppel, ran her house 'as a work of art in itself'.[23] The Hon. Mrs George Keppel, married to the third son of the seventh Earl of Albemarle, was among the many rich hostesses in London who entertained King Edward VII.

The indulgent life of the king centred around a strict succession of entertainment and travel. Under his guidance, the Season took on a renewed purpose. Christmas and New Year he spent at Sandringham, a large estate in Norfolk purchased with the revenue he received as Duke of Cornwall.

The Duchy of Cornwall, established in 1231 by Edward III for the monarch's eldest son, comprised more than 100,000 acres throughout several counties in the west of England. When the eldest son of the sovereign became Duke of Cornwall, he was presented with a bundle of firewood, a goat skin, one hundred silver coins, a pound of pepper, and a pound of mixed herbs, each in a silver casket. He was given a pair of falconer's gauntlets, a pair of gilt spurs, a hunting bow, a salmon spear, and two greyhounds. Such gifts, while welcomed by the heir to the throne, Prince Edward, Prince of Wales, when he became Duke of Cornwall, were also a symbolic link with his particular interest in shooting. The purchase of Sandringham had been solely for this purpose. The isolated house with its landscaped gardens was set in the middle of a pine forest, around which he and his guests could spend days shooting the pheasants which had been specially reared for them.

In January, King Edward spent a week shooting with the Duke of Devonshire at Chatsworth in Derbyshire, or a week with the first Lord Iveagh, who in 1890 had purchased the Elveden estate in Suffolk for sporting purposes. At the end of January the king moved to Buckingham Palace. February was spent in London. At the beginning of March he moved to Paris or to Biarritz and then might cruise in the Mediterranean. The beginning of May saw the start of the Season. He moved to Windsor Castle for the Ascot races in June, and then in July to Goodwood to stay with the seventh Duke of Richmond for the race week there. At the beginning of August the king viewed from the royal yacht the sailing regatta at Cowes on the Isle of Wight and then spent some weeks in Marienbad in Germany for a cure. October was spent in Scotland.[24] An article in *The Times* described the end of the Season:

> The great whirlpool of the city, which three months ago sucked everything and everybody to itself, and has kept them whizzing round and round in its vortex, has somehow lost its velocity. Now it is as if the coils had begun to unwind; the thrust of the current has become centrifugal and out we go, mere jetsam, flung first to Goodwood, then Cowes, then out into the far still waters of the Scottish moors.[25]

When he stayed on the Scottish moors, King Edward VII felt happiest in the shooting lodge in Inverness-shire rented by his friend Arthur Sassoon. On the accession of Queen Victoria in 1837, Arthur Sassoon's father had joined in the chanting of 'God Save the Queen' played by a military band.[26] That Arthur Sassoon's father should have done this in Bombay, wearing the flowing robes that he and his Sephardic Jewish ancestors had worn in Baghdad, was an indication of the openness of the king to rich newcomers to London, an openness which shocked many members of English landed society. Soon after the Sassoons had moved to London, they had been introduced to the king when he was Prince of Wales by the Rothschilds; their daughter Hannah had married the fifth Earl of Rosebery at a synagogue in London in 1878 with the Prince of Wales among the guests. The king, 'bored with a feudal hierarchy' and the 'gloomy protocol of royal castles or some of the draughtier stately homes'[27] preferred to spend his time with rich financiers and their entertaining wives, with whom he could discuss racing and shooting and gambling in warm smoke-filled rooms.

Before he succeeded his mother Queen Victoria in 1901, Marlborough House in Pall Mall had been the London residence of Prince Edward, Prince of Wales. Not far from Marlborough House in Pall Mall and in St James's Street were a number of peculiarly English havens, gentlemen's clubs. To be a member of a club in London allowed the free interchange of opinion and information in an atmosphere that was calm and congenial. In dining rooms and in bars, in dark silent sitting rooms, these clubs provided an escape from the whirl of the hot summer Season. In St James's Street, White's Club, 'an oasis of civilisation in a desert of democracy',[28] was not far from Boodle's, named after the head waiter, which was not far from Brooks's, whose design was like a small country house.[29]

Some clubs were political, some literary. The Athenaeum demanded high academic qualifications for membership, the Turf and the Cavalry clubs did not. The Carlton Club in St James's was Conservative, the Reform Club in Pall Mall was Liberal. A Liberal government had been returned in 1892. When after April 1894 the Liberal Chancellor of the Exchequer Sir William Harcourt dined at the Reform Club, surrounded as he was by political allies, it must have been none the less with a certain amount of trepidation. For in April 1894 he had introduced a levy on estates passing at death, referred to as death duties. Such taxation at death was to contribute to the gradual and relentless erosion of English landed society in the twentieth century.

* * *

Was it a cruel turn of the wheel of fortune that Sir William Harcourt should, so soon after introducing death duties, have become a victim of his own tax? For in 1904 he unexpectedly inherited his nephew's Nuneham estate in Oxfordshire. His nephew had sold Harcourt House in Cavendish Square in London to pay for the upkeep of the estate in Oxfordshire, but the capital had been swallowed up by death duties. In 1904 Sir William Harcourt 'threw himself into the heavy task that had fallen on him with unfailing courage'.[30] He wrote: 'Landowning is a more troublesome and less profitable business even than public affairs. . . .It is the least restful of all occupations.' Hour after hour Sir William Harcourt sat turning the pages of the large ledger books of the estate, 'terribly depressed by the despairing revelation of its impoverishment'.[31]

Harcourt's Nuneham estate in Oxfordshire was one of many in that county and throughout England which had suffered from the depression in agriculture since 1879. A few miles to the south of Nuneham the first Lord Overstone wrote that the alarm of landlords 'seems to be daily increasing', and that the ninth Duke of Bedford's decision to surrender the whole of his Lady Day rents had created 'a perfect panic'.[32] The first Lord Overstone was a banker who had purchased the Lockinge and Ardington estates in the middle of the nineteenth century. For him the prospect of falling rents did not cause him too much dismay: 'the sacrifice will fall upon unnecessary luxuries, and the trouble may prove a healthy exercise of the mind to ward off insidious lethargy'.[33] Such sentiments were not echoed by many other landowners in England during this time.

When the first Lord Overstone had purchased the Lockinge and Ardington estates it had been during the golden age of farming. This time of prosperity for farmers in the middle of the nineteenth century was an interlude between the repeal of the Corn Laws in 1846 and the market being flooded with cheap corn. The new cereal-producing areas which were opening up in Russia and North America at this time had been dependent upon the development of internal transportation systems and cheap long-distance shipping. When the new supplies of cheap corn from overseas did arrive, English arable farmers suffered some of the worst harvests of the century. Wet summers continued from 1878 to 1882. With falling rents, the purchase of land as an investment was 'no longer safe, and the bloom has been altogether rubbed off the peach', noted Randolph Churchill, the brother of the eighth Duke of Marlborough, in 1884.[34] The following decade, there were severe droughts between 1892 and 1895.

Not all parts of England were equally affected by the depression.[35] Much depended on the foresight and ingenuity of estate managers as on differences in soil and climate.[36] On the Duke of Sutherland's Shropshire and Staffordshire estates the agent correctly appraised the situation as early as 1879 and much arable land was converted to pasture. On the Duke of Bedford's Buckinghamshire and Bedfordshire estates, however, the duke decided to continue to grow corn, where the extremes of heavy clay and light sands made it difficult to make the costly conversion to pasture pay.[37] On the Marquess of Bath's Longleat estate in Wiltshire severe depression was felt on the chalkland with its sheep and corn farming, but on the dairying parts there were few signs of strain.[38]

Despite falling income from their land, landowners still spent the same proportion of their gross rents on their estates during the agricultural depression. This meant that actual money spent on maintenance fell, which slowed down any chance of future recovery on farms. On the Duke of Bedford's Woburn estate £278,000 of rent was simply not collected from his tenants during the worst years of the depression and he distributed over £152,000 in voluntary payments to churches and schools, pensions, charities, and donations.[39] At the Grimsthorpe estate in Lincolnshire the first Earl of Ancaster had spent more than £1 million between 1872 and 1893 on his Rutland, Derbyshire, and Huntingdonshire estates. Expenditure included new buildings, repairs, fences, insurance, drainage, allowances for grass seeds, embankment rates, tithes, land tax, local rates, management expenses, pensions, allowances, subscriptions, and donations.[40] It was during this time, therefore, that landowners began to invest in the Stock Exchange and in securities. The sixth Duke of Portland invested in breweries, collieries, South African goldmines, and Burmese, Indian, and South American railways. Until the 1880s it was unusual for peers to become directors of companies, yet by 1896 over a quarter of the peerage held directorships, usually in companies in which they had a direct or indirect interest.[41]

Before the depression in agriculture was over, Sir William Harcourt had imposed his death duties, which he fixed at 8 per cent on estates of £2 million. Although few boasted such wealth, these death duties were seen as an attack on the landed interest. Indignation was voiced by Henry Chaplin, a landowning Member of Parliament who was 'one of the last, almost the last, of the fox-hunting country gentlemen who also wielded political influence'.[42] During the debates in the House of Commons in 1894 he referred to Sir William Harcourt's measures in a speech expressing sentiments destined to be repeated in one form or another throughout the twentieth century. He said that houses owned by large landowners were maintained 'at a cost largely exceeding the income of the whole estate to which they belong':

> They employ hundreds of people and labourers of every description, and they give amusement and enjoyment to thousands. In the summer months the means of conveying the people who go to see these places become absolutely an industry in itself. But if properties like these, which are blessed or encumbered with a Chatsworth, are to be mulcted in the manner which you propose, the inevitable consequence will be that one after another they will be shut up, their contents will be sold and dispersed, the whole army of people to whom they give occupation throughout the year will be dismissed and their employment gone, and money will no longer be attracted to the neighbourhood.[43]

The owner of Chatsworth, the eighth Duke of Devonshire, was equally perturbed by Harcourt's measures. At a presentation in the town of Buxton not far from Chatsworth the duke observed that 'the clouds of increased taxation were gathering' and 'painted a gloomy picture of the prospect which awaited large-landed proprietors, and the likelihood that in future Buxton would not receive the same amount of assistance from him that it had done from his predecess-ors'.[44] The duke saw the possibility of three of his other residences, Hardwick Hall in Derbyshire, Bolton Abbey in Yorkshire, and Lismore Castle in Ireland all having to be closed. The Earl of Ancaster also expressed concern saying that 'the imposition of these duties must in the end prove to the disadvantage of the tenants and labourers' and that it would be impossible for his son to keep up the buildings 'even in a tenantable state of repair'.[45]

The loyalty of landowners to their tenants was recalled by Anthony Eden, the second son of Sir William Eden of Windlestone Hall in Durham. At the celebrations of his parents' silver wedding in 1911, the atmosphere among tenants from all over the estates in Durham was 'relaxed, even intimate, as among a closed company of friends':

> I encountered many cronies, the men and women on whom the smooth functioning of the Windlestone estate depended. They in turn knew that they could count on my father to see that they were well housed and well paid, and on my mother to make sure that they were looked after in sickness and adversity. If they con-sidered that my parents were fulfilling their side of the bargain, they would anticipate that they and their descendants would work on the estate for generations, as indeed many of them had.[46]

Country Life, the magazine subscribed to by almost every land-owning family in England, observed in 1908 that

> a tenant must be very much at odds with his landlord, or a very ill-conditioned person, if he does not wish that the landlord should live in the big house and find his pleasure on the land. All the interests and many of the amusements of the farmer depend upon the help and support of the resident gentlefolks. The cricket, the point-to-point, the local show, in fact, a great part of the lighter side of the farmer's life depend on there being one or two residents with some means and leisure.[47]

In 1909, there occurred another attack on landowners under the aegis of another Chancellor of the Exchequer, David Lloyd George. A deep-seated hatred of large landowners felt by the Welsh Chan-cellor stemmed from his upbringing in rural north Wales. He recognized only two classes: landowners and everyone else. For him, land reform was 'an ideal, a goal to be reached. . . .But how all this was to be done, how these dreams were to be turned into legislative reality, Lloyd George never made clear because he did not know.'[48] He made a start by adding on to the Finance Bill of 1909 four new land taxes, all equally complex to implement.[49] These measures were defended at the time with characteristic vigour by Winston Churchill, then a Liberal Member of Parliament.

> We say that the State and the municipality should jointly levy a toll upon the future unearned increment of the land. The toll of what? Of the whole? No. . . .Of a fifth – that is the proposal of the Budget. . . .Such is the increment tax about which so much chatter and outcry are raised at the present time, and upon which I will say that no more fair, considerate, or salutary proposal for taxation has ever been made in the House of Commons.[50]

The land taxes, destined to raise a mere 3 per cent of a budget deficit of £16 million, from which agricultural land had been exempted, were a means of diversion from what really outraged landowners everywhere. For the implementation of such taxes required the valuation of all land. It was this systematic enquiry into such a sensitive issue, paving the way, so landowners thought, for future taxation of a far more devastating nature, which caused such anxiety.

A landowner who represented exactly the class which Lloyd George most despised was the nineteenth Baron Willoughby de Broke. In his memoirs he recalled that it was not until Lloyd George brought in his budget in the spring of 1909 that rural Conservatives 'began to realise that the landslide of 1906 might after all mean something very awkward'. An old farmer having told him that everything he had would be taken away from him, Lord Willoughby de Broke recalled: 'But, of course, I did not believe a single word of it, and went on hunting as if nothing were going to happen.'[51] Indeed, the cost of the valuation for the land taxes outweighed the revenue that would have been gained and in 1920 the Act was repealed.

One of the first of the large landowners to take action and sell land before the First World War was the ninth Duke of Bedford, who 'regarded it as modern and up-to-date to sell off landed property and buy stocks and shares because the return was greater'.[52] In 1909 he sold estates in East Anglia and in Devonshire. He then turned his attention to his immensely valuable Covent Garden estate in

London. It was with cheerful irony that he noted that the valuation undertaken as part of the 1910 Finance Act actually enhanced the price which he finally received at the sale.[53]

The Duke of Bedford was one of several landowners with land in London. Before 1914 other such landowners included Lord Howard de Walden and the Duke of Westminster, the Marquess of Northampton and the Marquess Camden, the Earl of Berkeley and the Earl of Harrington, the Earl of Ilchester and Earl Cadogan, Viscount Portman and Lord Southampton. Several large industrial towns in England also had links with landed society. Liverpool was dominated by three peers: the Earl of Derby, the Earl of Sefton, and the Marquess of Salisbury. The Duke of Norfolk and Earl Fitzwilliam owned much of Sheffield, the Ramsdens much of Huddersfield, and the Duke of Sutherland owned land in a number of Staffordshire towns. The Earl of Dartmouth and the Earl of Dudley both owned urban estates in the west Midlands, while the Calthorpes had slowly built up their influence in Birmingham.[54]

Resort towns too were associated with landed families. Moving from west to east along England's southern coastline, the Haldons at Torquay, the Tapps-Gervis-Meyricks at Bournemouth, the De La Warrs and Brasseys at Bexhill, and the Radnors at Folkestone were the principal landowners in these seaside towns. Eastbourne had been created by the Dukes of Devonshire, while Skegness in Lincolnshire and Southport in Lancashire were two resorts on the north-east and north-west coasts of England owned by titled families, the Scarbroughs, the Scarisbricks, and the Heskeths. But before 1914 titled families had begun to withdraw from the towns. As early as 1885 the Haldons had begun to sell off their holdings in Torquay, a process which was completed before the First World War. The Sutherlands too had abandoned public life in Staffordshire, Lord Radnor no longer resided in Folkestone, and Earl De La Warr had leased out his manor house at Bexhill.[55]

Landowners whose estates had coal beneath them benefited from another important source of income. They included the Duke of Devonshire, the Marquess of Bute, the Earl of Lonsdale, and the Marquess of Londonderry. The Earl of Durham at Lambton Castle in Durham owned coal beneath 12,000 acres and on the Duke of Northumberland's estates coal had been worked since the thirteenth century.[56] It was the largest landowners with estates all over England who were more likely to possess such incomes. Like the

London landowners, their numbers were few but their influence considerable. For untitled landowners whose income derived solely from farm rents, diversification into stocks and shares was an alternative to company directorships, as companies sought titled directors to lend prestige to their company reports. The land sales evident before the First World War were a practical response to financial difficulties.

For the owner of an estate faced with financial problems of ownership a classic solution lay in marriage to an heiress. Such a move was spectacularly shown in 1895 by the marriage of the beautiful American heiress Consuelo Vanderbilt to the ninth Duke of Marlborough. Although the marriage was to end eventually in divorce, it served its purpose during the short time it lasted: Consuelo brought with her to the declining fortunes of Blenheim £20,000 a year and income from a fund of £500,000.[57] Consuelo recalled her introduction to her mother-in-law, the Dowager Duchess of Marlborough, who 'bestowed a welcoming kiss in the manner of a deposed sovereign greeting her successor'. The Dowager then

> expressed great interest in our plans and made searching inquiries concerning the manner of life we intended to live, hoping she said to see Blenheim restored to its former glories and the prestige of the family upheld. . . .Then fixing her cold, grey eyes on me she continued, 'Your first duty is to have a child and it must be a son, because it would be intolerable to have that little upstart Winston become Duke.[58]

As Consuelo returned to Blenheim from London in cold isolation, the palace in which she lived, with its high ceilings and little heating, was isolated too. The village of Woodstock was only a short distance away, but in the middle of a landscaped park Blenheim could have been in another world. So too were other country houses throughout England.

* * *

At the second Earl of Londesborough's Blankney Hall in Lincolnshire, the house, the church, the stables, and the kennels were a colony in a 'flat landscape that did not exist: the village was somewhere near, yet out of reach as the equator'. In the winter Blankney Hall was brilliantly lit inside and 'seemed to exist solely as a cave of ice, a magnificent igloo in the surrounding white and mauve negation'.[59] In Sussex, Petworth House was almost in the town of Petworth and yet separated from it by a high park wall 'solid enough to suggest a fortress and so high that even the Sussex hay-waggoner perched on the top of his load, can get no glimpse of the sacred precincts within'.[60] At Powderham Castle in Devon, home of the Earl of Devon, there was 'all the charm of country silence over the woods and meadows that surrounded it'. Here, strange 'sub-tropical flowers grew in profusion in that gentle climate'. Walking to the cliffs near the Earl of Devon's summer home at Salcombe the path lay 'through a tunnel of green. . .where the sunlight filtered through the laced branches, and on days of sunshine the sea glittered with a million diamonds far below'.[61]

Powderham had been the childhood home of Lady Halifax, whose family made visits to Devon every summer. The Halifax estates were in Yorkshire, centred on Hickleton Hall and Garrowby. The second Viscount Halifax's son remembered as a child Hickleton being surrounded by a grass field which after haymaking was fenced with sheep hurdles. He regretted his father creating a formal entrance with 'enclosing walls and outer lawns' so that 'the cry of the corncrake was no longer heard by the children at their lessons, and the games in the hay were a thing of the past'.[62] At Garrowby, there was at all times 'a profound silence in the park and gardens, a hush rare in the modern world'.[63]

Not far from Garrowby was Carlton Towers, originally the home of the tenth Baron Beaumont. Perhaps its remoteness from the public gaze was no great loss, for here:

> First sight of the house is staggering, concrete-faced, ivy-grown, 1870-early-Tudor bristling with gargoyles, heraldic animals carrying fully emblazoned banners, coroneted ciphers; an orgy of heraldry. . . .The inside gives every evidence of semi-amateur planning; space where none is needed, cramped arches and windows where one cries out for space, harsh light everywhere from bad stained glass. . . .All state bedrooms face north over stable yard while servants' quarters command the south terrace.[64]

Indeed, some country houses, lavishly decorated, appeared incongruous in the English countryside. Vita Sackville-West, daughter of the third Baron Sackville of Knole Park in Kent, observed that

> they were not true country houses at all, but a deliberate attempt to reproduce in the country the wealth and fame which their

owner enjoyed in town. . . .Thus, although Chatsworth, Stowe, Blenheim, Welbeck, Bowood, Castle Howard, Wentworth Woodhouse. . .have their splendours, they cannot be said to melt into England or to share the simple graciousness of her woods and fields. They are as much out of place here in England as Versailles or Vaux-le-Vicomte are in place in France.[65]

For the Countess of Warwick, Wentworth Woodhouse, seat of Earl Fitzwilliam and the largest country house in England, was 'ugly and uncomfortable, noteworthy only because of its useless size'. The Duke of Devonshire's Chatsworth 'needed all the hospitality of its host and hostess, and all the *objets d'art* within its walls, to atone for its shortcomings'. The Duke of Westminster's Eaton Hall was 'a Victorian monstrosity in which you could lose yourself quite easily'.[66] Where their design had not taken into account the English climate the most beautiful houses seemed out of place. While Boughton was 'a miniature Versailles. . .and surrounded – as in Versailles – by star-shaped avenues', at Kedleston in Derbyshire the cold house faced north, where it was as if some of the ceremonial rooms had been designed to offer 'cool relief from a burning Italian sun'.[67]

At Lord Lyttleton's Hagley Hall in Worcestershire, the house and garden which replaced the old Elizabethan manor were among the supreme achievements of eighteenth-century English architecture and landscape gardening. The house, with its ornate rococo decorations, looked out on a Gothic 'ruin' and a Grecian temple in the grounds. These were favourite devices used by landowners in the eighteenth century, who had wanted to recreate in England the romantic Italian landscapes depicted in the paintings of Claude Lorraine, Gaspard Poussin, and Salvator Rosa. In parks, streams became serpentine lakes, hills were created, and trees were planted on them. On islands in the middle of lakes small Greek temples were built. Practically every large country house in England had its park landscaped along these lines.[68] So it was that 'dealing in none but the colours of nature, and catching its most favourable features, men saw a new creation opening before their eyes'.[69]

Smaller country houses might have a moat or a lake covered in water lilies, smooth lawns with formal yew hedges between which peacocks strutted, birds from the east which, with their imperious heads held high, added an aristocratic air to the most modest garden. From one country house its heir recalled looking out onto the fountains and pools, the hedges of yew, the abrupt fall of the land, and the watery expanse of the lakes beyond, with their woods and to me well-known tracery of fields, now covered with the burnished glow of the harvest, and, in places, with their clothing of light mists, the hills rising almost to be mountains.[70]

While Osbert Sitwell looked out on such a view from Renishaw Hall in Derbyshire, another writer recalled looking across to the Duke of Norfolk's Arundel Castle in Sussex:

on the other side of the tidal river there stretched away for miles, with its sweeping uplands, its beech clumps, its wild deer, its bracken, its rare beds of Atropa Belladonna. . .Arundel Park. No English castle, except perhaps Windsor itself, looks as impressive from a distance as Arundel Castle. You see it standing on the edge of its park, above its river, with the silvery gleam of the Channel a few miles behind it, and you feel that Sussex can boast her 'melancholy seignorial woods' as well as any chateau on the Loire.[71]

* * *

It was in castles, palaces, and houses such as Arundel and Renishaw, Blenheim and Hagley, Hickleton, Garrowby, Petworth, and Stowe that members of landed society entertained themselves with guests during the winter. Guests were invited for a 'Saturday to Monday', with emphasis on the word Monday and its implicit reference to the absence of a working week. Entertaining was on a large scale. At Blenheim, lengthy meals consisted of two soups, hot and cold, two fish, hot and cold, an entrée, a meat dish, and then a sorbet to precede the game, which in the shooting season was varied, comprising grouse, partridge, pheasant, duck, woodcock, and snipe. An elaborate sweet followed and then a hot savoury. 'The dinner ended with a succulent array of peaches, plums, apricots, nectarines, strawberries, raspberries, pears and grapes, all grouped in generous pyramids among the flowers that adorned the table.'[72]

For women the day required four changes of clothes, an elegant dress of velvet or silk at breakfast, after which the morning was spent around the fire, reading the papers and gossiping. They then changed into tweeds to join the guns for luncheon. An elaborate tea gown was donned for tea, after which they played cards until it was time to dress for dinner, when they wore satin or brocade and a display of jewels.[73] The number of trunks and hat boxes which accompanied guests and their entourage for stays at country houses was considerable. One observer recalled the arrival of guests at a station in Suffolk in 1904:

> I have seen mountains of luggage turned out there in a dark November evening, to be sorted out by a willing, but, on these occasions, a totally inadequate, staff of porters, and destined for four or five different houses. You are really very lucky if you reach the right one yourself, much less your baggage. On one of these occasions I saw the stalwart host of one of the places named, who had come down from the station to receive his guests, forcibly drag off a lady he knew, but who was not this time one of his party, and put her in his own carriage; and it was only by his returning to effect a fresh capture that she was able to escape.[74]

Guests who arrived to stay with the second Baron St Levan, at St Michael's Mount in Cornwall, arrived by train at the fishing village at Marazion.

> Buffeted by a howling wind and lashed with rain, they were escorted by those stalwart fishermen who lived in the village at the foot of the Mount and had rowed over to meet them, down steep rocky pathways to one of the primitive landing-stages hewn out of the rock. . . .Once down, the visitors were wrapped in heavy coarse serge boatcloaks, helped aboard sturdy sea-going rowing-boats and then, perched precariously across the thwarts or on the gunwales, they were rowed by the same stalwarts dressed in oilskins and sou'westers across the quarter-mile of rough seas, the boat pitching about and its occupants being dowsed by spray time and time again.[75]

On arrival, guests had to climb up some 200 feet to the castle itself. 'Not the sort of experience really expected by those smart London guests.'[76] Yet wherever they were in England guests treated their stays away from London as 'a kind of sorting house for information'. 'Did Gertrude mention to you darling, what Geraldine said to Campbell-Bannerman at the Opening of Parliament?' 'No, *do* tell, *do* tell. . . .And then I'll tell you about Muriel and the German Emperor.'[77]

The second Baron St Levan had married in 1892 a daughter of the fourth Earl of Mount Edgcumbe, whose estate was not far from St

Michael's Mount in Cornwall. Marriages could link estates all over England. Lady St Levan's mother was one of the seven daughters of the first Duke of Abercorn. By the time of his death in 1885, the Duke of Abercorn had seen his seven daughters unite estates all over Great Britain, together comprising some 700,000 acres. His daughter Lady Katharine had married the fourth Earl of Mount Edgcumbe in 1858. Another daughter, Lady Beatrix, married the second Earl of Durham of Lambton Castle in Durham, and Lady Harriet married the second Earl of Lichfield of Shugborough Hall in Staffordshire. Lady Maud Hamilton married the fifth Marquess of Lansdowne of Bowood in Wiltshire and Lady Georgiana the fifth Earl Winterton of Shillinglee Park in Sussex. The fourteen-year marriage between Lady Albertha and the Marquess of Blandford, later eighth Duke of Marlborough, was dissolved in 1883, but in 1884 another sister, Lady Louisa, became Duchess of Buccleuch, when her husband, the sixth duke, inherited estates of almost half a million acres.

Such family connections required lengthy journeys to country houses all over England to visit sisters, cousins, and aunts. At such gatherings at the beginning of the twentieth century a new diversion was to go out in a motor car. Before 1914 some country houses had set up 'motor stables' for cars. 'I shall never forget climbing up the several steps into that very high, open conveyance, and waiting with a tremulous sense of expectancy for it to start.'[78] Returning to the house, there was the familiar warmth, 'the fumy feathery scent of logs and wood ash, and a lingering odour, perhaps of rosewater, or some perfume of that epoch, a fragrance too of Turkish cigarettes'.[79] Such lives of luxuriant ease were maintained for hosts and guests by another community hidden away in the house itself, the servants.

The community of servants was strictly hierarchical. When Lord Lascelles, who had married the Princess Royal, stayed at Lowther Castle with the fifth Earl of Lonsdale, below stairs 'the Princess's personal maid was led into dinner on the arm of the House Steward. They were followed by Lascelles's valet on the arm of the House keeper.'[80] The house steward was in charge of the running of the house. He paid the bills and wages, ordered supplies, and kept the accounts, while the house keeper engaged and dismissed women servants below stairs. The house steward and house keeper were intermediaries between their employers and the rest of the servants. Those working closest to the family, the lady's maid, the nanny, the valet, and the butler, had working beneath them footmen, an under-butler, the young lady's maid, a housemaid, scullery maids, kitchen maids, laundrymaids, and dairymaids. Outside were coachmen and grooms. There were also lamp-and-candlemen, who 'polished and scraped the wax off the candelabra, cut wicks, poured paraffin oil and unblackened glass chimneys all day long'.[81] There was a 'gong man' who rang the gong for luncheon, dressing-time, and dinner, watermen who filled the baths each morning, and coalmen who replenished the coal buckets in the bedrooms. At Belvoir Castle in Rutland, hidden away in the upholsterer's room was a man who mended the different kinds of flags which flew from above the turrets; slim flags for windy days, smaller ones when it rained, large ones for sunshine, and hunting flags.[82]

> The timing of the household was such that the schoolroom maid climbing the back stairs with the children's breakfast would pass the valet on his way down to the brushing-room with his master's suits. While the brass cans of hot water were carried from bedroom to bedroom, the butler would be removing the top sheet of blotting paper from all the writing tables so that indiscretions penned the day before might not be held up to a looking-glass to be read by an under-housemaid.[83]

At Longleat, loose change was washed daily, the Marquess of Bath's bootlaces were ironed before he dressed, and the morning papers toasted and ironed before being placed on the breakfast table.[84]

* * *

Longleat had been inherited by the fifth Marquess of Bath from his father, the fourth marquess, in 1896. Inheritance by the eldest son meant that landed estates in England remained intact. It also meant that while younger sons were consigned to lives free of the responsibilities of ownership they had to make their own way in the world, whether in the army, the diplomatic corps, or occasionally the Church. Yet it was never certain that this would be their fate until their elder brother had a son and heir. Many younger sons could live

> on tenterhooks for years, depressed by news of the pregnancy of their brother's wife and then elated by her miscarriage or still birth; depressed by a successful birth and then elated again by the early death of the infant in the cradle; elated at the death of a

childless sister-in-law, and then depressed by their brother's remarriage with a nubile young girl.[85]

Through the unexpected death of his brother, the fourth Earl Amherst succeeded to the title in 1910. Returning to Montreal Park in Kent he was 'almost childishly happy to be back in his old home'.[86] When the Hon. Hugh Lowther, a younger son of the third Earl of Lonsdale, unexpectedly succeeded his brother at the age of 25 in 1882, he brought to Lowther the flamboyant outlook which he had adopted as a carefree younger son. With the prospect ahead of him of spending the rest of his life as brother of the fourth earl he had broken loose and joined a circus. As the fifth Earl of Lonsdale, he delighted in displaying the tricks he had learnt. Taking a cigar-case out of one pocket, 'a gold Fabergé cigarette-case out of another pocket, a gold pencil and a gold cigar-cutter out of another. . .he did several forward "roll overs", very neat and quick'.[87] But, lamented the fifth son of the fifth Earl Cadogan, younger sons 'who had been brought up in the same extravagance and luxury as the eldest, found themselves with only a few hundreds a year to marry, to make a home and to rear children'.[88]

At the beginning of the twentieth century a chance of a new beginning for some younger sons occurred with the opening up of Kenya by the third Baron Delamere. In 1910 *Country Life*, under the heading 'The colonies and the younger son', announced that

> that great regiment of youths who have no particular genius for anything, and are, as a rule, healthy and good-natured, who play cricket and football and other athletic games, and who frankly recognise themselves that they are not highly intellectual, will find in Colonial life much that will satisfy their desires.[89]

Denys Finch Hatton, the talented second son of the thirteenth Earl of Winchilsea of Haverholme Priory in Lincolnshire, declared 'England is small – much too small. I shall go to Africa. I need space.'[90] In Kenya there was a chance for him and others to imitate on a large scale the life that had been left behind. The second Baron Cranworth, whose decision to go to Kenya was prompted by 'love of sport. . .and shortage of cash' recalled seeing mango trees and palm trees on his arrival at Mombasa 'where the water was a glorious blue'. The tract of land which he bought looked towards Mount Kenya. 'Behind us rolled plains on which herds of game fed, the zebras barked and the lions grunted. . . .It was a pleasing spot in 1907.'[91] Other members of landed society who purchased land in East Africa were the first Baron Armstrong of Bamburgh Castle in Northumberland, the eighth Viscount Cobham, the first Lord Waleran, the fifth Earl of Warwick, and the second Duke of Westminster.[92]

Such landowners had initially been attracted to Kenya by the excitement of big-game hunting. Hunting expeditions were organized by the firm of Newland Tarlton, who became the biggest employer of labour in Kenya at this time. The firm's clients 'would have excited the jealousy of any climbing hostess in Mayfair'.[93] The men and women who arrived to shoot lion, elephant, rhino, and buffalo were accompanied on their expeditions by porters 'carrying everything from collapsible baths to cases of champagne'.[94] At the Christmas and July races in Nairobi, women wore hats more suitable for Ascot. During the race weeks, Nairobi was filled with sunburnt Englishmen wearing broad-brimmed felt hats and carrying revolver holsters, who paraded through the streets or lounged over their drinks on the verandah at the Norfolk Hotel. During the race weeks, a good night's sleep was 'the most difficult thing to obtain at the Norfolk. It was nothing to have an Italian baron or an Austrian count thrown through the window onto your bed in the middle of the night.'[95]

Not far from Nairobi, jackal-hunting took place at dawn, when the scent still lay on the ground with the dew. The master of the hunt in 1905 had been a contemporary at Eton of Lord Delamere, fox hounds had been imported from England, and hunting coats were worn. 'The clear notes of an English horn sounding along cultivated valleys. . .echoed strangely on ears attuned to the hollow pulse-throb of an African drum.'[96]

In England, hunting became an obsession with some families. During house parties at Blankney in Lincolnshire 'No small creature on small feet, no feathered thing with wings, as it ran over the snow, was safe; neither the fox. . .nor hare, nor pheasants.' After a day spent hunting, guests seemed 'scarcely at ease out of the saddle and tended to fall asleep if they entered the house and sat for a moment, except at meals'.[97]

Blankney had been the home of Henry Chaplin, whose children had been taught to 'think, speak, and dream of hunting and riding almost like a religion'.[98] In neighbouring Leicestershire, a county where farmers thought of their acres in terms of 'runs', 'jumps', and coverts', the son of the first Viscount Churchill remembered his initiation into fox-hunting. Present at the killing of the fox, he was 'blooded':

> The recollection was vivid of the huntsman, grinning, in his red coat, coming towards me on foot out of the struggling mass of the hounds. He had the dead fox's 'brush' in his hand. . . .I grinned too, pretending that I liked it, and men on horses leaned over and patted me on the back.[99]

The Marquess of Worcester, born in 1900, heir to the ninth Duke of Beaufort and called 'Master' as a boy, later remembered the exhilaration and the excitement of being in a successful hunt, which for him came from 'a subtle combination of being at one with both horse and hounds'.[100] And Siegfried Sassoon, whose father's family had been so closely associated with King Edward VII, was able to capture the hold which hunting had on English landed society:

> The mornings which I remember most zestfully were those which took us up onto the chalk downs. To watch the day breaking from purple to dazzling gold while we trotted up a deep-rutted lane; to inhale the early freshness when we were on the sheep-cropped uplands; to stare back at the low country with its cock-crowing farms and mist-coiled waterways: thus to be riding out with a sense of spacious discovery.[101]

The part of Sussex where Sassoon was riding was not far from the English Channel.

> On the wind was a mutter and pulse, a throb which seemed to be in it and yet not of it, like the beating of a great heart, strangely remote from all the gleam and softness of spring sunset, pale fluttering cuckoo-flowers, and leaf-sweet pools of rain. A black-bird called from the copse by Cowlease Farm, and his song was as the voice of sunset and April and pooled rain. . .still the great distant heart throbbed on, its dim beats pulsing on the wind, aching on the sunset, over the fields of peaceful England dropping asleep in April.

> 'You hear 'em pretty plain tonight. . .the guns in France.'[102]

2

The dark colours of mourning, 1914–18

On Salisbury Plain in Wiltshire, the Royal Artillery practised military exercises. In villages close by their inhabitants were used to hearing 'the distant boom of big guns'. For them the sound was associated 'with gardening and with the scent of flowers; and that long sustained rumble was in itself drowsy and peaceful'.[1] From the moment of the declaration of war on 4 August 1914, landowners in Wiltshire and throughout England attempted not only to get to the western front as soon as they could but encouraged their estate workers to join the colours too. In Wiltshire, on their way to the front, soldiers visited Salisbury Cathedral, where they 'continued to come through the Close gates to drink in this miracle of celestial quietude'.[2] Everyone was certain that the war would be over by Christmas. Four years later, when the armistice was announced in 1918 on the eleventh hour of the eleventh day of the eleventh month, the high officer casualty rate throughout those long years had brought bereavement and loss to every landed family in England. In November 1915 D. H. Lawrence wrote to Lady Cynthia Asquith:

When I drive across this country, with autumn falling and rustling to pieces, I am so sad, for my country, for this great wave of civilisation, 2000 years, which is now collapsing, that it is hard to live. So much beauty and pathos of old things passing away and no new things coming. . .the past, the great past, crumbling down, breaking down, not under the force of the coming birds, but under the weight of many exhausted lovely yellow leaves, that

24

drift over the lawn, and over the pond, like the soldiers, passing away, into winter and the darkness of winter. . .where all vision is lost and all memory dies out.[3]

That the world that existed before the Great War of 1914–18 had been irretrievably lost has been echoed by numerous writers and historians. In every country that shared the experience of war 'the equanimity of all classes was deeply and permanently disturbed'.[4] Throughout Europe, the years before 1914 and the period after 1918 were divided 'like a band of scorched earth'.[5] They were 'distinct from each other as are two Geological Periods'.[6] In France, the phrases 'avant la guerre' (before the war) and 'jadis' (as it was), became interchangeable.[7] After several years of political turbulence in England, for one writer the death of Rupert Brooke in 1915 was the point at which the 'old order' finally ended.

Standing beside that moonlit grave, one looks back. All the violence of the pre-war world has vanished, and in its place there glow, year into backward year, the diminishing vistas of that other England, the England where the Grantchester church clock stood at ten to three, where there was Beauty and Certainty and Quiet, and where nothing was real. Today we know it for what it was; but there are moments, very human moments, when we could almost find it in our hearts to envy those who saw it, and who never lived to see the new world.[8]

Landed society lost many of its heirs on the fighting fronts: an implicit and yet little explored theme of English history. The task of discovering the exact number of men throughout Britain killed during the conflict has been undertaken by the Cambridge historian J. M. Winter. He has shown that of the 6 million men in Britain who served during the Great War, 723,000, one in eight, were killed. From these statistics there emerges that a man's social class largely determined the risk he faced of becoming a casualty. In the first year of the war, one in seven of the officer corps were killed, against one in seventeen of the rank and file. Of the British and Irish peers and their sons who served during the First World War, one in five was killed.[9] The rolls of honour at Eton and at Harrow and at Oxford and Cambridge colleges were unprecedented testaments to this loss of life among the country's elite, evident in every public school and every university which had an officers' training corps.

Among titled families many lost the direct heirs to their titles and estates. There were, however, younger sons and close male relations to inherit both land and title and thus preserve continuity. The 1919 edition of *Debrett's Peerage and Baronetage* listed all the sons of dukes, marquesses, earls, viscounts, barons, and baronets who were killed in the Great War. Of the titled families who owned at least 3,000 acres in 1883, almost one in ten lost the direct heir to their estates during the First World War.[10] Among these, about half had younger sons to inherit both land and title. In most of the remaining cases, a grandson became the new heir. Of the rest, an uncle, a nephew, or a distant kinsman succeeded to the title. Just three titles out of 558 which had been linked with estates of at least 3,000 acres in 1883 became extinct as a result of the First World War.[11] Despite the death of three-quarters of a million men during the war and the legend of a lost generation, war losses had extraordinarily little impact on estate inheritance in England. Where a direct heir was killed, in practically every case there was someone in line to inherit. Some of the English estates of 10,000 acres or more owned by peers who lost heirs would underline this story of aristocratic continuity in the countryside.

Such families resided in counties all over England, from Durham to Cornwall and from Shropshire to Sussex. At Raby Castle in Durham the ninth Baron Barnard, owner of 100,000 acres throughout England, had three sons who served during the war. The eldest, the Hon. Henry Vane, died in 1917 of illness contracted on active service. When Lord Barnard died the following year, the title and estates were inherited by his second son, the Hon. Christopher Vane. In Shropshire at Powis Castle, Viscount Clive, the eldest son of the fourth Earl of Powis and heir to 60,000 acres, died of wounds in a hospital in London in October 1916. A second son, the Hon. Mervyn Herbert, then became the heir.[12] In Warwickshire, the eighth Earl of Aylesford of Packington Hall near Coventry lost his only son Lord Guernsey in the second month of the war. The 19,000-acre estate was later inherited by the earl's grandson Heneage, whose father had been killed in 1914.

In Lincolnshire, the 50,000-acre Brocklesby estate was deprived of its heir when the fourth Earl of Yarborough's son, Lord Worsley, was killed in action in September 1914. Here, two younger sons remained in line, the eldest of whom was the Hon. Marcus Pelham. In Cambridgeshire the sixth Viscount Clifden, who owned the

Wimpole estate, lost his eldest son and heir, the Hon. Thomas Robartes, who died of wounds in 1915. Four more sons were in line to inherit the title and estates: the Hon. Francis Robartes, the Hon. Arthur, who was wounded twice, the Hon. Cecil, and the Hon. Alexander Robartes, who was also wounded. Sometimes it could take several decades for the title to be assured; it was not until 1946 that a son and heir was born to the sixth Marquess of Northampton, whose younger brother and heir presumptive was killed in 1915. To the south of Northamptonshire in Buckinghamshire, the first Marquess of Lincolnshire owned an estate, as well as land in Lincolnshire. His only son, Lord Wendover, a lieutenant in the Royal Horse Guards, died of wounds in 1915.

At Lord Wendover's funeral in Buckinghamshire, the plain oak coffin which had been brought back from France was wrapped in the Union Jack and covered with flowers. At the grave the Last Post was sounded. Lowered into the grave with the coffin was a heart-shaped wreath from his parents.[13] Although the marquessate of Lincolnshire became extinct after Lord Wendover's death, the estates and barony of Carrington were later inherited by an uncle of Lord Wendover.

The second Baron Redesdale, who owned land in Gloucestershire centred on Batsford Park, succeeded to the title when his father died in 1916. His elder brother and heir to the title, the Hon. Clement Freeman-Mitford, had been killed in action in 1915 and five Freeman-Mitford brothers served during the war. To succeed him Lord Redesdale had one son, the Hon. Thomas Mitford, who had four sisters: the Hons Nancy, Pamela, Diana, and Unity Mitford, and later two more, the Hons Jessica and Deborah Mitford. As in so many families where a war death caused an unexpected change of fortune, Evelyn Waugh later reminded the Hon. Nancy Mitford that 'if your uncle had not been killed in 1915 and your posthumous cousin had been a boy, then you would never have had the title Hon'.[14]

Not far away from Batsford Park in Gloucestershire the tenth Earl of Wemyss at Stanway lost two of his three sons in 1915 and 1916, Lord Elcho and the Hon. Ivo Charteris. The estates in Gloucestershire and Scotland which amounted to some 60,000 acres were later inherited by a grandson, born in 1912. In Wiltshire Viscount Weymouth, heir to the fifth Marquess of Bath's 50,000 acres in England and Ireland centred on Longleat, was killed in 1916. The viscount's younger brother, Lord Alexander Thynne, was killed in

1918 seven weeks before the armistice. But there remained a third brother, Lord Henry Thynne, born in 1905, who later inherited the land and title. In Dorset the Hon. Gerard Sturt, heir to the second Baron Alington's Crichel estate, died at home on armistice day at the age of 25 where he had remained an invalid since the beginning of the war, having been seriously wounded. His brother the Hon. Napier Sturt then became the heir. And when the second Earl of Feversham of Duncombe Park in Yorkshire was killed in action in 1916, he had a son to succeed him. The obituary written for Captain Reggie Wyndham, heir presumptive to Lord Leconfield and killed in action in November 1914 (at which his younger brother became the new heir), was reminiscent of thousands written at the time:

> Through his shrewdness were constantly breaking his love of adventure, his thoughtfulness for others, his forgetfulness of himself – all, indeed, that may be summed up in the old word chivalry – while along the paths of Colonial life, the Turf and Society he maintained those high standards of conduct and honour that are looked for from the stainless knight.[15]

* * *

The enthusiasm with which the announcement of war was greeted on 4 August 1914 was remembered with tragic disbelief as the war went on. The long-established links between landed society and the army meant that every family had a connection with some regiment. The military fervour which emerged in the middle of a tranquil English summer in August 1914 was recalled by the Hon. Lionel Tennyson, who held a commission in the Rifle Brigade. His battalion was based in Colchester in Essex, but weekends he spent away from the barracks at an apartment in a hotel in Piccadilly. On the night of 3 August:

> It was about two o'clock in the morning and I was sound asleep, and dreaming one of the dreams that ardent cricketers know. . . . Down came the ball, my bat swung and caught it truly, and then it soared far away over the heads of the crowd on the leg side to give me my century. A tremendous burst of applause followed which, though I acknowledged it in the orthodox fashion by repeatedly raising my bat, refused to stop. The scene of my dream grew dim, and I gradually awoke to the fact that the noise was that of someone banging loudly on my door.

'What the hell's the matter?' said I, turning on the electric light and shouting 'come in!'

This invitation was quickly followed by the appearance of the night porter's head in my open doorway.

'A telephone message for you, sir,' he said.

'A telephone message!' I exclaimed, 'at this time of night! Who is it from?'

'From Captain Liddell, sir, Adjutant 1st Battalion The Rifle Brigade.'

' 'Snipe' Liddell,' said I. 'What the devil does he want at two o'clock in the morning?'

'The message says,' replied the night porter, 'that war has been declared on Germany and that you are ordered to return to duty immediately.'

War! Of course I and all my brother-officers had been expecting it for some time. This summons in the middle of the night had been, however, in the nature of a surprise. All trace of sleepiness nevertheless vanished directly at the news. I leapt out of bed. . . .

I remember dressing and packing with the night porter's help in feverish haste, so anxious was I not to run any chance of missing the war; and a very few moments later saw me speeding through sleeping London on my sixty-mile taxi drive back again to Colchester.[16]

The Marquess of Tavistock's reaction to the national call to arms meanwhile was one of unashamed horror. For him,

in addition to a purely personal aversion to re-entering what was to me the slavery of Army life, two other feelings began to take shape with increasing clearness in my at first tortured mind. The first was that, quite apart from anything to do with selfish personal inclination, it would be definitely wrong for me, after my known and proved incapacity to do the right thing in a sudden emergency, to take a commission and then, by some blunder on the battlefield, perhaps sacrifice the lives of my men uselessly and needlessly. The second was that in this great time of crisis I ought to go and find *some* way – exactly what I did not know – of serving my fellow-men in no matter how humble a capacity.[17]

When he informed his father that he would not serve, the Marquess of Tavistock was disinherited by the eleventh Duke of Bedford, but legal difficulties ultimately prevented him from being deprived of an income. He spent the war working in a centre for troops in Portsmouth, cleaning and washing dishes. Describing his companions, the marquess said 'Socially of course they were not of the same class as I but what did that matter? I had had enough and more than enough of the "Upper Ten" both at Eton and in the Army!'[18]

The Duke of Bedford's determination that his son should serve was equalled by the Duchess of Rutland's determination that her son should not. She wanted the direct heir to the dukedom to have a staff job where he would be in relatively little danger. This she achieved through the charms and connections of her daughter, Lady Diana Manners, 'and the results were excellent. John got on the staff, wore a red and gold band on his hat and was a bit despised.'[19] A close friend of Lady Diana's, Raymond Asquith, enlisted in the London Volunteer Defence Force, which, 'since it did not exist and would probably never be allowed to exist by the War Office, guaranteed its members the certainty of staying alive at least until after Goodwood, 1915'.[20] Despite such exceptions, Viscountess Barrington remembered 'the pride and exaltation of fond parents and wives, their willing offering of their sons and husbands to fight in so great a cause in the early days of the War'.[21] At a dinner at Petworth House in August 1914, the party was much diminished because of the departure of so many men. One or two of the guests 'were chiefly concerned to think that they would not be able to do their "cures" in Germany – Lady Blandford ceaselessly harped on the fact that all the men who had gone off that morning "looked so serious, even sad, which was so strange!"'[22]

Landowners who were too old to serve on the fighting fronts encouraged their estate workers to enlist. Lord Leconfield had a scheme whereby he discharged men in his employ who were of an age to serve. If they joined the army he kept their jobs for them. So too the fifth Earl of Lonsdale on his Cumberland and Westmoreland properties. If single men did not enlist, they might lose their jobs. The Duke of Bedford organized a depot for the Bedfordshire Territorial regiment, of which he was Colonel, and presented the gift of a pair of binoculars to every officer leaving the camp. On his estate, employees who volunteered were promised that half their weekly wages would be paid to their dependants at home while they were away. The Marquess of Lincolnshire allowed dependants of estate workers who were left behind to live in their cottages rent-free. The second Earl of Ancaster of Grimsthorpe Castle in Lincolnshire outdid them all; not only did he send a circular letter to all his employees explaining that their jobs would be kept for them, but he guaranteed an income for the wives and families of married men while they were away. Families of volunteers would be allowed to live in their cottages rent-free, and any man prepared to enlist was given a bonus of £5. In Wiltshire, Lady Glenconner personally conveyed volunteers to Salisbury in her motor car.[23]

At recruiting meetings in villages it was often landowners who presided. At Arundel in Sussex speakers addressed the crowds from a farm waggon. The Duke of Norfolk said that he was 'proud to know that Arundel had shown a very fine spirit' and expressed 'sincere gratitude for the great number of men working for him who had gone away to serve their country'.[24] Not far away Lady Cowdray supported the Women's Emergency Corps, whose work included the training of women into a disciplined body like the police. The women learnt to march, drill, shoot, and signal. This was one of the many uniformed women's organizations which emerged during the early weeks of the war, each founded by two or three strong-willed women, whose motives seemed to consist of a 'genuine desire to help the national effort, a liking for uniform. . .and a passion to compete with anyone else who had the temerity to set up an organisation of their own'.[25]

In late 1914 a thousand officers and men from the Gordon Highlander and Bedfordshire regiments were billeted near Cowdray Park in the estate village of Easebourne for three weeks. The village hall, sawmill, and barns were turned into sleeping accommodation and Lady Cowdray spent £1,200 on 500 bedsteads, mattresses, pillows, and blankets. For the Duchess of Bedford, the war required a doubling of her efforts for the local community at Woburn, where she had already designed a hospital. It became a military hospital in 1914, while the riding school and tennis court were converted into another hospital. The duchess eventually devoted some thirty years to this work, doing everything from being a probationer scrubbing floors to acting as theatre nurse. The Duchess of Westminster meanwhile was among the first to go to France with a Red Cross unit where she nursed the wounded at Boulogne and where she had her own hospital. The Marchioness of Exeter at Burghley House in Northamptonshire was also an energetic worker for the Red Cross and superintended her own small hospital.[26]

While some hospitals were set up near country houses others moved in to the houses themselves. At Longleat the 'Bath' bedroom became an operating theatre, nurses were moved into rooms on the top floor, and beds were put in the Saloon. In Buckinghamshire, Taplow Court was converted by the first Lord Desborough into a rest home for Red Cross nurses where in these restful surroundings they had 'every opportunity of recovering from the nerve strain and shock of war'.[27] Robert Graves found himself in Osborne House on the Isle of Wight. His bedroom had once been the night nursery of King Edward VII.

> This was the strawberry season and fine weather; we patients could take all Queen Victoria's favourite walks through the woods and along the quiet seashore, play billiards in the royal billiard-room, sing bawdy songs in the royal music-room, drink the Prince Consort's favourite Rhine wines among his Winterhalters, play golf-croquet, and visit Cowes when in need of adventure.[28]

In London the Hon. Lionel Tennyson, who was wounded three times, felt quite at home in the hospitals run by Lady Carnarvon and Lady Ridley, which he pronounced 'the best in London'. 'No attention was too much trouble, the nursing was wonderful and the food given us exquisitely cooked and served.'[29]

Entertainments for the wounded were provided by some owners of country houses on a large scale. At Arundel Castle in August 1916 the Duke and Duchess of Norfolk entertained 700 wounded soldiers. Entering the castle, the soldiers 'found their way to the green shelters of the private grounds, where, amid all that makes English home parks lovely, and under a summer sun, they found rest, refreshments, music, singing'.[30] Some houses looked out on temporary army camps. At the third Earl Brownlow's Belton Park in Lincolnshire almost 20,000 men were housed in tents and corrugated iron huts:

> Here at first. . .all was peace; the Dutch garden slept in the sunlight, the peacocks, with sadly depleted tails, took their accustomed walks, the park looked deserted. Then, far away against the background of encircling woods, there appeared a long brown line, at first dim and hard to discern. . . .The lines grew nearer and plainer; soon the words of command could be heard. . . .Gradually the park became full of soldiers. . .[31]

Entertainments for the wounded and nursing of the wounded brought home the gradual realization of the horrors of trench warfare. This realization was temporarily eclipsed by the social activities which went on throughout the war. In London, the eighth Duke of Rutland's daughter combined her work as a nurse at Guy's Hospital, and later at a hospital for officers in her London home, with a heady social life. One evening she attended an officer who had to have a rib cut out of his side – 'and from his side came a cataract, two basins full of flowing poison, and now he's gasping relentlessly poor man'. She then went to a dinner at Wimborne House and a ball given by the Duchess of Sutherland.[32] Lady Diana Manners recalled the many evenings spent with friends who might never be seen again:

> We dined at any time. The long waits for the last-comers were enlivened by exciting, unusual drinks such as vodka or absinthe. The menu was composed of far-fetched American delicacies – avocados, terrapin and soft-shell crabs. The table was purple with orchids. I always sat next the host, and the dancing, sometimes to two bands, negro and white (and once to the first Hawaiian), so that there might be no pause, started immediately after dinner.[33]

After his marriage to the daughter of the first Baron Glenconner in 1918, the Hon. Lionel Tennyson rented a house in Lincolnshire where they entertained house parties at weekends. Tennyson and his army friends gambled far into the night. He also rented a shooting estate. 'I believe that my friends and myself, in our determination to get our money's worth, shot practically every living thing on the place.'[34]

In January 1915 *Country Life* observed that for soldiers who did some shooting on leave, the war seemed to have had 'a disastrous effect on their marksmanship'. It was ascribed to 'a little natural "jumpiness" of the nerves after listening to the shells screeching around them for so many days'.[35] But for those who carried on shooting on their estates they found 'a keener pleasure in the conditions of their shooting during the war than they did in those halcyon days preceding it'. For them the difficulties gave 'a zest to shooting that was not there in the days when all, in the mechanism of life, went on wheels perhaps too smoothly oiled'.[36] Tenant farmers too, felt a somewhat keener pleasure in shooting when, during the food campaign of 1917, they were allowed to shoot any birds which came onto their land. This was in response to pressure from farmers and the Board of Agriculture. The cereal shortage also threatened the procurement of feed for hunters, but eventually such horses were allowed a fixed ration, on the understanding that they would be placed at the disposal of the military authorities should they be required.[37]

In his memoirs, *Men and Horses I Have Known*, the Hon. George Lambton recalled that his brother, many years after he had given up hunting, and no one else being available in Northumberland, 'took hounds again, hunted them himself, and with the assistance of one old Whip, kept the whole thing going for three seasons'.[38] In Essex the hunt attracted large fields when yeomanry or cavalry regiments were stationed in that county.[39] And on the fighting fronts too it was possible to go hunting. In 1915 Lord Winterton sailed for Gallipoli with the Sussex Yeomanry and then served in Egypt. Here he wrote that despite the slaughter, the heat, the stench, the flies, and the shells the Sussex Yeomanry was still itself. 'After lunch to my great joy the faithful Alfred Pankhurst, former whip of the Crawley and Horsham Hunt and later Lord Winterton's Canterbury Beagles, met me with a hack.'[40] Under heavy fire in France, a company commander recalled Lord Desborough's son, Julian Grenfell, walking up to him and introducing himself, saying 'You once gave me a mount with the Belvoir Hunt.'[41]

While he was in France, Julian Grenfell was visited by the Duchess of Sutherland from her hospital in Boulogne. She took him out in her motor car with her entourage. Grenfell wrote that 'all the picture-postcard people were there. . . .I spent the day with them; it was rather amusing. Millie looking *too* lovely!'[42]

At home, glimmers of the grand society occasions which had taken place before the war emerged from time to time throughout the four years from 1914 to 1918. In November 1916 the seventh Duke of Richmond's granddaughter was married in Mayfair. She wore a gown trimmed with silver lace and white fox furs and carried white lilies. The bridesmaids wore dresses of pale gold satin, sashes of gold, gold shoes and stockings, and carried red roses. In July 1917 there were two large society weddings: at the Guards' Chapel the Hon. Sybil Cadogan, daughter of the late Viscount Chelsea, married Lord Stanley, the son of the seventeenth Earl of Derby, and Lady Bridget Coke, daughter of the third Earl of Leicester, married the ninth Earl of Airlie at St George's, Hanover Square.[43] Before the war, families such as these had seen each other constantly at the same venues throughout the London Season. Now, as they received news of the deaths of sons, brothers, fathers, fiancés, cousins, husbands, and friends it was with a common sense of loss. Because everyone knew everyone, they suffered bereavement as one. But there remained, too, despite the relentless toll of war losses, an English stoicism, which only occasionally lapsed into open grief. Lady Diana Manners treated sorrow 'like an illness which had to be got over as soon as possible, doing all she can to be cheerful, laughing and talking till tears come like a sudden seizure and she has to give way'.[44] When told that his grandson had decided to join the Flying Corps in France, Sir Oswald Mosley cried openly. 'I should have explained in warm and passionate words all that I felt for him. But I was just a frozen young Englishman; I could not move, I could say nothing.'[45] Lady Desborough, who later lost her two sons, Julian and Billy Grenfell, was reminded by a friend of

> the morning in May when I was with you in the London Hotel and you suddenly burst into tears and cried out 'Oh! I am so frightened about them!' and then a few minutes later with wondrous courage you lifted up your head, dried your eyes, and with a strange wonderful smile said 'Well, they could not do more than die for their country'.[46]

Writing to Lady Desborough after Julian's death the Hon. Charles Lister stated that he had 'stood for something very precious to me – for an England of my dreams made of honest, brave, and tender men, and his life and death has surely done something towards the realization of that England'.[47]

The Hon. Charles Lister had enlisted at the beginning of the war with the First County of London Yeomanry but then decided to join his Balliol friends who had commissions in the Royal Naval Brigade. He was gazetted into a battalion where he met still more friends from Eton, Oxford, and Cambridge. His early letters home described an experience of war quite different from any other:

> We have been joy-riding about the Mediterranean under conditions which, up till now, made the idea of active service seem very remote. A Cunarder with its American bar, six-course dinner, and other accessories does not connect itself in my mind with anything but a transatlantic trip to Newport.[48]

The sons of landed society who served on the western front were, like everyone else, incapable of describing the horrors of trench warfare in letters home.[49] Letters published in newspapers perpetuated this censorship. In *The Times* in November 1914 one soldier wrote: 'I've never felt so well or so happy or enjoyed anything so much. . . .The fighting excitement vitalizes everything, every sight and word and action';[50] and in a letter to the Sussex newspaper the *Chichester Observer* in May 1915:

It's a simply gorgeous afternoon, in fact the whole day has been tip top, and we are all in the highest spirits! I sit with my back to the foe, facing the blue sky and sun-lit pines. . .though few of the pines have escaped the ravages of shot and shell. As I look up I see trees broken off half way up, boughs hanging limply down, yet all looking cheerful.[51]

The reality could not have been more different.

Burial was impossible. . . .And where we fought several times over the same ground bodies became incorporated in the trenches themselves. In one place we had to dig through corpses of Frenchmen who had been killed and buried in 1915.[52]

In between these battles were days and days of waiting,

waiting for Mills bombs to come, or for jam, or for generals, or for the tanks, or transport, or the clearance of the road ahead. You waited in offices under the eyes of somnolent orderlies, under fire on the banks of canals, you waited in hotels, dug-outs, tin sheds, ruined houses. There will be no man who survives of His Majesty's Armed Forces that shall not remember those eternal hours when Time itself stayed still as the true image of bloody War![53]

When the armistice was announced in November 1918 there were scenes throughout England reminiscent of those when war had first been declared in August 1914. After demobilization there were more celebrations. In the summer of 1919, the Duchess of Norfolk hosted one of the many days of festivities organized by landed society in England. At Arundel Castle there was a dinner in the baronial hall of the castle for returned soldiers and their wives and children, as well as for farm tenants from the Sussex and Surrey estates. The following day the Duchess invited every 'man, woman and child in

Arundel' to tea in two large marquees, and there were clowns, sports, and dancing. In the evening there was a firework display. Rockets 'emitting myriads of multi-coloured stars' were of brilliant colours, with diamond sprays, magenta, and emerald clusters. There was a bouquet of red, white, and blue, a lattice of gold and coloured jewels, snow crystals, 'a salvo of victory bombs'.

> Hundreds of rockets whizzed into the sky emitting brilliant stars, and among grand devices were the words 'Victory', 'Thanks to the Boys' (carried out in large letters of vari-coloured fire), a colossal portrait – wonderfully faithful – of the King, and the word 'Peace' in large letters of vari-coloured fire, set in a frame of gold.[54]

A few miles from Arundel Castle at the Goodwood races at the end of July 1919 the thousands who flocked to see the revival of glorious Goodwood were disappointed if they had expected to see 'anything like the dazzle of pre-war gaiety and colour'.[55] With a cold north wind and the absence of royalty that year, the crowds looked drab. While attendance in the members' enclosures was sparse, the lower priced enclosures were more packed than ever, and motor cars now filled the nearby fields. In the ladies' elegant costumes, black was predominant. In the grandstand could be seen the dark colours of mourning.

3

The burdens of estate ownership

The view from the grandstand at Goodwood at the height of summer is one of the most beautiful in England. Looking across the clear vista of woods and fields in the summer of 1919, the farms on the Goodwood estate of the seventh Duke of Richmond, on neighbouring estates in Sussex and beyond them, and beyond the horizon on every landed estate in England, were in a more prosperous condition than they had been for decades. The prosperity was principally due to the drive for home-grown food during the war (in order to counter the submarine menace to imported food) on which the survival of the population depended.

At the start of the First World War little had been done to help farmers; a report in July 1915 recommending guaranteed wheat prices for farmers for four years had been rejected by the government, who thought that the threat to grain-carrying ships by German submarines had abated. But in the late summer of 1916 the poverty of the American harvest and a renewed submarine menace prompted the government to reappraise its agricultural policy once more. When in December 1916 Lloyd George took over from Asquith as prime minister, he appointed the eleventh Duke of Bedford's agent, Rowland Prothero, as President of the Board of Agriculture. Prothero saw the threat to food supplies by submarines as 'an opportunity to re-establish agriculture under a system of state support which would secure good farming by the farmer and good estate management by the landlord'.[1]

The food campaign of 1917 was launched when food supplies were at their lowest ebb, when there were greater shortages and higher prices than ever before. The campaign aimed to increase the acreage on which wheat was grown, which had decreased steadily since the onset of the agricultural depression at the end of the nineteenth century. The Corn Production Act became law in 1917, its passage having been secured by 'sheer force of will' by Lord Milner through 'a jaded House of Commons'.[2] Under this Act, landlords were prevented from raising agricultural rents and powers were given to agricultural departments to enforce cultivation. The cropping and stocking of land was regulated, neglected land was cultivated, and inefficient farmers and landowners could be dispossessed. This indeed was a revolution in the countryside, for the landed interest was now being made accountable in its methods of estate management to the government. A telling example of wartime governmental interference was when the eighth Earl of Aylesford of Packington Hall was fined £70 with £5 costs for failing to comply with the order of the county agricultural executive committee to cultivate a field on his estate.[3]

While landowners were prevented from raising the rents on their estates during the wartime food campaign, their tenants, particularly in arable areas, were benefiting from the high corn prices. With such profits, tenant farmers were keen to purchase their farms when landowners started to put portions of their estates on the market after the war. The tenth Duke of Leeds wrote to his Yorkshire tenants to explain his reasons for selling up:

> As you are probably aware, the heavy burdens thrown upon landed proprietors throughout the country, caused by high taxation and an increase in every department of expenditure have rendered it necessary for many of them to part with their estates. Having regard to the friendly associations which have for many generations existed between my family and the tenants of the West Riding estate, I should be extremely reluctant to have to sever this connection. . . .Should it be necessary I should afford all of you an opportunity of acquiring your holding on terms to be arranged, and if this cannot be done the estate will have to be submitted to auction.[4]

With the rising cost of estate maintenance after the war, net rents gave a very poor return on the capital invested, and an even poorer return – if any at all – on money spent on capital improvements. Farmsteads tended to fall into disrepair. In 1913 the net income on the third Baron Leconfield's 25,000-acre estate in Sussex had been 10s an acre. By 1920 it was only 5s an acre. While the sale value of such land had doubled, its income had been halved. A tenant on an old estate where rents were low knew that if his farm were sold his rent would probably be increased, perhaps to double its previous level.[5] With high product prices and high levels of income both during and immediately after the First World War, tenants were anxious to buy the farms which landlords were equally willing to sell. The result of this activity on the estate market after the First World War was that by 1927 a quarter of the rural land of England and Wales had changed hands. This twentieth-century break-up of estates in England has been put in its historical context by Professor F. M. L. Thompson.

> Such an enormous and rapid transfer of land had not been seen since the confiscations and sequestrations of the Civil War, such a permanent transfer not since the dissolution of the monasteries in the sixteenth century. Indeed a transfer on this scale and in such a short space of time had probably not been equalled since the Norman Conquest.[6]

While many small estates were sold in their entirety, others were completely broken up. One-third of Derbyshire's original twenty-nine estates were broken up after the First World War.[7] The owners of large tracts of land in counties throughout Great Britain sold distantly located parts of their estates in a calculated and businesslike way. They were seizing on the opportunity at last, after years of depression in agriculture, of transferring their capital into lucrative stocks and bonds. This did not mean that there was a complete withdrawal of landowners from the countryside. The eagerness with which country houses surrounded by several thousand acres were purchased by newcomers in some counties underlined the importance still attached to the perpetuation of the landed way of life in postwar England.

Despite the sales, large landowners perceived little change in their standing in the countryside. Whether they owned 40,000 acres or 20,000 made little difference if it meant that their finances were in a healthier state than they had been for decades. Since the end of the nineteenth century they had endured falling rental incomes with little opportunity of selling their land. Now they sold it while the going was good. Then in 1921, in the midst of falling world prices, farmers were no longer guaranteed government support. The postwar boom in land sales came to an end.

Apart from taxation and rising costs, landowners had to contend with the added burden of increased death duties. In 1919 the Chancellor of the Exchequer increased the rate to 40 per cent on estates of £2 million. But the majority of land sales after the war were not directly the result of death duties.[8] They were part of the long-awaited opportunity for England's large landowners to rid themselves of some of the burdens of estate ownership. To observers it appeared that all England was changing hands. It was however only far-flung sections of estates that were sold. Generally, the core remained in their original ownership.

A quarter of the rural land of England was in the hands of landowners who owned at least 10,000 acres. Among these land-owners one of the first sales during the postwar boom was by Lord Aylesford, who sold outlying portions of the Packington estate in Warwickshire. The sale of nearly 2,000 acres brought him £65,000. This still left Lord Aylesford with 17,000 acres. In Lincolnshire, the fourth Earl of Yarborough sold nearly 2,000 acres, but this made little dent in the 50,000 acres he already owned throughout the east of England. By selling just 346 acres in Grimsby in Lincolnshire, he was able to raise £41,000.[9] The Duke of Sutherland, the largest landowner in Great Britain, continued sales started in 1917, when the 17,000-acre Lilleshall estate in Shropshire had been disposed of. At the time of this sale the duke had been on active service, but left instructions that all the cottages on the estate tenanted by men on active service or their dependants be reserved from the sale. Lilleshall House, which was only used by the family at Easter, was sold two years later in 1919, while in Staffordshire the sale of the duke's Trentham estate yielded £333,000.[10] Such sales made little change in the Duke of Sutherland's standing in the landholding ranks. With the future so uncertain, he thought it unwise to have so much of his capital tied up in land. 'I likewise made some readjustments regarding my homes, though not so much for financial reasons as for convenience.' He gave up his London house in Portman Square and bought Hampden House in Mayfair, and after selling Lilleshall in Shropshire he bought Sutton Place near Guildford in Surrey.[11]

Other large landowners who sold outlying portions of their estates after the war included the fourth Marquess of Cholmondeley, who lived at Houghton Hall in Norfolk and who sold 2,000 acres, one-eighth of his estate, in Cheshire. The sixth Marquess of Northampton sold part of his Long Compton estate in Warwickshire and 3,000 acres in Devon. The fifteenth Earl of Pembroke sold 7,000 acres of his 40,000-acre Wilton estate in September 1919, while not far away in Wiltshire the fifth Marquess of Bath sold off more than one-third of his Longleat estate.[12] The eighth Duke of Rutland was perhaps the most prominent among those who chose to divest themselves of large parts of their estates in the immediate postwar years. Land in the town of Bakewell, 'handy for Haddon Hall, Chatsworth and other places', was auctioned in July 1919 and this, along with 13,000 acres on the Belvoir estate and almost 15,000 acres in Derbyshire, together comprising half the land he owned in these two counties, realized £1.5 million.[13] Much of this money was spent on the careful restoration of Haddon Hall in Derbyshire, whose simple medieval architecture stood in quiet contrast with the Italianate extravaganza of Chatsworth close by.

Where estates changed hands in their entirety during this time it brought about an end to centuries of landownership by one county family in a few short years. Most of the 3,000-acre Rolleston estate in Staffordshire was sold by Oswald Mosley's father in 1919, and later the hall and its surrounding 600 acres. Oswald Mosley had persuaded his father to sell the estate, 'foreseeing the ruin of agriculture which politics were bringing'. For him,

> it was a terrible uprooting, causing me much sorrow at the time, and I have sometimes regretted it since. . .but it appeared then a mistake to maintain in post-war circumstances an unmanageable pile of a Victorian house together with a way of life which seemed gone for ever.[14]

Yet amid these sales of small estates and outlying portions Lord Leverhulme, the soap manufacturer, bought the whole of North Harris Island in Scotland and others off the coast of Inverness – altogether some 60,000 acres.[15] Lord Brownlow at Belton Park in Lincolnshire meanwhile, who felt 'the ownership of a vast, rambling estate to be a great and costly mistake', sold one-fifth of his Shropshire acres.[16] In Shropshire one of his tenants said that he had hoped to remain there all his life as a tenant of a good landlord, 'but times had changed sadly, and good old English estates had to be broken up'. Instead of letting the tenants be 'bought out by rich men', Lord Brownlow had given them the right of first option of the freehold.[17]

Disparaging references to 'rich men' who bought up land were frequent during the turnover of land after the war. Such sentiments were evoked by the fifth Earl of Warwick, who welcomed the possession of much land by a few people.

> I have never met a tenant who would willingly exchange a landlord of the old school for one of the business men who has bought a big estate and conducts it to bring in a safe five or six per cent on capital outlay. He lacks tradition, and the lack, as the farmer knows instinctively, is fatal.[18]

A landowner who, like Lord Leverhulme, certainly lacked 'tradition' was Sir Weetman Pearson, later first Lord Cowdray. In 1909 he had purchased the 17,000-acre Cowdray estate in West Sussex. By looking at this one county in particular, despite the unusual presence of a landowning businessman such as Lord Cowdray, some light can be shed on the geography of the break-up of large estates in England after the First World War. For here, as in many other counties, the principal landowners owned estates throughout Britain and Ireland. The six principal landowners in West Sussex could lay claim to half a million acres throughout England, Wales, Scotland, and Ireland; and this was before the advent of the wealthy businessman Sir Weetman Pearson. These particular representatives of English landed society contributed to the transfer of land which occurred after the First World War by holding on to their principal estates in the south of England and selling off land in the north of England, Scotland, and Ireland.

* * *

The picturesque county of West Sussex, directly south of London and with a coastline overlooking the English Channel between Portsmouth and Brighton, gave the impression in 1919 'more of an aristocratic and middle-class county of pleasure than of real agricultural work. In many cases oak trees stand casually in the middle of fields. It is very charming, but hardly conducive to good farming.'[19] As far as its residential attractions were concerned,

Sussex is, or has been, too much in possession of rich people who do not depend on the cultivation of the land for their livelihood. This tendency has, of late years, been increased by a fashion with a group of literary men, who have come to live in Sussex, of extolling this county in verse and prose, thus attracting other invaders.[20]

One inhabitant who for a long time extolled the virtues of the Sussex landscape was Hilaire Belloc, who described the most notable feature of the county, the South Downs, as

the great line of chalk hills which stand steep up against the Weald, that is, with their escarpment facing northward, and which slope gradually towards the sea-plain upon the south. A section taken anywhere in the range resembles in form a wave driven forward by the south-west wind and just about to break over the Weald.[21]

In this wooded landscape were ancestral houses which were the homes of some of the oldest families in England. On the southern flanks of the South Downs overlooking the coastal plain to the Channel, the Duke of Richmond's Goodwood House near Chichester was not far from the Duke of Norfolk's Arundel Castle. Three impressive residences to the north of the Downs were Lord Egmont's Cowdray Park near Midhurst, Lord Leconfield's Georgian Petworth House, and Lord Zouche's Elizabethan Parham Park. This area was closely surrounded by other ancient parks, whose inhabitants constituted the inner core of landed society in the county.

By the beginning of the twentieth century there had begun an infiltration of businessmen from London into the county, who, building country houses surrounded by several hundred acres, sought to emulate their long-established landed neighbours. The north-eastern section of the county around Horsham had initially attracted the new rich from London into West Sussex. They included the French ostrich-feather importer, Philip Saillard, who built a large mansion 'in hot red brick and yellow stone' where the hall had ostrich feathers discreetly painted on the high ceiling.[22] The part of the county midway between the capital and Brighton had for long been largely inaccessible because of its undulating woodland, but soon roads were built by the new landowners themselves.[23] At

1 Bridesmaids and a sister of the bride at the wedding of the Hon. Sybil Cadogan and Lord Stanley at the Guards' Chapel, Wellington Barracks (*Tatler*, 25 July 1917).

2 The memorial room in Castle Drogo, Devon, of Adrian Drewe, killed in action in July 1917. (© National Trust)

3 The Elveden war memorial on Lord Iveagh's Suffolk estate commemorating the war dead from three surrounding parishes. (Courtesy of Dr Adam Strevens.)

NINETEEN DAYS' SALE AT STOWE

By direction of the Right Hon. The Baroness Kinloss, C.I.
The Rev. The Hon. L. C. F. T. Morgan-Grenville, Master of Kinloss, and the
Trustees of the will of the late Duke of Buckingham and Chandos, G.C.S.I.

THE DUCAL ESTATE OF STOWE
NEAR BUCKINGHAM.

The Historical Seat of the Dukes of Buckingham and Chandos
and for some years the residence of the late Comte de Paris.

MESSRS. JACKSON STOPS

WILL SELL BY AUCTION, AT STOWE HOUSE,

On Monday, July 4th, 1921, at 1 o'clock
THE FREEHOLD OF THE HISTORIC
MANSION & ESTATE

Extending to about 1,400 acres, including the World-famous Grounds, and
Temples, Surrounding Park Lands, and the Picturesque Village of Dadford,

The Estate will be first offered as a whole, and, if not then sold, in 67 lots, including
24 First Pasture Farms and Small Holdings, chiefly with vacant possession; Houses
and Freehold Ground Rents, at or near the Town of Buckingham.

On the eighteen days following (from July 5th to July 28th
excluding Saturdays, at 11 o'clock precisely each day) will be sold the

Contents of the Mansion

Including the Supremely Valuable Collection of

Heirloom Pictures, Tapestries and Historic Furniture,

by the World's Greatest Masters, Superb Statuary and Metal Work, important collection
of Rare China, Porcelain, an immense assortment of other Objets d'Art, the Contents
of the Magnificent Library, fine collection of Historic Letters and Manuscripts, the
Valuable Gold Plate, Carvings and Panellings by Grinling Gibbons,

FAMOUS CLASSIC TEMPLES

and other Buildings and Bridges luxuriously
built to designs by famous architects.

Finely Illustrated Catalogues, with Historical Preface, Plans and Particulars (which
will admit three persons to sale) price 25/- may be obtained from

MESSRS. JACKSON STOPS, F.S.I., F.A.I., Northampton and Towcester.

MESSRS. SMALL & BARKER, Solicitors, Buckingham.

MESSRS. WITHERS, BENSONS CURRIE WILLIAMS & CO., Solicitors, Howard House,
  4, Arundel Street, Strand, London, W.C. 2.

JUDGE PATTERSON, City Hall, Philadelphia, U.S.A.

4 The 1921 sale of the house and estate of Stowe in
Buckinghamshire. By this time a quarter of the rural land of
England had changed hands since 1919.

5 A gathering on the steps of Longleat in 1926 for the 21st birthday party of Viscount Weymouth (seated, front row) later sixth Marquess of Bath. (© Daphne Fielding 1954, reprinted by kind permission of Curtis Brown Ltd.)

6 (top right) The funeral cortège of the second Viscount Cowdray leaving Cowdray Park, 1933. (Records of S. Pearson & Son, Box A.24, Science Museum Library. Reproduced by kind permission of Pearson Plc.)

7 (right) Cowdray estate employees follow the cortège through the village of Easebourne. (Reproduced by kind permission of Pearson Plc.)

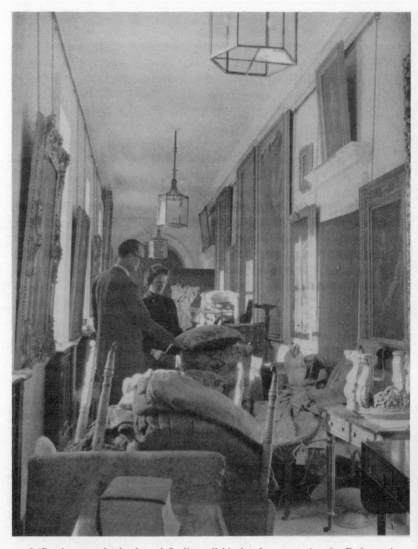

8 'Sorting out the junk and finding all kinds of treasures' – the Duke and Duchess of Bedford at Woburn Abbey after the Second World War. (Reproduced by kind permission of the Marquess of Tavistock, and the Trustees of the Bedford Estates, Woburn Abbey.)

9 (top right) Landowners in the library of the Royal Agricultural College in Cirencester listening to a lecture on taxation, 1949. (Reproduced by kind permission of International Thomson Publishing Ltd.)

10 (right) A farm tour near Cirencester, 1949. (Reproduced by kind permission of International Thomson Publishing Ltd.)

11 Sir Harold Bowden,
August 1947.
(Reproduced by kind
permission of *The Field*.)

12 Gainsborough's *Mr and Mrs Andrews* – also with gun and dog
(Reproduced by courtesy of the Trustees, The National Gallery,
London.)

The ninth Earl of Portsmouth on his
Hampshire estate in 1947. As in
Gainsborough's portrait, the ricks have
been tied by hand. (Reproduced by kind
permission of *The Field*.)

14 Lord Bingley outside Bramham Park
in Yorkshire, 1947. (Reproduced by kind
permission of *The Field*.)

Sir Cecil Newman at Burloes in
Hertfordshire, 1947. (Reproduced by
kind permission of *The Field*.)

16 The first Baron Bicester, chairman of
Morgan Grenfell bank, in front of
Tusmore Park in Oxfordshire, 1947.
(Reproduced by kind permission of *The
Field*.)

17 The east front of Henham Hall in Suffolk, home of the fifth Earl of Stradbroke. (Reproduced by kind permission of the Royal Commission on the Historical Monuments of England.)

18 Preparation for the demolition of Henham Hall in 1953. (Reproduced by kind permission of the Royal Commission on the Historical Monuments of England.)

19 Henham Hall from the south. (Reproduced by kind permission of the Royal Commission on the Historical Monuments of England.)

20 Workmen among the ruins. (Reproduced by kind permission of the Royal Commission on the Historical Monuments of England.)

21 The last remains of Henham, originally built between 1793 and 1797. (Reproduced by kind permission of the Royal Commission on the Historical Monuments of England.)

22 The thirteenth Duke of Bedford guides visitors around Woburn Abbey, first opened to the public in 1955. (Reproduced by kind permission of the Marquess of Tavistock, and the Trustees of the Bedford Estates, Woburn Abbey.)

23 Viscount Weymouth, Lord Christopher Thynne, and Sir Mark Palmer, 1969.

24 Mentmore in Buckinghamshire, home of the De Rothschilds and the Earls of Rosebery before its sale in 1977 in order to pay death duties. Rich arable farmland lies close to the mansion and park. (Cambridge University Collection: copyright reserved.)

25 The 1987 Annual General Meeting of the Historic Houses Association, founded in 1973. From left to right: the Marquess of Tavistock of Woburn Abbey, Bedfordshire, Hon. Treasurer; the Duke of Grafton of Euston Hall, Suffolk, Patron; Commander Michael Saunders Watson of Rockingham Castle, Northamptonshire, President; the Earl of Shelburne of Bowood, Wiltshire, Deputy President; Norman Hudson, Technical Adviser. (Reproduced by kind permission of the Historic Houses Association.)

26 The Hon. Simon Howard, owner of Castle Howard, 1985. (Reproduced by kind permission of *The Field*.)

27 John Clotworthy Talbot Foster Whyte-Melville Skeffington, thirteenth Viscount Massereene and Ferrard, 1986. (Reproduced by kind permission of *The Field*.)

the same time, the wooded north-western corner of the county, with its spectacular views across to the Downs, was an attractive area for new estates. Here the poet Alfred Lord Tennyson built Aldworth House in the style of a French chateau and replaced the surrounding gorse with pine trees; the Aldworth estate was later bought by the Maharajah Gaekwar of Baroda. Close neighbours included the merchant banker Sir Felix Schuster at Verdley Place, and Sir Frederick Philipson-Stow, a co-founder with Cecil Rhodes of the De Beers mining company in South Africa, at Blackdown House. To the south, in the area bordering Hampshire, the Downs became less wooded. The large residences here were Uppark – a windswept Jacobean edifice and home of the Hon. Keith Turnour-Fetherston-haugh, and Stansted Park, home of Lord Bessborough.

In 1909 the international engineering contractor, Sir Weetman Pearson, purchased the Cowdray estate from the eighth Earl Egmont. When Sir Weetman was created a peer in 1910 he took the title Baron Cowdray which was raised to a viscountcy in 1917. He was one of only three very wealthy British businessmen who, having made their fortunes in industry, invested in land on a very large scale in the twentieth century. The other two were Lord Iveagh the Guinness brewer and Lord Leverhulme the soap manufacturer.[24]

Sir Weetman Pearson had slowly expanded his father's Yorkshire-based firm of builders. In the 1880s and 1890s the firm had constructed the docks in Milford Haven and Southampton and the Halifax docks in Nova Scotia. Having completed the construction of the East River tunnel in New York, Pearson was asked in 1889 by the President of Mexico, Porfirio Diaz, to drain Mexico City. This formidable task, only attempted once since the arrival of the Spanish conquistador Hernan Cortes, was completed in 1896. Meanwhile, a contract for the Blackwall tunnel in London had been won in 1890 and was completed in 1897, after which Pearson received a knighthood. By this time he had purchased 6,000 acres in East Sussex.[25]

In 1901, while travelling from Mexico City to New York, Sir Weetman Pearson was delayed for nine hours at the railway station at Laredo, where the town was in the middle of an oil boom. Such was the excitement there that he immediately decided to try his hand at this new venture. He had already formed a close friendship with the President of Mexico and was granted concessions by him to drill on state lands in four oil-bearing provinces in Mexico. During these unpredictable years Sir Weetman decided to purchase the 17,000-acre Cowdray estate in West Sussex.

Sir Weetman Pearson was known internationally throughout the engineering world for his supreme confidence in his own powers, not only to direct vast operations successfully but to predict with uncanny accuracy the cost of damming the Nile or building a railway or an underwater tunnel, yet finishing with a profit. In a brief moment of pessimism he wrote to his wife from Mexico City:

> I cannot help but think what a craven adventurer I am compared to the man of old. I am slothful and horribly afraid of two things – first that my pride in my judgement and administration should be scattered to the winds and secondly that I should have to begin life again. These fears make me a coward at times. I know that if my oil venture had to fizzle out entirely that there is enough left for us to live quietly at Cowdray say on £40,000 a year [*sic*]. Yet until our oil venture is a proved success I continue nervous and somewhat despondent.[26]

Pearson's nervousness and despondency soon disappeared when a few months later his firm struck on the single most productive oil well in Mexico.

Concerned as he was with all his business interests Sir Weetman Pearson spent little time at Cowdray Park. It was his son Harold, educated at Eton and Christ Church, who began to play a leading part in county society. At Christ Church he was a contemporary of the Hon. Edward Turnour, later sixth Earl Winterton, from the neighbouring estate of Shillinglee in Sussex. In 1906 Turnour was invited to Mexico by Sir Weetman Pearson and was present at the inauguration of the Tehuantepec railway. Joining the towns of Salina Cruz and Coatzacoalcos, it linked the Atlantic and Pacific seaboards of the Mexican peninsula. Pearson had built the railway and modernized both towns.[27]

In West Sussex, a businessman who had bought a small estate bordering the Cowdray estate was Sir James Buchanan, later first Lord Woolavington. In 1880 he had founded the whisky distilling firm of James Buchanan & Co., purveyors of Black and White and House of Commons whisky, and had created a new demand for Scotch whisky in England.[28] He bought the Woolavington estate in the late 1890s as well as land in Scotland, British Columbia, and East Africa. His 3,000-acre Lavington estate near Petworth on the northern scarp of the Downs was surrounded by parkland. Here he developed a racing stud, thus forging a link with the Duke of Richmond at Goodwood nearby.

In 1918 Sir James Buchanan put his two Ross-shire estates in Scotland on the market. Then in 1922 his 17,000-acre Ross and Cromarty estate was put up for auction with its 'thirty to forty stags in season, salmon and sea trout fishing, and plenty of mixed shooting'.[29]

Lord Cowdray meanwhile was actively buying up land. Dunecht Castle in Aberdeenshire had been purchased in 1910 and after the war Cowdray added almost 13,000 acres to his Scottish landholdings. These included Castle Fraser, home of Cowdray's second son, the Hon. Clive Pearson. In West Sussex the Hon. Clive Pearson lived at Parham Park, purchased in 1922 from the Hon. Darea Curzon, sister of the late Baron Zouche. In 1915 Clive Pearson had married the Hon. Alicia Knatchbull-Hugesson, the daughter of the first Baron Brabourne, and they carefully restored Parham to its former Elizabethan glory.[30] In Scotland it was alleged that Lord Cowdray spent £250,000 on Dunecht Castle alone. He created an island with a temple and a boathouse on it in the middle of a loch, and in the village of Echt provided a water supply and a sewerage system. He built cottages, shops, garages, new roads, and dykes. Sawmills and workshops were centralized while every year a hundred acres of land was planted with Scots fir.[31] Between 1909 and 1924 Lord Cowdray had spent more than £1 million buying up land. In West Sussex he owned as much land as the Duke of Richmond and throughout Great Britain he owned more land than the Duke of Norfolk.

Among the long-established landowners in West Sussex such as the Duke of Norfolk and the Duke of Richmond, Lord Leconfield, of Petworth House, owned a 25,000-acre estate in Yorkshire, 11,000 acres in Cumberland centred on Cockermouth Castle, and over 40,000 acres in Ireland as well as his Sussex estate.[32] He spent most of the year at Petworth, where his main preoccupation was fox-hunting, reputedly hunting for four days a week from 1901 to 1942 throughout his long mastership of the Leconfield Hunt. In 1920 he sold 20,000 acres, four-fifths of his estate, in Yorkshire. He gave his tenants the opportunity to buy their holdings and publicly outlined his reasons for parting with his Yorkshire property, the most valuable of all his land in England and Ireland. He told his tenants that all attempts to obtain justice as regards taxation of landed property and proper protection for home-grown produce had failed.

> I feel very strongly, therefore, that the only means by which there can be any hope of getting justice done to agriculture is by increasing the number of occupying landowners to the greatest extent possible, and so providing an opportunity for them to combine and present a united front to the government.[33]

Having sold valuable land in Yorkshire, Lord Leconfield also sold his birthplace, the 'comfortable old Georgian residence' of Drove House near Goodwood, with 1,000 acres of 'first rate sporting land'.[34] But apart from this sale, his estate in West Sussex remained intact.

South of Petworth, Arundel Castle was the principal seat of the Duke of Norfolk, who owned three other residences in England, Derwent Hall in Derbyshire, Beech Hill in Sheffield, and Norfolk House in St James's Square. The trustees of the young Duke of Norfolk, whose father, the fifteenth duke, had died in 1917, sold only a few properties in West Sussex.[35] The sale of outlying portions of the Sheffield estates produced £80,000 from private negotiation and at auction. Agricultural land in Yorkshire yielded up to £120 an acre for some lots and the auction total here was between £54,000 and £70,000.[36] In 1920 Derwent Hall in Derbyshire was obstructing a Midland water scheme. The boroughs of the towns of Derby, Leicester, Nottingham, and Sheffield succeeded in getting a Bill through Parliament which involved the submerging of Derwent Hall and some villages. Eventually Derwent Hall was to be 'deep down below the surface of what may be, in some ways, a very pretty lake. . . .But none who has ever known Derwent Hall will look upon the surface of the waters without thinking regretfully of the necessity of sinking such a fine old house below it.'[37]

To the west of the Duke of Norfolk's Arundel Castle in Sussex the Duke of Richmond at Goodwood owned an estate of 17,000 acres which included some of the richest farmland in England. He also owned nearly 300,000 acres in Scotland where he spent part of the year at Gordon Castle in Banffshire. In 1922 the Duke of Richmond rid himself of one-fifth of his Scottish acres.[38]

Among the small estates in West Sussex, those which were sold were soon bought without being broken up. Burton Park was purchased by a brother of Samuel Courtauld, chairman of the family firm of rayon manufacturers. Major Courtauld represented Chichester in the House of Commons from 1924 until his death in 1942. A neighbour was the Hon. Charles Bigham, later second Viscount Mersey, who in 1926 purchased Bignor Park and 500 acres. He recalled:

> I could have had another 500 acres and have since regretted not buying the whole property, though the balance was outlying land and not essential. But I was fortunate in having two neighbours, Lord Leconfield and Major Courtauld who took over much of the remainder of the estate; the danger of having it turned into building lots was thus avoided.[39]

The continued attractions of counties near London such as West Sussex were alluded to in the sale particulars of the Bignor estate. An excerpt from an 1832 guide to the county described the view across to the Downs from the Hon. Charles Bigham's Bignor Park.

> The most striking features are the South Down hills, which fall away abruptly on this side and present a great variation of outline. . . .The whole level which occupies the centre of the view, to the extent of more than a thousand acres has then the appearance of a large lake or of an inlet of salt water, the limits of which on the one side are marked by the noble ruins of Amberley Castle. Broad masses of woodland, interspersed with rich meadows fill the intermediate space between Bignor Park and the river and give effect to the other parts of the landscape which, on the whole have more the air of an Italian distance than is usually to be met with in England.[40]

*   *   *

While many large landowners were selling outlying portions of their estates in counties miles away from their principal county of residence, there was also a move to rid themselves of their urban estates. Near Birmingham, outlying portions of the Edgbaston estate were sold by the Calthorpes and in 1920 Lord Radnor began his sale of Folkestone. In the same year the Ramsden estate in Huddersfield was sold to a corporation for £1.3 million and Lord Derby began to dispose of his Liverpool ground rents.[41] Between 1926 and 1927 the Scarisbricks and Heskeths auctioned off their holdings in Southport in Lancashire. At the same time the Dudleys started their sale of

4,000 acres in the west Midlands. The Fitzwilliams in Sheffield, having begun their development of the Eccleshall estate on a traditional leasehold pattern, laying out roads and letting on the market plots to tenant builders, had begun to find this policy inflexible by the early 1900s. It now seemed preferable to sell to developers. Thus by the 1920s, 'at the very time of unprecedented suburban expansion, the aristocracy, frightened by the risks more than entranced by the prospects, opted for sale rather than leasing'.[42]

In London there was a similar story of the decline of aristocratic dominance after the First World War. Several distinctive parts of the capital belonged to members of the peerage. Almost a hundred acres of quiet, residential, tree-lined streets and squares in Bloomsbury was owned by the eleventh Duke of Bedford, who sold £2 million worth of ground rents here in 1919.[43] The Bloomsbury estate bordered Lord Howard de Walden's 200 acres of densely packed residential streets centred on Portland Place, inherited from the Duke of Portland in 1879. To the west was Viscount Portman's estate centred on Portman Square, whose grey brick and white porticos were similar to the Duke of Bedford's Bloomsbury. Lord Portman's estate comprised 250 acres stretching from Regent's Park down to Oxford Street. Directly south of the Portman estate and stretching from the southern side of Oxford Street, the Duke of Westminster resided in, and owned most of, Mayfair. This was the most exclusive residential part of London at the beginning of the twentieth century, and included Park Lane, where large houses overlooked Hyde Park. To the east, Mayfair was bordered by the Earl of Berkeley's twenty-acre estate centred on Berkeley Square.

The Duke of Westminster owned an even larger area of London than Mayfair, centred on Belgravia, which comprised land stretching from the south-eastern tip of Hyde Park down to Pimlico and the River Thames. Immediately to the west of the Belgravia estate, Earl Cadogan owned much of Chelsea, from Fulham Road in the north down to Cheyne Walk, another smart residential part of London with views through plane trees to the river. In 1880 his estate had comprised 200 acres, including Sloane Street near Cadogan Square, named after Elizabeth Sloane, who had married into the Cadogan family in 1717. Another member of landed society with a London estate close by was Lord Ilchester at Holland Park who had bought the estate in 1874 from a distant relation, Lady Holland.

In north-east London, far away from the West End, the Marquess Camden owned land in Camden Town and the Marquess of Northampton land in Canonbury, Islington, and Clerkenwell. Numerous street names on all these London estates were taken from towns and titles associated with these families: Eaton Square in Belgravia was named after the Duke of Westminster's estate in Cheshire, and Bryanston Square was named after Viscount Portman's Bryanston Manor at Blandford in Dorset; hence also Blandford Street and Dorset Street. There is a Woburn Place, Bedford Square, and Tavistock Square in the Duke of Bedford's Bloomsbury. Between them, therefore, these landowners owned practically all of the most valuable parts of residential London at the beginning of the twentieth century, their presence a constant reminder in many of the most exclusive addresses in the West End.

Of all the London landowners the second Duke of Westminster was the most prominent, owning most of Mayfair and Belgravia. After the First World War he sold small sections of his London estates. His grandfather, the first Duke of Westminster, had died in 1899 leaving death duties of £600,000.[44] For the first time in the history of the Grosvenor estate, sales were resorted to to meet taxation. Two small properties had been sold near Victoria Station and a site at Hyde Park corner was bought by St George's Hospital. Between 1920 and 1923 there were sales by the second duke of portions of the Pimlico properties near Victoria, which raised £1.1 million.[45] Outside London, in 1921 the duke sold just over 7,000 acres of his Eaton estate in Cheshire comprising 'fifty-five of the best equipped farms in Cheshire, twenty-six small holdings, the "Grosvenor Arms" Pulford, and a hundred and forty eight model cottages'.[46]

The Berkeley estate, which bordered the Duke of Westminster's Mayfair estate, was sold in its entirety by the eighth Earl of Berkeley to Sir Marcus Samuel, later Lord Bearsted, in 1919. Describing the estate as 'compact rectangular blocks of the most valuable residential district in existence', *Country Life* was relieved to observe that, if London land had to be sold, 'we can desire nothing better than that it should pass into the hands of men of the standing and personal repute of Sir Marcus Samuel'.[47] Yet such a complete change of ownership was unique as far as the sales of London estates were concerned. Most landowners sold small sections of their estates. The fourth Marquess Camden sold £94,000 worth of sites and ground rents in Camden Town after the war while Viscount Portman gained a similar sum for 300 houses, five public houses, and thirty shops on seven acres of his Marylebone estate. The fourth Baron Southampton, who owned land near Euston Station, sold sites on Euston Road for £73,000, between £10,000 and £11,000 an acre being paid for favoured positions.[48] Such changes of ownership made little difference to Londoners. To them it was the fate of the private residences of some of English landed society in London – that is, the demolition and conversion of their London mansions – which was the most poignant indication of changing times after the First World War.

Writing of London in 1908 E. B. Chancellor, the chronicler of, in his terms, the capital's 'private palaces', observed that Paris, Berlin, and Vienna had more splendid streets than London, small towns on the continent had better churches, Brussels and Paris had parks and open spaces just as impressive. Yet London's 'great palaces. . . compare with those palaces for which Venice was once famous'.[49] It was the collections of pictures, furniture, and china that these houses contained which prompted such praise. The appearance of the mansions, whether they overlooked Hyde Park or Green Park, whether they were in Mayfair or St James's, was not usually notable. Money was lavished on their interiors, where entertaining took place during the London Season in the summer, when landed society spun out its time between hunting seasons in the shires.

The Duke of Westminster's house on Park Lane had probably the finest collection of Rembrandts in the country, as well as pictures by Salvator Rosa, Claude Lorraine, Murillo, and Velázquez. In the dining room there were Rembrandts and a Rubens, as well as pictures by Claude. In the saloon there were Italian, French, Spanish, Dutch, and Flemish pictures. All the doors of the house were of solid mahogany picked out in gold. There were mantelpieces of Carrara marble, Louis XIV cabinets of exquisite porcelain, and tables of lapis lazuli mounted on ormolu.[50] In 1926, Grosvenor House was pulled down and the picture collection dispersed. In its place the modern Grosvenor House Hotel was built, topped by apartment towers in red brick.

Not far from Grosvenor House on Park Lane, Brook House had been purchased by the financier Sir Ernest Cassel, who had imported marble from Italy for the grand staircase, hall, and galleries.[51] In 1931 the house was demolished and a block of flats built in its place. At the top, a penthouse provided the London home for Sir Ernest Cassel's granddaughter and her husband, Lord Louis Mountbatten. Also overlooking Hyde Park, Dorchester House was perhaps the most spectacular of London mansions, although not inhabited by a landed family. Its demise however was symbolic, as it too was demolished soon after Grosvenor House, and with it 'its stately staircase of white marble, resplendent with alabaster balustrading'.[52]

The last of the large houses to be built in Mayfair was Sunderland House on Curzon Street. It had been given to Consuelo Vanderbilt by her father as a wedding present in 1895 when she had married the Duke of Marlborough, and this house survived the interwar period. At the other end of Curzon Street, at Lansdowne House, the reception held in 1920 after the marriage of the ninth Duke of Devonshire's daughter Lady Dorothy Cavendish to Harold Macmillan was the last big society function held. In 1935 the main façade of Lansdowne House was rebuilt, two wings having been demolished. Two rooms decorated by Robert Adam were salvaged and transported to America. Not far from Lansdowne House, Chesterfield House on Curzon Street, a masterpiece by Robert Adam, was entirely demolished in 1937.[53]

The conversion and demolition of London mansions in the 1920s and 1930s were outward signs of changes throughout the whole of Mayfair, where a large proportion of English landed society had traditionally claimed a residence. Between 1921 and 1939 the Duke of Portland and the Duke of Somerset, Earl Fitzwilliam and the Earl of Durham all left Grosvenor Square. By 1939 four of the eight resident peers lived not in houses but in apartments.[54] The demolition of Devonshire House on Piccadilly was the first and most significant of all these changes in London. A costume ball was held there in 1924, but soon afterwards 'the sight of an historic 18th century house being pulled down by a gang of 20th century English workmen was sufficiently novel for artists to come and draw the scene'.[55] Contemporary commentators were distressed both at the sight of Devonshire House's demolition and at the prospect of a block of apartments being built in its place. The owners of Devonshire House, the Cavendishes (the family name of the Dukes of Devonshire), were described as

representatives of a great class and a great social system which they utterly failed to maintain – where they were hopelessly beaten; and it is this utter failure which is personified by the destruction of their old house in Piccadilly. This house has been demolished and rebuilt by their conquerors, the new plutocrats who have made their money by trade instead of by the cultivation of land. The old Devonshire House represented the earlier country gentleman's agricultural England; the new block of flats are the very living symbol of the manufacturers' and traders' England.[56]

The question was asked:

Was one family of cultured, well-behaved aristocrats really more dangerous to the populace than the great mass of stock brokers, idlers, company promoters, night-club dancers, and all the variegated throng. . .who will take the Cavendish place? Will they turn out between them a producer of Ben Jonson's masques, a second wrangler or eighth classic, a Georgiana or a Bess of Hardwick, or a fraction of all the stately honest figures of public life that have come along the line of Cavendish tradition?[57]

Meanwhile, E. B. Chancellor quietly observed that with the 'disappearance or the conversion into other uses of London's private palaces, something of the grace of life seems to be departing'.[58]

'Something of the grace of life' had departed for another peer, Viscount Churchill. Well before the imposition of high taxation and high death duties his father had sold up the ancestral house and estate in Wiltshire in an apparent gesture of abandonment. His son began a life of aimless wandering, which took him eventually to the beaches of California. The effects of the sudden reversal of centuries of planning and development of estates, reversals which for many families occurred throughout England immediately after the First World War, were described by the viscount:

All [my ancestors'] planning and maintaining and preserving, done so carefully for themselves and their descendants, had come to nothing. The pedestals and the props which they had passed on so conscientiously from one to the other had been knocked away. They were destitute now, living only through me, depending on me, sleeping where I slept: on sea beaches, in ships and in hotel bedrooms, homeless, their house no bigger than my skull, the chances of their memory surviving no greater than my wits.[59]

4

Fast living and feudalism, 1919–39

The guilt of survival seemed to dominate the decades between 1919 and 1939 after the Great War. Among the men who returned from the war there emerged a conspiracy of silence, a mutual and unspoken understanding that the horrors witnessed on the battle-field should appear to be forgotten. The silence lasted for ten years, for it was not until 1928, ten years after the armistice, that there was a new deluge of literary descriptions of trench warfare. Among such books written by officers educated at public schools and with whom landed society identified were Siegfried Sassoon's *Memoirs of an Infantry Officer*, Robert Graves' *Goodbye to All That*, and Edmund Blunden's *Undertones of War*. In 1929 R.C. Sheriff's play *Journey's End*, set entirely in a trench, ran at the Savoy Theatre in London for 600 performances. For the Great Interruption, which had brought bereavement and loss to every family in England, had been exactly that – a tragic and incomprehensible interlude, which had shattered for a short while the tranquil world of Edwardian stability.

For landed society the happy world of the years before the war was transformed into one of cynical detachment, not only from what was happening on their estates, but also from what was happening on the international scene. Adaptation to the loss of those who had been closest to them, the financial difficulties of the late 1920s and the early 1930s, and then the possibility of another war brought about a retreat into their enclosed and uncaring world, a retreat which continued until 1939.

The realization that landed wealth and influence were no longer unassailable seemed to engender among the survivors a brittle, frenetic outlook. Daring and constant diversions were looked for by those who emerged from wartime England. A new flippancy and sophistication emerged too, an attempt to show that in fact nothing had changed, that the old order of upper-class ascendancy had returned. But the very need to assert this apparent continuity was itself indicative of collapse. Parties became louder, exploits wilder, laughter became sharper, and the obligatory accent more pronounced. Jazz and cocktails from America, cars, films, and London nightclubs were the heady means of obliterating the dark years of bereavement and quiet restraint which had been the lot of landed society throughout the war.

The Season started with a flurry of activities after the armistice. Dancing became 'a sort of mystical religion'. 'Supported by nothing but tea or coffee (a glass of sherry would have turned it into an orgy), we fox-trotted tirelessly till it was time to dash home and change into evening dress for a real dance.'[1] The patriotic fervour of the armistice attached little place to social distinctions. Before the war the officer corps had been the exclusive preserve of the upper classes. After 1918, any man with the title of Major or Captain was accepted as an equal.[2]

For landed families who could draw upon incomes from investments, from town property, or from mines, their way of life altered little. Country houses were still run on the old lines, with large staffs employed in the house, in the garden, and on the estate. Yet throughout the two decades which separated the two world wars, many ancient landed families abandoned their houses and estates. Ascribing the traditions of landed connections to sentiment but prompted by the financial collapse of 1930, many such families exchanged a country house and its parkland for an apartment in London and a fast car. In the country they were replaced by newly rich families who perpetuated the continued prestige of landed living, and purchased estates for hunting and for shooting. While motoring through the north of England in 1926, J. Fairfax-Blakeborough was struck by 'the unlovely country houses which have been erected in recent years. . .they are gaudy, pretentious or vulgar, and savouring of urban villadom. . .such eyesore abominations are now springing up all over rural England'.[3]

Throughout rural England estates suffered the worst depression in farming since that of the late nineteenth century. This was brought about by what was referred to by farmers everywhere as the 'Great Betrayal' of 1921. Quite suddenly and quite unexpectedly, the government had reversed its policy of guaranteeing corn prices, a wartime measure which had temporarily restored prosperity to farming. Unable to afford the payments to farmers necessary after a price fall in 1921, the Cabinet made the decision to revert to the free market, and arable farmers throughout England were left to suffer in silence. Another sharp price fall in the early 1930s made matters even worse, and farming had to wait for a second world war to be given whole-hearted government support once more. As in the late nineteenth century, farming in England was hardest hit in the corn-growing areas in the east of England, whereas livestock farming fared better.

Former tenants who had purchased their farms during the land sales immediately after the war were faced with coping with unpredictable price falls alone. Those who remained tenants did not have the added burden of maintaining farm buildings, walls, and fences. Yet because of the depressed economy, landowners them-selves were hard-pressed to undertake all the duties of estate maintenance required of them. Farm buildings, walls, and fences gradually deteriorated, thatched roofs caved in to exude 'the rotting smell of failure', bricks and rubble became overgrown with nettles.[4] Less and less arable land was to be seen in the English landscape, 'the number of derelict fields, rank with coarse matted grass, thistles, weeds and brambles multiplied; ditches became choked and no longer served as effective drains; hedges became overgrown and straggled over the edge of fields'.[5] During these years, the rela-tionship between landlord and tenant was never more important, as agreements were made to lower rents and to keep estates maintained in a minimum working condition. On some estates, tenants were allowed to farm rent-free.

In Yorkshire, the 12,000-acre Birdsall estate had belonged to the eleventh Baron Middleton's family since the early eighteenth cen-tury. Its gross rental income had continued to rise until the mid-1920s, following the general increase in rents during the prosperous conditions after the war. Between 1928 and 1929 its rental income dropped from £14,000 to £6,000.[6] On only two previous occasions, in 1898 and 1904, had the estate yielded a rent of less than £10,000. By 1930, arrears on the estate totalled two-thirds of its rental income and Lord Middleton and the newly formed

Birdsall Estate Company offered 10,000 acres of land for sale. With no satisfactory offer, the property was taken off the market after four months. Had the sale proceeded, Birdsall House and most of the southern part of the estate would have been disposed of.

The decision by Lord Middleton to hold on to the Birdsall estate demanded careful management. So that the land could still be farmed, co-operation with tenants became particularly important. When one tenant threatened to leave in 1933 he was offered rent for 5s an acre instead of 8s, no more than had been paid in 1889 or 1898. The terms of entry for new tenants had seldom been more favourable, and one was allowed to farm 800 acres rent-free for two years from 1931. By the end of 1931 nearly 3,000 acres of the Birdsall estate were without tenants. Lord Middleton's home farm had once had a wide reputation for its pedigree hunters, shire horses, beef shorthorns, and Leicester sheep, run as much for pleasure as for profit. But in 1925 the shorthorns were sold, the stud farm was discontinued, and only 300 acres of the home farm's original 2,000 were farmed by Lord Middleton. For him, having a number of farms in hand acted as a stimulus to the purchase of machinery. By 1934 there were four tractors on estate farms, but much of the work was still performed by shire horses.[7]

The slowness of the adoption of tractors and of milking machines long after their invention at around the turn of the century was another feature of the decline in farming on landed estates during the depressed years between the wars. It was not until the Second World War that farms became mechanized. Horses were a cheaper source of power than tractors, as much of the running cost of horses came off the farm itself as grazing, oats, and straw. If dairy farmers without arable land purchased maize for their work-horses, this was cheaper than buying petrol or paraffin for a tractor. In 1935 a new Fordson tractor cost £140, the same price as a pair of good horses with their gear. Horses had a working life of ten years but a tractor only four or five.[8]

Although tractors had been introduced onto farms during the First World War, this had been well in advance of their competence to stand up to the work required of them. Their frequent breakdowns had caused farmers to lose confidence in them. Gateways to fields and entrances to cattle yards and cowsheds had all been designed to accommodate horses. Landlords were not inclined to provide a new building for a tractor or a milking machine. While owner-occupiers could rip out hedges or knock larger holes in their walls to accommodate machines, tenants on estates had to work with existing buildings and gateways.[9]

At Birdsall, Lord Middleton was particularly interested in farming, but many landowners remained unaware of what was happening on farms on their estates during these years. The countryside came more and more to be a temporary setting for long weekend house parties rather than for the lengthy stays which had been the feature of entertaining in Edwardian days. The war had brought with it a new freedom, particularly for women, who were determined to obliterate the long years of devastation and bereavement. The countryside was there for hunting and shooting, for country walks and for entertaining. Overgrown and dusty lanes were no more than the means of access to house parties. Watched by onlookers, their fast and noisy cars sped through rough lanes and small villages on their way to urgent destinations at country houses. For the motor car had opened up new vistas for the survivors of the Great War, providing a means of quick and independent escape from London and from one house party to another.

Hostesses were less likely to write to their guests giving them the times of trains. Although train journeys were more comfortable, to arrive by car was considered more chic.[10] During long journeys by motor car in the 1920s, tyres had to be changed frequently and tanks refilled with petrol from cans. Luggage, strapped precariously to the outside platform, arrived crumpled and mud-stained if it didn't actually fall off. 'The fact that the car has made an average of twenty-five miles an hour is no solace to the woman whose gown is ruined and whose hat has been assaulted by every blast from heaven.'[11]

Travel could be more sedate, however, when a new addition joined the ranks of the estate staff, that of the chauffeur. The choice of this word was ascribed to the altogether foreign nature of this method of conveyance. 'French, it was recognised, would constitute the medium between driver and motor, could it talk – in short, English for horses, French for motors. No Englishman could be found tricky enough to manage such a novel and temperamental contraption.'[12] Chauffeurs fell into two distinct classes, young mechanics who wore blue suits and caps, and ex-coachmen, who dressed themselves to look like their Edwardian predecessors with leather leggings and long coats and 'who sat at a wheel of a car very much as on the box of a carriage, urging on a recalcitrant and sometimes refractory machine with encouraging cries'.[13] With the advent of the motor car, stays in the country could be abbreviated at a moment's notice. Lord Ernest Hamilton lamented:

> You come down to breakfast and find that your charming neighbour at dinner the night before has gone off in her car to some other country house 200 miles away. Somebody else – probably a complete stranger – arrives during breakfast and introduces a discordant note that does not, perhaps, even begin to blend in with the general harmony for two or three days. It is upsetting.[14]

The speed of transportation from one country house to another was extravagantly demonstrated by Philip Sassoon, who lived at Port Lympne in Kent. His sister had married Lord Rocksavage, later fifth Marquess of Cholmondeley, of Houghton Hall in Norfolk. Sassoon used to fly in a small aeroplane to breakfast with his sister at Houghton and then perhaps to Paris to see the opening of a new play. From his house in Trent Park near London he could fly to Kent 'just to see how the flowers are doing at Lympne' and hurry back to London for a concert.[15]

The depressed condition of the farms over which Philip Sassoon flew was eventually brought home to those who had remained aloof from these difficulties by the sudden collapse of the New York Stock Exchange in October 1929. The crash had repercussions throughout the world and in London share prices fell dramatically. So too did farm rents. In 1928 there had been a bumper wheat crop in North America which was still largely unsold before there was another bumper crop in 1929. By the spring of 1931 farmers in England held meetings of protest all over the country demanding that the Labour government, which had been elected in June 1929, stem imports and maintain prices of agricultural products, or else subsidize wages in order to save the farming community from bankruptcy. Such was the crisis that seldom before in the history of agriculture had landowners, farmers, and labourers been so clearly of one mind. In addressing a meeting in Chichester in West Sussex, Lord Leconfield had lamented in 1921 that being a landlord was 'no longer the fun that it used to be'.[16] His remarks would have appeared even more poignant in 1933, when the price for wheat reached its lowest level since the sixteenth century.[17]

The events which followed the crash of the Stock Exchange in New York in 1929 made innumerable inroads into the finances of landowners everywhere. The crisis of September 1931, when Britain came off the gold standard, seemed to be the final chord of the heady days of the 1920s. 'The minstrels packed their instruments and went the way of the pound.'[18] Until about this time the small estate owner, with centuries of association with the land, had still been 'a power to be reckoned with, despite progressive adversities'.[19]

Where landed families were forced to abandon their houses, these stood as the first memorials to the lost age of landed living. At one deserted country house in Suffolk the old lodge keeper who remained to show around potential buyers opened the wrought iron gates 'and bustled about to undo them as though a fine equipage and impatient horses fumed outside'.[20] In the garden, the paths were overgrown with roses, yet the edging of the lawn that curved in front of the house was clean cut. At the entrance to the house two sheep scrambled to their feet and clattered down the steps, while the lodge keeper, 'a prophet in the wilderness trusting still in the return of that earthly patrician Messiah to set up his kingdom there', proudly displayed the house.[21]

Throughout England, some 130 houses were pulled down during the two decades between the wars, and after 1930 a thousand families were missing from Burke's *Landed Gentry*.[22] While numerous families abandoned their houses or sold their estates, the statistics from one county, Shropshire, put these interwar upheavals in perspective. Here, of the county's 173 principal seats, almost one-third found new owners between 1922 and 1934, eight were converted into institutions, and just seven were unoccupied.[23]

Mansions which before the First World War had been emblems of family pride became 'incubuses sitting heavily upon impoverished acres which could no longer support them'.[24] It was therefore the smaller landed families without alternative sources of income who were knocked out by the financial crisis of 1930. If the payment of death duties coincided with this period, this could provide the final blow. In some cases, where it had taken just one generation to make a landed family, so also in the 1930s it took one generation to unmake one. Many such families joined London society, in the 'rootless, restless, social world which never had contact with earth'.[25] Yet with the insecurity of investments in the City many estate agents at this time recommended the purchase of land as a sure means of investment whose value was bound to recover. A well-chosen property, if judiciously purchased in the right locality, was regarded as a gilt-edged security, not subject to fluctuations in stocks and shares, and 'worth the attention of the shrewd and far-seeing investor'.[26]

By the time the financial crisis had passed, the new poor had, it seemed, quietly changed places with the new rich in the countryside. The old mansions of ancient landed families were now owned by 'merchant princes and manufacturers' who were 'a very agreeable and generous-hearted crowd'.[27] But to become established in county society these new squires, 'the fathers – or the great-grand fathers – of the old squires of the future' were unlikely to be accepted by their tenants immediately. If they attempted to patronize and to appear 'superior', if generosity to their employees was seen as 'charity' rather than as 'tactful presents', and if they tried too hard to take up 'the proper position' of the squire and his lady, then their acceptance by their adopted village communities took many years.[28] Throughout England, farmers and labourers bewailed 'the loss of the old squire and the advent of his successor, the commercial magnate'.[29] But if these newcomers farmed their land well and did not let the shooting rights to millionaires this, in village eyes, could cover a multitude of sins.[30]

The land sales immediately after the First World War saw the advent of the owner-occupiers who were eventually to take over two-thirds of the farmland of England. At the same time there was an exodus of farm labourers from the land in search of better paid work in towns; one-fifth of all farm labourers left the land between the wars. This was prompted also by the reversion of labour-intensive arable land to grassland, and the inability of many farmers to pay the minimum wages set up by the Labour government of 1924. There was still a wide disparity between low farm wages and higher wages in industry.[31]

The many families of farmers and farm workers scattered over rural parishes in receipt of outdoor relief from the poor law received less publicity than the unemployed in towns. Unemployment insurance introduced in 1920 had not been extended to agriculture.[32] In one county town in Suffolk, the unemployed happened to gather in the winter opposite an electrical showroom whose central attraction was a modern electric fire. They stood gazing apathetically at it, through the plate-glass window which was like 'that invisible barrier which starves the world in the midst of its plenty'.[33] For landed society, the subject of unemployment used to come up at every lunch party. The Duchess of Westminster could not help being 'struck unpleasantly by the bejewelled. . .ladies and their affluent consorts smugly declaring over the caviar that there was no solution to the problem'.[34]

In the midst of these economic difficulties there emerged once more another political attack on the landed interest. Before the war it had been Lloyd George's attempted valuation of all land which had engendered such outrage among landowners. This time the attack came from the Labour government. In the spring budget of 1931, in the middle of the crisis in farming, the Labour Chancellor of the Exchequer, Philip Snowden, attempted to impose a land value tax. As far as the 1931 land value tax was concerned, it was admitted that revenue considerations were not its only rationale, for the valuations were to be open to public inspection. The ultimate end in view was the nationalization of all land. This was claimed by Snowden to be 'one further stage towards the emancipation of the people from the tyranny and injustice of private land monopoly', a radical cause which he had cherished all his life.[35] In 1931, the threat of the Bill had 'a disturbing effect on the minds of owners and potential buyers in property'.[36]

In 1932 Lord Ashburton drew attention to the potentially devastating impact of death duties on his estate in Hampshire. He said that the only way to avoid the taxation was to destroy his house, the Grange, in order to reduce the duties payable on the assessment value of the property. By proposing to sell the 8,000-acre estate, and mansion with seven reception rooms, fifty bed- and dressing rooms and ten bathrooms, Lord Ashburton underlined the plight of many landowners.[37] In Sussex, the eighth Duke of Richmond's decision to sell the magnificent beech timber from the woodlands surrounding Goodwood in 1930, following the death of the seventh duke in 1928, was described as 'evidence of the vindictive policy which successive Governments have pursued against landowners'.[38]

In 1934 the problems of maintaining a historic house were raised at the annual general meeting of the National Trust, a charity set up in 1895 to preserve places of historic interest and natural beauty. The owner of Blickling Hall in Norfolk, the eleventh Marquess of Lothian, proposed several measures to help save country houses, suggesting that owners be subject to various types of fiscal relief.[39]

The Marquess of Lothian had inherited Blickling Hall in 1930, as well as two residences in Scotland. In order to pay death duties, most of the valuable contents of the library at Blickling had been sold in New York.[40] Yet under the marquess's guidance, the National Trust Act was passed in 1937, enabling houses such as Blickling, along with its gardens, parks, woods, and farms, to be handed over to the Trust while the Marquess of Lothian continued to live there.

If the seventh Earl of Warwick had married the richest and most dazzling of interwar débutantes, Margaret Whigham, then his estate's financial difficulties might have been solved. The young earl, an officer in the Grenadier Guards, had proposed to her in Egypt in 1932 while the couple walked across the Aswan Dam. When later she visited the Warwick estate Margaret was greeted by cheering crowds on her way to the castle but was somewhat perplexed when her fiancé greeted her. He said that not he but the head guide would show her the castle, as 'He knows the place so much better than I do.' For the rest of her stay Margaret received little attention from Fulke Warwick. Somewhat bemused, she said to her maid on the last night: 'Well. . .I don't think I can see myself sitting around here.'[41] Twenty years later when she married the eleventh Duke of Argyll, it was Inverary Castle in Scotland which was repaired and restored thanks to the Whigham fortune.

The predicaments of the heir to Warwick Castle, the Marquess of Lothian, and Lord Ashburton emphasized that alternative sources of income other than farm rents were crucial for the survival of estates between the wars. Yet while the possession of home farms prompted some landowners to join in the chorus of complaints about the state of agriculture in the early 1930s, many of them took little interest in these farms. Bailiffs employed to look after home farms were given little financial help to make them profitable. Owners remained 'wonderfully undisturbed by the losses on their home farms', many regarding them as 'a necessary expense in order to secure a guaranteed milk supply'.[42]

On some estates, pedigree herds were still kept as expensive and prestigious features of home farms. On a tour of West Sussex by 'farmers from the empire' in 1928, visits were made to the Duke of Richmond's herd of Aberdeen Angus cattle at Goodwood, the Derby winner at West Grinstead Park, Dexter cattle on Lady Loder's Leonardslee estate near Horsham, the pedigree stock farms at the

Burrells' Knepp Castle, Colonel Ulric Thynne's Hache herd of Friesian cows at Findon, as well as the Rt Hon. Walter Guinness's dairy cattle at Bailiffscourt.[43] On the second Duke of Westminster's Eaton estate in Cheshire, the Duchess of Westminster was asked by the agent to view a cow which had won an award at the home farm. She and the duke visited the farmyard where the agent proudly showed them the cow. The duke and duchess told him 'how perfectly marvellously he'd done. Neither of us knew a thing about it. I said, "What beautiful eyelashes it has" or something feeble like that.'[44]

The incongruity of the Duke and Duchess of Westminster viewing a cow in the farmyard at Eaton and the unease with which they did it encapsulated the detachment of landed society from all that went on on their estates between the wars. And in the House of Commons, where successive parties sought to grapple with the economic problems which dogged the interwar years, the nature of the House had changed beyond recognition by 1939 as far as its representation by landed society was concerned. Although in 1914 there had been thirty-two large landowners among Conservative Members of Parliament, nineteen small landowners, and sixteen heirs to estates, together comprising almost a quarter of all Conservative MPs, by 1939 there were just seven large landowners, sixteen small landowners, and fourteen heirs to estates – just one-tenth of Conservative MPs.[45] Yet in the Conservative governments between the wars many landed peers and members of landed families held high office. The Duke of Devonshire could 'survey the long line of Secretaries of State sitting beside him to the farthest limits of the Upper Chamber and could almost think that the happy past had returned'. The dust

> danced in the golden sunbeams; from the benches rose the buzz of conversation which is never hushed by their Lordships except to hear a member of the Government. . .a dewy-feathered and hereditary slumber weighed down the eyelids of the Duke, and Britain seemed to be sailing along her ancient course of prosperity and glory.[46]

Stanley Baldwin, prime minister from 1924 to 1929 and from 1935 to 1937, romanticized the countryside at every opportunity. At the annual dinner of the Royal Society of St George, held at the Hotel Cecil in 1924, he said that to him England was the tinkle of the hammer on the anvil in the country smithy, the corncrake on a dewy morning, the sound of the scythe against the whetstone, and the sight of a plough team coming over the brow of a hill. . . .The wild anemones in the woods in April, the last load at night of hay being drawn down a lane as the twilight comes on. . .and above all, most subtle, most penetrating and most moving, the smell of wood smoke coming up in an autumn evening.[47]

Despite the prime minister's sympathy with the countryside, the Conservative Party in the House of Commons had changed. It derived its mass support and finance not from the ancestral acres of England but from 'business, manufacturing, and commercial interests whose political passions were fired by the menace of socialism in industrial areas'.[48]

Not only were the members of landed society increasingly removed from the political confrontations of the House of Commons, but the houses in which they lived still symbolized their detachment from the modern world. In Suffolk, 'For a little while we were beside fields where men hoed and gathered clover-hay, or ploughed the sudden wintry square of a bare fallow. But then the landscape of labour gave way to park and woodland.' The river which had turned the water mill in a village close by became an ornamental lake, 'a white stone bridge spanning it with a lissom bow giving a cool light of stone under the tree shadows' with a Graeco-Georgian temple near by. Over the river was a rose garden and beyond that Euston Hall, seat of the Duke of Grafton.[49]

In Wiltshire Daphne Vivian, later Marchioness of Bath, saw Longleat for the first time in the 1920s. The house was 'bathed in the sunshine of a June afternoon, which gave the stone a honey glow'. The 'great golden house, built in an Italianate style, lay cradled in the lap of a broad valley of wooded parkland, looking like a fairy-story palace'.[50]

On the other side of England the Duke of Rutland's Belvoir Castle looked like a fairy-story palace in 1935 when it was floodlit for a hunt ball. The castle stood on the top of a hill, and at night could be seen for miles around. The road leading up to it was bordered with coloured lights, 'a sight that, for once, put anything in the movies to shame'. The morning after the hunt ball the Belvoir pack met on the snow-covered lawn in front of the castle. The 'fairy castle of the night before went on looking like a fairy castle in the pale, rose-tinted winter sunlight. . .with footmen rushing about with huge trays of cherry brandy in the cold morning air'.[51]

At Arundel Castle in Sussex it seemed that the world before the war had never departed. In June 1929 the coming of age of the sixteenth Duke of Norfolk was celebrated for several days. There was a lunch for more than a hundred tenants and their wives, a fête in the castle grounds, a firework display, and a party for children. On the top of a hill near the castle a fire was lit which could be seen from Sussex, Surrey, and Hampshire and from ships in the Channel. Bury Hill was 'a natural crown, set with innumerable gems, the lights of about a thousand cars and topped with a flaming diadem'. The fire was lit amid the cheering of a large crowd singing 'For he's a jolly good fellow'.[52]

At the funeral of the second Viscount Cowdray in 1933, the horsedrawn cart carrying the coffin processed from Cowdray Park to the parish church a mile away, all the estate workers walking behind it six abreast.[53] In Yorkshire in the same year thousands of tenants from the seventh Earl Fitzwilliam's Rotherham estate were transported to Dublin to attend his son's lavish wedding in St Patrick's Cathedral.[54] On the return of the Duke and Duchess of Norfolk from their honeymoon in 1937 the bells of the parish church at Arundel pealed their welcome and the duke and duchess were greeted by cheering crowds.[55] At another ducal residence, Chatsworth in Derbyshire, Christmases between the wars were like 'another world, almost as remote from present day England as the descriptions of Count Rostov's family in *War and Peace*'.[56]

While hunt balls, comings of age, and Christmas gatherings continued in style after the war, there was also a reaction by landed society against the old prewar world. Many expressed boredom with the life accepted for so long. London society and county society now merged with greater frequency. At country-house parties in England the tenor of social life changed. Gramophones and cocktails, treasure hunts and car chases, jazz musicians at parties, even if they played from Gothic galleries, were all reminiscent of London nightclubs, of the metropolis after dark. As lucrative investments were to be had not in land but in the City, so the inhabitants of country houses came to identify less with their estates and more with London. The new speed and ease with which one life could be exchanged for the other, while still maintaining the important prestige of landed connections, brought about an unlikely combination of London sophistication and county patronage, of fast living and feudalism. It was an age of transition, in which 'the remaining dignity of an aristocratic order combined with the luxuries of a cosmopolitan machine civilization; the Spanish Embassy *and* the Embassy Club, Norfolk House *and* the Blue Lantern'.[57]

* * *

The Embassy nightclub was a favourite haunt of the Prince of Wales and his brother. When the two princes arranged one evening for the band from the Embassy to play at a court ball at Buckingham Palace, guests were somewhat perturbed when a 'blonde in a skin-tight sequin dress' stepped to the fore and began a rendition of 'You're my baby' until a hasty message silenced her.[58] Throughout the Season in May, June, and July 'the awnings stretched outside the houses of Mayfair, Belgravia and Westminster'. All the lovely débutantes and 'the bored and eligible young men' were at the conservative and grand coming-out balls. There were 'the badly dressed duchesses with tiaras on slightly skew-whiff, heavily tasselled curtains, very polite conversation. . .and at the buffet, a slight perfume of methylated spirit and molten silver'.[59]

After the opening parties of the Season there was racing at Ascot, but now the road back was one long line of cars.[60] Then at the races at Goodwood, where the atmosphere was reminiscent of the end of a school term, holiday time began 'for the very few who are on a perpetual holiday'.[61] From the grandstand in 1930 parties could be seen arriving from country houses nearby. The Cowdray party arrived from Cowdray Park, Lord Woolavington and his party from Lavington Park, Lord and Lady Leconfield with a party from Petworth, and Lord and Lady Bessborough from Stansted Park. The eighth Duke of Richmond entertained his many guests at Goodwood House itself.

Goodwood was still followed by the post-Season escape to Scotland. On the platforms at Euston Station in London were piles of luggage, gun cases, and shooting-sticks labelled for the Scottish moors, alongside groups of servants all waiting to go north to the grouse moors. The popularity of Scottish shooting seemed to be 'increasing rather than falling off'.[62] For others, the Golden Arrow train took travellers from Victoria Station to the south of France, while the Orient Express provided the height of luxurious travel. The Countess of Rosse spent her honeymoon in China, crossing Siberia on the Shanghai Express. 'It was the most luxurious, Marlene Dietrich, train that you can imagine. . . .Of course, coming back from Siberia we had caviar practically every day. . . .There was even a bath. I adored it all.'[63]

Back at home there emerged a new informality as old traditions were adapted to modern needs and more sophisticated entertainments. At Ernest Guinness's country house in Ireland, in front of which a 'great brown lake lapped the glistening mica-strewn sand with froth like Guinness's stout', guests spent their days by the lake 'in dressing-gowns and pyjamas, fancying that we looked like the photographs we had seen in *The Tatler* of smart people at the Lido'.[64] The Guinness family also owned Bailiffscourt near Littlehampton in West Sussex, a house reconstructed in 1929 in a medieval style indistinguishable from the original. Here guests stayed for the Goodwood races nearby. Inside, Bailiffscourt was a mixture of genuine furniture of the period, while upstairs there were modern bathrooms and every possible luxury.[65]

Not far from Bailiffscourt lay the West Dean estate, purchased in 1891 by the James family, whose fortune had been founded in timber production in New York State and through marriage into the Phelps Dodge metals and mining company. Edward James, who came into his inheritance in 1929, was an early patron of surrealism and a friend of Salvador Dali and Magritte. In 1935 he moved out of West Dean House, which he found too large for his tastes and began converting the shooting lodge into 'the first surrealist abode'.[66] This rural retreat, created by a somewhat disillusioned member of landed society, was approached by a 'two-mile drive through sinister woodland'.[67] It had plaster mouldings underneath the windows in the shape of towels hung out to dry, while the drainpipes were made to look like bamboo. The front door was flanked with two large palm trees carved from wood, the entire house painted a dark purple while the interior was a surrealist creation.

Edward James's grandfather had played a leading role in the development of the United States railway system, in particular the Santa Fé railway. It was also American money which financed a unique experiment in the regeneration of the countryside in England when Leonard and Dorothy Elmhirst purchased the Dartington estate in Devon in 1925. Leonard Elmhirst was from an old landed family in Yorkshire. After Trinity College Cambridge he studied agriculture at Cornell University in 1919. There he met the widowed Dorothy Straight, heiress to the vast Whitney fortune, her father having made his money from the Metropolitan Street Railway Company in New York. It was therefore New York City's subway system which subsidized the Dartington experiment, part of which was to create a school whose classrooms were to be 'a farm, a garden, workshops, play grounds, woods and freedom'.[68]

When Leonard Elmhirst first saw Dartington he wondered whether his wife, 'the grand lady from Fifth Avenue', would be able to picture herself 'in a rambling, almost derelict house in Devon'.[69] But by the time the Elmhirsts had moved in to Dartington, they had modernized their new home entirely and their household staff was on the same scale as in their two other homes on Park Avenue and Long Island. In Devon they employed the Marquess of Bute's former butler, the Duke of Portland's former chauffeur, and the Earl of Yarborough's former gardener. When in 1935 Dorothy Elmhirst's son by her first marriage married the daughter of the fourteenth Earl of Winchilsea, Daphne Finch Hatton, seventy-three members of the Dartington estate staff travelled to London to attend the wedding; it was unusual for an American marrying into a landed family to be able to match the retinue of estate employees from his bride's family with some of his own.[70]

The aim at Dartington was to create a thriving rural community on an estate which had suffered financial ruin in the 1920s. Since 1554 it had been the property of the Champernowne family. Many such estates would have been sold for speculation, sport, or social prestige at this time, but the Elmhirsts, using the expertise of the School of Agriculture at Cornell, wanted to put farming on a profitable basis. By refusing permission for hunts to ride over their land and by paying higher wages they antagonized their landed neighbours. But by providing employment for 600 people Dartington was 'an unprecedented effort to create a new source of income and amenity in the countryside at the depth of the depression'.[71] Apart from the farmland and woodland, there was a poultry unit, orchards, a cider plant, a sawmill, and a textile plant. There was an agricultural science laboratory and departments of agricultural and woodland economics. Medieval buildings were restored and an arts department for dance, music, design, and drama was set up. In 1927 the Elmhirsts were asked to back a play by the unknown author

R. C. Sheriff called *Journey's End*. With the success of the play, their
£400 advance brought them a vast return.[72]

In Kent the sale of Vita Sackville-West's bestselling novel *The
Edwardians*, published in 1930, helped to finance the restoration of
Sissinghurst Castle. Sissinghurst was not far from the author's
ancestral home of Knole Park, upon which her novel had been
based. Vita Sackville-West was the daughter of the third Baron
Sackville. In 1913 she had married Harold Nicolson. Their decision
in 1930 to purchase Sissinghurst was a bold one. Like Dartington,
the place was a ruin. There was no water or electricity and not a
single habitable room. For more than a hundred years the discon-
nected fragments of the ancient red brick castle had been used as
stables and housing for farm labourers. Yet when Vita first saw
Sissinghurst on a spring day in 1930 it 'caught instantly at my heart
and my imagination. I saw what might be made of it. It was
Sleeping Beauty's Castle.'[73] The castle was furnished with Persian
rugs, glass, silver, ebony mirrors, Jacobean chests, and a portrait of
Charles Sackville from Knole. The garden became one of the most
famous in England, designed by Harold Nicolson and planted by his
wife.

> In the firm perspectives of the vistas, the careful siting of an urn or
> statue, the division of the garden by hedges and walls and
> buildings into a series of separate gardens, the calculated alter-
> nation between straight lines and curved, one can trace his
> classical hand. In the overflowing clematis, figs, vines and
> wistaria, in the rejection of violent colour or anything too tame or
> orderly, one discovers her romanticism.[74]

The Nicolsons, the Elmhirsts, Edward James, and the Guinnesses
could afford each in their own way to adapt their houses to a more
relaxed way of life. Where landed families clung on to the old
traditions, they were at times quietly ridiculed by guests. 'What a
bore week-ends are, forty-eight hours social crucifixion', moaned Sir
Henry Channon in his diary in 1936. Weekends for him that
summer had been spent with the Marquess and Marchioness of
Dufferin and Ava in 'a hideous villa, with cocktails, gramophones,
pekes and bridge', and at Tredegar, 'glorious house, but the feel and
even smell of decay, of aristocracy in extremis'.[75] For Harold Acton,
weekends in the country meant sleeping in a strange bedroom
among disturbing pictures, where the bath tap was turned on before

71

he was awake, and where he was expected to contribute in unexpected ways to the general entertainment; all this was 'more toil and trouble than repose'.[76] At Cliveden, Harold Nicolson recalled a cold and draughty weekend with more than thirty people staying in the house; 'Great sofas in vast cathedrals: little groups of people wishing they were alone'.[77]

The daughter of the second Baron Redesdale, the Hon. Nancy Mitford, warned readers of *Vogue* what would await them at weekends in the country, where meals had to be endured in cold dining rooms with guests who had been chosen for their skill with the gun rather than for their personal charm. Luncheon next day would be near a windswept haystack, after which guests accompanied the guns to a bleak hedgerow. Here they would have to stay very still, for a long time, in silence. 'When the man with whom you are standing breaks a heavy silence by saying angrily, "Shut up and lie down", remember that he is most probably addressing not you, but his dog.'[78] After each drive, guests would be expected to search the ground for dead birds. In spite of the fact that even if one was found 'no bribe would induce you to touch it', it was 'better to appear happy and occupied for fear that your hostess should think that you are bored'.[79]

Boredom was one of the principal reasons for another, ultimately devastating break with tradition when the Prince of Wales chose to move in social circles outside the court, finding witty American hostesses more fun than the staider members of landed society. His association with the divorced Wallis Simpson, to whom he had been introduced at a country-house party in Leicestershire by another American, Lady Furness, could not be reconciled with his destiny as monarch.[80] He became king in 1936 but his determination to marry Mrs Simpson after her divorce from her second husband eventually led to his abdication. His lord-in-waiting and close friend was the sixth Baron Brownlow of Belton Park in Lincolnshire, who had the task of attempting to prevent such a crisis. When Mrs Simpson decided to leave the country, Lord Brownlow accompanied her, suggesting on the way to Newhaven that she stay at his Belton estate, thus allowing easier communication with the king. But she was determined to get as far away as possible and so began a dramatic trip through France to Cannes, where they were to stay with friends. Lord Brownlow 'became the centre of the world's interest and perhaps for some days the whole fate of the Monarchy hung on him'.[81] But in December 1936 Edward VIII renounced the throne in favour of his brother, who became George VI, and the couple were married in France, taking the titles of Duke and Duchess of Windsor.

The ex-king and his bride spent their time on the continent, being received on one occasion, against Foreign Office advice, by Hitler. When Lord and Lady Redesdale visited their daughter Unity in Germany, they too met Hitler. During their stay, a German general asked at a dinner if in the event of war the English would fight. There was evident consternation when Lady Redesdale said that they would fight, and if necessary for ten years at sea.[82]

When in September 1938 the Prime Minister returned from Germany after meeting Hitler, he was greeted as a hero who had saved the world from war. But Neville Chamberlain was naïve about international affairs. To him the dictators of Germany and of Italy might have different views, but were 'fundamentally reasonable, decent men like himself'.[83] In February 1938 the Foreign Secretary, Anthony Eden, had resigned in open disagreement with Chamberlain's foreign policy. Lord Cranborne, heir to the Marquess of Salisbury and Eden's Under-Secretary of State, resigned with him. In Eden's place Chamberlain appointed the third Viscount Halifax, who shared his views. But Lord Halifax had always been more at ease on his Yorkshire estates than fulfilling his ministerial duties in London, once saying that he would rather be a master of fox-hounds than prime minister.[84]

In the summer of 1938, while Lord Halifax and Neville Chamberlain grappled with the growing international crisis, Anthony Eden and Winston Churchill were both guests at a ball at Blenheim Palace. The two spent the evening on the terrace discussing the burning international issues of the moment. Oblivious of the floodlit palace, the trees decorated with coloured lights, or the orchestra playing Viennese waltzes in the candlelit ballroom, Churchill and Eden talked on, while between them Viscountess Weymouth looked from one to the other in silence.[85] For Churchill, Eden's resignation as Foreign Secretary in February 1938 had caused the only sleepless night he remembered. Throughout the war as Prime Minister he recalled that he awoke refreshed to tackle whatever was before him. Yet when Eden resigned over the policy of appeasement he claimed it was the one occasion when sleep deserted him. To Churchill, Eden had been 'one strong young figure standing up against long, dismal, drawling, tides of drift and surrender, of wrong measurements and feeble impulses'. Looking at the morning light coming through his window, Churchill saw before him 'in mental gaze the vision of Death'.[86]

For Churchill and for landed society in England the eve of the Second World War was like the end of an era:

> It had died away – the old bluff, hospitable life of the countryside – like a summer's day. . . .It died slowly, like a cloudless afternoon, splendid to the last. Fewer grew the company that followed the hounds over the fields. Memory contracts the years, and I see the pink coats in successive waves through the meadows and up the hill, and always they seem to melt and melt before the unseen enemy, until sometimes it appears as if only the few leaders remain.[87]

5

Dark days of war and peace, 1939–51

The grim forebodings of Winston Churchill were proved correct in 1939, and during the Second World War landed society in England took on a new purpose. Country houses were again transformed into hospitals and schools or were taken over by troops. In villages and parishes throughout England landed society assumed roles of command in the urgent war effort on the home front. Here, the meagre rations of wartime could be supplemented by an unending supply of vegetables, eggs, and dairy produce from home farms and from kitchen gardens. Deprived of most of their servants, who had been called up to join the armed services or who had found employment in war industries in towns, the wives and daughters of landed society now cooked and gardened and worked on the land which had been theirs for centuries.

After six long years of war, the victorious Prime Minister, Winston Churchill, was defeated in the general election of 1945. A Labour government, with a massive majority in Parliament, heralded an era which demanded further adaptations by landed society. For the socialist government's determination to perpetuate both a state-controlled economy and the apparent burial of class differences in wartime was considered by landed society to be a prospect worse even than the war itself. Legislative measures put through by Labour between 1945 and 1951 included the nationalization of coalmines in 1945, very high charges put on the development value of land in 1947, continued high taxation, and, perhaps most significantly, the attempt in 1949 to abolish fox-hunting. Yet, unseen by many, there occurred too the beginnings of the salvation of landed society in England in the twentieth century. In 1947 the government committed itself to state support of agriculture in peacetime, and in 1949 death duties on agricultural land were charged at just over half the normal rate. Slowly, agricultural land increased in value, and went on increasing throughout the decades that were to come. Yet the impact of the war, breaking down the class system and with its high taxation, meant that life in country houses and on country estates was never quite the same again.

The military fervour that had swept through Britain on the outbreak of the First World War was singularly lacking in 1939. With just two decades to recover from the Great War of 1914–18 landed society, along with everyone else, was loth to hurl itself into another conflict. Although centuries-old connections with county regiments had been retained with training at summer camps throughout the 1920s and 1930s, the general mood in September 1939 was one of a lack of preparedness and of stifled resentment at the inevitable disruption of war. Yet those whose families and contemporaries had all lost brothers, fathers, and friends between 1914 and 1918 rejoined their regiments or banded together in new fighting units in 1939.

In 1914 there had been a place to go and a definite mission to pursue, but the early months of the Second World War were a time of waiting and of training for the army, the navy, and the air force. During this time of unknowing, schemes and ideas were formulated and suggested by military heroes of the First World War such as Colonel Laycock, who formed a unit in 1940. Among his officers were Lord Stavordale, the sixth Earl of Ilchester's son and heir, and the seventh Earl Fitzwilliam's heir, Lord Milton. Describing the early days of training with Colonel Laycock's unit, Evelyn Waugh wrote that his fellow officers 'drink a very great deal, play cards for high figures, dine nightly in Glasgow & telephone to their trainers endlessly'.[1] Numerous contacts among high and landed society enabled many aristocrats to join congenial fighting units such as these.

Certain yeomanry regiments attracted their elite. The fifth Marquess of Bath's son and heir Viscount Weymouth joined the Wiltshire Yeomanry, which was then encamped on Wincanton racecourse. The wives of officers used to gather in the town of Wincanton at weekends. Wearing diamond regimental badges on the lapels of their tweed suits and sitting in squadron cliques, they sat 'drinking pink gins in the cold lounges of uncomfortable hotels, warding off thoughts of the future while knitting for the regimental comforts fund and discussed the latest rumour'.[2] In 1940, the town of Warminster was packed with troops after the retreat at Dunkirk. Among them were officers of the Fourth City of London Yeomanry, who prided themselves on having the biggest mess bills in the army. Here they gave a series of parties in Warminster 'at which an exceptionally beautiful camp-following of wives and girl friends always appeared'.[3]

Slowly, the countryside in England became like a huge armed camp. Between high flowering hedges and through winding village streets, military convoys passed in procession. Slow-paced towns were transformed with the arrival of troops, where carts, cattle, and military vehicles became entangled. Planes were lined up on parklands, 'prehistoric monsters, dispersed, tethered by the nose'.[4] After the war country houses requisitioned by the army emerged in a damaged condition. Meanwhile, they became the centre of military activity. Ornamental lakes designed by the great landscape architects of the eighteenth century, and which since then had provided classical outlooks and walks for their owners and guests, were now used as bathing pools for troops. Surrounding parkland became the setting for assault courses and mortar ranges. When Evelyn Waugh's Brideshead was revisited soldiers had been billeted in the house and the magnificent fountain was full of cigarette ends and remains of sandwiches. A painted and pillared room in the grounds had become a signal office, where 'they made absolute hay of it; rather a shame'.[5]

At Brocket Hall in Hertfordshire, the James Paine bridge was disfigured by Canadian troops cutting their names and addresses inches deep into the stonework. Yet, commented James Lees-Milne, a unique observer of country houses during this period, such a memorial was quite in keeping, 'like the German mercenaries' names scrawled in 1530 on the Palazzo Ducale in Urbino'.[6] In Northamptonshire, Deene Park was occupied by six different army units between 1940 and 1945, including a Polish, a Czech, and an Indian regiment. From his portrait above the mantelpiece in the ballroom, the seventh Earl of Cardigan 'looked down at night on rows of sleeping soldiers'.[7] Other country houses, such as Hatfield House in Hertfordshire, became military hospitals. Narrow iron hospital beds lay side by side in the great state rooms against the carved panelling. The characteristic odour of beeswax and wood smoke was replaced with that of disinfectant.[8] At Longleat an American general hospital was built in the hollow of the park, consisting of wooden huts on concrete foundations and a large encampment of Nissen huts.

Soon after war was declared in 1939, children were evacuated to the countryside in anticipation of air raids on large towns. Their physical condition shocked the families who took them in and it was with mutual relief that some of the young evacuees returned home. Some schools and orphanages took up permanent residence in country houses. At the first Earl of Bessborough's Stansted Park in Sussex sixty orphans who played cricket on the lawn in front of the house 'were carefully excluded from the main part of the house itself, which remains as cheerful and comfortable as ever'.[9] In Oxfordshire, Blenheim Palace became the new home of Malvern boys' college. The magnificent tapestries, damask curtains, and mahogany doors were all carefully protected and the floors covered with linoleum. The state rooms and long library were turned into dormitories, the old laundry became a laboratory, and school meals were eaten in the great entrance hall.[10] At the tenth Duke of Devonshire's Chatsworth in Derbyshire the state rooms were turned into a girls' dormitory; the pictures began to suffer from mildew, so unaccustomed were they to human breath. In Wiltshire, the Royal School at Bath for the daughters of army officers was moved to the Marquess of Bath's Longleat, where he now lived in three rooms. In his loneliness, the old marquess welcomed 'this surge of young life which pulsed through the house'.[11]

Some houses made few concessions to the war, such as Renishaw Hall in Derbyshire. Although its lawns became overgrown and its hedges unkempt, inside there were no dust sheets, except in the ballroom. The house was full of 'potted plants & bowls of roses; piles of new & old books & delicious cooking'.[12] Good cooking was a memorable feature of James Lees-Milne's visit to the Hoares at Stourhead in Wiltshire in 1942. Despite rationing, he was given a sumptuous dinner of soup, whiting, pheasant, apple pie, a Rhine wine, and port. While Lady Hoare had to do without a housemaid she still had a cook and a butler, declaring with satisfaction that not far away the Duchess of Somerset had to do all her own cooking.[13]

78

At Badminton in Gloucestershire the old style of dining was rigidly maintained, for it was here that Queen Mary spent the war. Arriving with seventy pieces of luggage and numerous servants, the Duke and Duchess of Beaufort's royal guest stayed with them for five years. Queen Mary spent much of her time at Badminton cutting down ivy; her request to have a cedar tree cut down close to the house was tactfully turned down by her hosts. In stark contrast with the scenes of disorder in country houses everywhere in England, both the interior and exterior of Badminton were meticulously maintained. In the hall, 'the white light radiating from the thin and scintillant layer of frost played on the dry, white Italian plaster work. . .and sparkled on the silver tops of the maces'.[14]

After twenty years of peaceful decline in the countryside, landed society at last had something to do in 1939. Women in particular, confined to their country estates by petrol rationing, launched the initiative for the war effort in villages close by. Houses were opened to a new role of charitable hospitality. Now there were soldiers in the hay loft, 'elderly ladies in odd corners brewing lotions and preparing bandages, hordes of children hurriedly gathered from threatened homes and guests who could stay for years'.[15] After months of waiting and of inactivity, the fall of France in May 1940 transformed the national mood. As the unheard-of prospect of invasion became probable, activity in rural areas took on a new lease of life. Cricket fields, parks, and areas where aircraft could land were scattered with benches, cricket rollers, or any obstacles which came to hand; signposts were taken down so that the enemy would not know where they were. And in the midst of all this urgent activity, the ruling classes in the countryside took up their responsibilities to their local communities by doing what they enjoyed – by organizing people.

Everywhere in England, the wives and daughters of landed families threw themselves into work on committees. They became secretaries and treasurers at preserving centres, dealing with the complicated permits for sugar and fruit. They attended ambulance classes, they became county organizers for the Women's Institute, they ran knitting groups, they arranged hot baths for troops.[16] As well as all this, gardening and farming, rural pursuits which would have been regarded with disdain as occupations for female members of the landed elite before the war, now became the most fashionable things to do in wartime, when tractors exercised 'an irresistible fascination over the women of the English countryside'.[17] This was a return to the land by landed society that would have horrified their landed ancestors; but it was advertised by one of the most renowned of prewar socialites, Lady Diana Cooper.

In 1940 Lady Diana moved to a cottage on the south coast of England near Bognor Regis which belonged to her mother, the Duchess of Rutland. Until then she and her friends had lived surrounded by scenes of 'expensive squalor' in the Dorchester Hotel in London.[18] Now her cottage in Sussex was littered with secondhand textbooks on chickens, cows, goats, and beekeeping. Lady Diana milked cows and made cheese, and found that 'the joy through surprise of the transubstantiation of milk into cheese quite transported me into nature-mysticism'.[19] Wearing dungarees and a straw hat, she appeared in the pages of *Vogue* looking after pigs and tending the roses in the garden, a sublime picture of rural domesticity. She recalled that early in the morning 'dressed as Babushka, I would go, lantern in hand, through the half-light of spring with the birds' first chorus to enliven me from bleary sleep, straightening up under my inevitable yoke'.[20]

Home farms and kitchen gardens provided all that landed society needed for the good life during the war, where away from large towns the possibility of bombing was remote. With all the vegetables, eggs, milk, and cheese they needed, landed society could take full advantage of an ample supply of such simple commodities which were now considered luxuries in wartime. The lengthy weekends of social gatherings which had been the norm for so long were now replaced by guests arriving just for a few nights, and who sometimes stayed at a nearby hotel. Whereas before the war gifts of chocolate and perfume had been received with perfunctory politeness, London guests brought lipstick refills, which were rapturously received in exchange for fresh eggs. Before the war, guests at country houses had been able to chop and change their plans with flippant ease. Now, in order to save petrol, arrangements were made well in advance and arrivals by train organized to coincide with the hosts' shopping trips to the nearest town. On arrival, guests helped with the running of the house, something unheard of before 1939. Then, decisions at weekends had revolved around what to do next; whether to swim or play tennis, or just sit in the sun. Now it was a case of deciding what to do first, whether to pick raspberries, water the lettuces, or take the youngest evacuee to school. Should you shell peas, make hay, or change for the benefit of the boys who were coming round from the local aerodrome?[21]

In London, those who stayed in the capital during the war had to adapt to the nightly prospect of air raids, and guests for dinner needed to be accommodated afterwards. Guests arrived early, 'hoping to cadge a bath, before dinner and the blitz', doing away with 'all that tiresome, superficial entertaining of semi-friends and near bores'. To be invited in for a bath rather than a drink was the new social gesture, 'soap and water being a far more pleasing offer than any amount of gin and lime, soda and scotch'.[22] During the blitz the dash and daring of the 1920s and 1930s in London became a macabre feast of entertainment. Almost recklessly, the social whirl in the capital moved from restaurant to nightclub to dinner party to bar. Despite the appearance of gaping ruins and piles of rubble the following morning, of choking dust, glass, and rescue squads, the defiant members of landed society who spent time in the metropolis went on being 'too, too normal'.[23] With true English phlegm, they demanded 'Where shall we eat? What's left?' while in 1941, when the blitz raged over London, there occurred the traditional start of the débutante season, Queen Charlotte's Ball at the Grosvenor House Hotel.[24]

This activity in London and in the countryside during the war was but a shortlived outburst of energy by landed society, a desperate and patriotic attempt to embrace all that their position could offer, which was so appropriately fulfilled in wartime. When victory was assured, the pace slowed and they started to lose direction. For the years immediately after the war were to bring greater changes than could ever have been imagined. A look at the largest estates in England owned by members of the peerage illustrates the blows and disruption to patterns of inheritance brought about by the war. Some peers had succeeded fathers and grandfathers as a result of a death in the First World War, when death duties on officers' estates had to be paid. By the time of the Second World War, officers joined the other ranks in being made exempt from death duties.

* * *

Among the large landowners in England, the ninth Duke of Northumberland was killed in 1940 at the age of 28, having succeeded to the dukedom when he was 18. The owner of Alnwick

Castle in Northumberland, Syon House near London, and Albury Park in Surrey, he had ceased to live at Alnwick Castle in 1939 because of the pressures of taxation, and moved to a house close by. But when the duke's flag with the blue lion rampant was flown at half-mast on the keep at Alnwick Castle the people of the town knew that the young duke had been killed, and the news spread over the town and countryside.[25] The heir to the dukedom was his younger brother, Lord Hugh Percy.

In August 1944 the seventh Marquess of Lansdowne was killed in action in Italy, eleven days after his younger brother, Lord Edward Fitzmaurice. The titles and estate at Bowood were then inherited by a cousin. In Worcestershire the tenth Earl of Coventry of Croome Court was killed in action in May 1940 and his son Viscount Deerhurst succeeded him. In neighbouring Warwickshire the ninth Earl of Aylesford, whose father had been killed in the Battle of the Aisne in September 1914, was killed at the age of 22 in May 1940. The Packington estate was then inherited by an uncle. So too when the sixth Duke of Wellington was killed in action in 1943 an uncle succeeded him.

The twentieth Earl of Suffolk of Charlton Park in Wiltshire, whose father, the nineteenth earl, had been killed in Mesopotamia in 1917, died on active service in May 1941. His obituary was somewhat unusual; he had a first-class degree in science, and a friend recalled an erudite Sorbonne professor being 'treated in rapid, fluent French' to a dissertation on pharmacology by him. The earl then entertained the company to 'a masterly and dramatic rendering of a dialogue between a Cockney using rhyming slang and a Chicago gangster conversing in his local idiom'.[26]

The third Baron Alington, whose elder brother had died at home on the Crichel estate in Dorset on armistice day in 1918, died in Cairo in 1940, when the title became extinct. Lord Alington seemed 'in appearance and character. . .to belong to an earlier age; to the eighteenth rather than the twentieth century'.[27] Two brothers, the second and the third Barons Shuttleworth, whose father had died in the First World War in 1917, died within two years of each other during the Second World War; the second Baron Shuttleworth in the Battle of Britain in 1940 and his brother the third Baron Shuttleworth in North Africa in 1942. The title and estate in Lancashire were inherited by a cousin, himself wounded in Libya.

Other peers who died in the Second World War included the sixteenth Baron Arundell of Wardour of Wardour Castle in Wiltshire, who was wounded and taken prisoner at Dunkirk. A Count of the Holy Roman Empire, this title had been conferred on Lord Arundell's ancestor in 1595 for services in the imperial army in Hungary, when he had taken the standard of the Turks with his own hand. In 1940 the barony, created in 1605, became extinct. In 1943 the sixth Baron Brabourne died at the age of 21, when an uncle inherited the estate in Kent. In the same year the owner of the Audley End estate in Essex, the eighth Baron Braybrooke, died and was succeeded by a cousin.

Among the heirs to estates who died in the Second World War was Viscount Lewisham, only son of the seventh Earl of Dartmouth of Patshull House near Wolverhampton, who was killed in action in Egypt in 1942. In the same year the seventh Earl Bathurst's son and heir Lord Apsley, of the Royal Gloucestershire Hussars, was killed in an aeroplane accident in the Middle East. He had served in Egypt and Palestine during the First World War and between the wars had been an enthusiastic airman, once making seven forced landings on a flight back from a shooting party in Poland.[28] At the time of his death Lord Apsley was the Member of Parliament for Central Bristol and the seat was taken over by his widow. When Lord Bathurst died in 1943 his young grandson, the son of the late Lord Apsley, inherited the Cirencester estate.

The Redesdale estate in Gloucestershire, centred on Batsford Park, was much diminished by the time of the death of the only son of the second Baron Redesdale, the Hon. Thomas Mitford, who died of wounds in Burma in April 1945. The Hon. Thomas Mitford's father had become second Baron Redesdale in 1915 as a result of the death of his elder brother in the First World War. As the Hon. Thomas Mitford had six sisters, the barony was eventually inherited by an uncle.

Living not far from the Mitfords' old home in Gloucestershire was the brother and unexpected heir of the fifth Earl Fortescue whose nephew, Viscount Ebrington, heir to estates in Devon, was killed in action at El Alamein in 1942. In Cornwall, the eighth Viscount Falmouth's Tregothnan estate was deprived of its heir when the Hon. Evelyn Boscawen was killed in action in Flanders in 1940. There were however three more brothers: the Hon. George Boscawen who became the new heir and who was himself wounded in the war, the Hon. Henry Boscawen who served at the end of the war, and the Hon. Robert Boscawen, who was wounded. This record of military service by the Boscawen brothers followed in the tradition of their father's brothers, both killed in the First World War.

Moving from Cornwall to Shropshire, the Hamilton-Russell family was dealt many blows. The eldest son and heir to the ninth Viscount Boyne, the Hon. Gustavus Hamilton-Russell, was a Lieutenant-General in the Grenadier Guards, 'a very gentle, perfect knight'[29] and killed in action in June 1940. His son, born in 1931, succeeded to the viscountcy after the death of his grandfather in 1942. The following year two uncles of the young Lord Boyne were both killed on active service. Before the war his sister and then his mother had died. Thus Lord Boyne, having lost his sister, his mother, his father, his grandfather, and two uncles within six years of each other was left to face life as a landed aristocrat after the Second World War in a tragically beleaguered state.

At Powis Castle Viscount Clive, the son of the fourth Earl of Powis, was killed in 1943. His elder brother had died during the First World War in 1916 and the earldom and estates at Powis were later inherited by a cousin. For Viscount Clive, who had enlisted into the ranks of the Royal Air Force and who was well over the age for a fighter pilot, his advance in the Royal Air Force had given him particular satisfaction, for he knew that a fighter pilot depended for success on his own merits, where 'mere social position counted for nothing'.[30]

On the other side of the country in Suffolk, the second Earl of Iveagh's heir, Viscount Elveden, was killed in 1945, leaving a young son and heir to the Guinness fortune. A service in memory of Viscount Elveden and his servant, John Stiles, who died with him, was held in the parish church at Elveden, near the family home.[31]

Perhaps one of the most renowned of war deaths among landed society during the Second World War was that of the Marquess of Hartington in 1944. Only a few months before he had married Kathleen Kennedy, the daughter of the former American Ambassador to the Court of St James. The registry office wedding had been held after strong reservations about the union by both families on religious grounds; a Protestant Cavendish was marrying a Roman Catholic Kennedy. A few months after the wedding, the marquess was killed. 'Leading the infantry forward, ahead of the tanks, completely calm and casual, carrying his cap and saying rather languidly, "Come on, you fellows, buck up!" death came to him instantly.'[32] Early in 1944 the Marquess of Hartington had fought a by-election at the Cavendish family seat in Derbyshire, which he had lost. This was regarded at the time as a defeat of great significance, and foreshadowed the far-reaching changes which the end of the war would bring.

* * *

For centuries the West Derbyshire constituency had been dominated by the Dukes of Devonshire at Chatsworth. Only once, between 1918 and 1923, had it been out of the family's hands. Its Member of Parliament since 1938 was Henry Hunloke, a brother-in-law of the ninth Duke of Devonshire. When in 1943 Hunloke, who was on active service, resigned, the tenth duke decided that it was time for his son, the Marquess of Hartington, to take over. The speed with which Hartington was adopted as a candidate generated much adverse comment in Westminster. Sir Richard Acland, a radical Devon landowner who was leader of the Common Wealth group, said that the Derbyshire constituents were being treated as if they were 'the goods and chattels of the Hartington family'.[33] But the council of the West Derbyshire Unionist League, chaired by the Duke of Devonshire, duly adopted his son as candidate. As the duke had arranged for his son to obtain leave from his reserve regiment for the election campaign, he was at hand to address the meeting there and then.

In order to prevent party political campaigns, by-elections were held during the war under an electoral truce. The Marquess of Hartington supported Churchill and the government and his opponent Charles White stood as an Independent. During the campaign the *Daily Mirror* declared that a way of life 'thought to have passed for ever' was flaunting 'its last challenge to democracy'. Eton and the Guards had given the Marquess 'a charm which can be switched on and off like an electric light, but sheer necessity [kept] his speeches short'.[34] Addressing a small gathering in the town of Bakewell soon afterwards, the Duchess of Devonshire defended her son's reported remark that he thought coalmines had already been nationalized. She claimed that the marquess had said that as the nationalization of coal had not been a success 'he did not see that it would be any more successful to nationalise the mines'. After smilingly removing a photograph of her son's opponent which someone had put on the back of her car, the duchess drove away with a cheery wave.[35]

In view of Hartington's appearances in uniform and his support of Churchill, his defeat at the by-election surprised the most cynical of observers. Indeed, the result caused 'a pall of the blackest gloom' to fall on Winston Churchill, who had earlier written a letter to the marquess praising the political record of the Cavendish family.[36] The Prime Minister said that at a time when national unity was essential and when the question of annihilating great states had to be faced, 'it began to look as if democracy had not the persistence necessary to go through with it, however well it might have shown its capacity for defence'.[37]

When in 1945 the Labour Party came to power with a landslide victory, this was for Churchill an even heavier blow to bear than any by-election defeat in wartime. He now took his seat in a transformed House of Commons where, such were their numbers, Labour members spilled over to the Opposition benches and gleefully heckled the Conservative leaders.[38] Many of Churchill's colleagues had lost their seats in Parliament in the general election, but rural constituencies on the whole remained Conservative.[39] Yet this first general election in ten years saw an even smaller number of Members of Parliament from landed aristocratic families. In 1935 there had been in the House of Commons just fourteen titled heirs to English estates. In 1945 there were only two titled heirs to estates in England out of some 600 Members of Parliament. They were Viscount Hinchingbrooke, who was the member for South Dorset and heir to the ninth Earl of Sandwich, and Lord Willoughby de Eresby, member for Rutland and heir to the second Earl of Ancaster of Grimsthorpe Castle in Lincolnshire. Even in 1952, by which time the Labour landslide had been countered by a return to power by the Conservatives, there were just six sons of English landed peers in the House of Commons.

In the countryside, country houses now seemed desolate and abandoned as troops departed, schoolchildren left, and hospital beds were moved out. Wartime conditions meant that many houses still inhabited by their owners contained rooms which had for years been swathed in dust sheets and where shutters had been drawn. As their owners adapted to peacetime, these temporary measures gradually became permanent. Taxation in wartime at 50 per cent, coupled with the difficulty of finding domestic staff and then paying their wages, were immense problems which for the majority of families could not be overcome. Having contributed to the war effort in villages and parishes close to their homes, landed society now found itself, quite literally, out in the cold.

* * *

Historic country houses could only function efficiently with the help of a large staff. Priceless pictures, glass, and china needed to be looked after with care while constant repairs to the interior and exterior of the house were always necessary. Fires had to be lit, furniture dusted, windows cleaned, and floors polished. Silver needed to be cleaned, meals cooked, and diners waited upon. These innumerable and constantly repeated tasks, carried out by a community of loyal servants under the supervision of butlers and housekeepers, no longer held their attractions after a war when class differences in England had been temporarily submerged. During the depressed years between the wars, domestic service had provided much-needed jobs, but full employment during the war had offered a better-paid and more independent alternative to the men and women who had for years worked in isolated country houses.

Their owners adapted to these changes, and moved the best paintings and the best carpets into a few rooms where the most valuable china and silver were still kept defiantly on display. In supervising the reorganization of pictures and furniture after years of inhabitation by soldiers or schoolchildren, owners started to scrutinize closely what they actually possessed. This process, as well as the need for finance, helped to nurture the idea of opening their houses to the public, and many families now turned to the National Trust, under the scheme initiated by the Marquess of Lothian before the war. The Trust's architectural adviser, James Lees-Milne, made visits to hopeful owners of country houses all over England during the late 1940s, observing adaptation to postwar conditions at first hand.

At Holkham Hall in Norfolk, a large Palladian house which looked out on views of lakes, woods, statues, and fountains landscaped by Capability Brown, Lady Leicester had had a nervous breakdown brought about by the anxiety of keeping up the house without servants. At Haigh Hall in Yorkshire, approached through a twisting road steeped in laurels and rhododendrons, there were hardly any servants at all. Lees-Milne and his host had to wait on each other at dinner. Surrounded by stacked pictures and furniture and 'utter muddle' the two talked until midnight over a rare rum, which was 200 years old.[40]

Wines, port, and rum were sometimes the last vestiges of grandeur which could be enjoyed by the beleaguered inhabitants of country houses in postwar England, consumed as they occasionally were after a meal of rabbit pie. At his house in Huntingdon, Viscount Hinchingbrooke tried to keep warm by a small fire while his wife scrubbed the kitchen floor. The couple were picnicking in the house, which was still full of hospital beds. At Gunby Hall in Lincolnshire, the 75-year-old Lady Montgomery-Massingberd polished the stairs every morning. The two remaining indoor servants were the butler and his wife. At dinner in the evening the butler, dressed in white tie and tails, served Lees-Milne and his host. At Uppark in West Sussex, Lady Meade-Fetherstonhaugh served cold coffee in the sitting room from a pot held over a log fire, while lunch and tea were served in the basement.

Living in large and draughty houses, landed society could hardly afford the expensive prospect of keeping warm let alone of entertaining large numbers of guests. The general election victory by the Labour Party in 1945, brought to power by an electorate determined to maintain the sudden equality and full employment of the war economy, was greeted by people such as the Leicesters, the Hinchingbrookes, the Meade-Fetherstonhaughs, and the Montgomery-Massingberds with a long intake of breath and a look of wide-eyed horror. Privations had been suffered almost gladly when the fate of the nation had been at stake but now the policies of a people's war were to be replaced by a people's peace. It was this, as far as landed society was concerned, which was almost harder to bear.

During the election campaign of 1945 both political parties offered the electors 'Food, Work and Homes', both offered a comprehensive system of national insurance, a national health service, and the development of provisions for education. Both recognized that industry should be more efficient. But the Labour Party contended that the Conservative Party could not be trusted.[41] The Conservatives had effectively been in power throughout the depressed interwar period, except in 1924 and 1929–31, when Labour had held office but not power. Remembering those depressed years, the voters returned the socialists, with their commitment to continued state control. And it was with undisguised glee that Emanuel Shinwell, the Glaswegian Minister for Fuel and Power, ordered the continued excavation of the parkland in front of the largest country house in England, Wentworth Woodhouse in Yorkshire, for opencast coalmining.

In 1947 an energy crisis coincided with the coldest winter for decades. Much hated attention was turned on the Minister for Fuel and Power, who, when the country was buried under snow and ice, ordered power cuts. After the enforced inconveniences of wartime, which had been a time of strain and frustration, of scarcities, restrictions, meagre rations, and of a nightly blackout, few welcomed the dark days of peace endured that winter – especially those in large and cold country houses. The decision therefore to dig up the parkland in front of Wentworth Woodhouse and other country houses for coal was seen as an unprecedented political attack on the landed interest.

Such was the size of Wentworth Woodhouse that when Lord Fitzwilliam's great-grandfather had lived in the great state rooms in his declining years his eight sons and six daughters could entertain their own house parties several at a time.[42] But since 1943 Lord Fitzwilliam had watched patiently his 'famed beeches, stud farm, fish ponds, woodlands, paddocks and avenues turned to black gaping wounds. . . .Peace, he hoped vaguely, might come in time to save his lawns and gardens.'[43] By 1947 every tree and shrub had been uprooted right up to the wall of the Vanbrugh front, which overlooked a scene far worse than 'the French battlefields after D-Day'.[44] Emanuel Shinwell had visited the sites in April 1946, claiming that his heart was heavy at the sight of so much destruction.[45] But as factories were running short of coal, the railways only had a few days' supplies, and more coal was needed for export, there was apparently no alternative.

Other parks in front of country houses requisitioned for coalmining included that at Winstanley Hall near Wigan. Here surface mining had been taken up to the front door and the park was 'the most appalling mess, a wilderness of dead earth in unsightly piles'. All the trees had been removed and the scenes had broken Lord Crawford's heart, who could talk of nothing else.[46] There was also a threat of opencast mining at the third Baron Newton's former home of Lyme Park near Stockport which had been taken over by the National Trust. The Minister of Town and Country Planning had agreed that it should be held in perpetuity for the benefit of the nation, a phrase given a somewhat different interpretation by Shinwell, and a vigorous protest followed.[47] On the small estate of Erdigg in Wales coal had been a valuable source of income since the eighteenth century. In 1947 officials from the Coal Board approached the owner, Simon Yorke, to warn him of their intention to undertake workings and that there was no exemption for buildings of historic interest. Yorke refused to have any dealings with the Coal Board and coal was worked directly beneath the house. Eventually the roof leads, instead of sloping to direct rainwater away to the gutters and downpipes, funnelled water towards the centre of the building, where it poured into the state rooms.[48]

Many landowners who had coal beneath their land lost an important source of income with the nationalization of coal mines in 1945, despite compensation. Families such as these included the Devonshires, the Northumberlands, the Butes, the Lonsdales, the Londonderrys, and the Durhams. The third Earl of Dudley in the Black Country was another coalowner; at his park at Himley Hall dust and dirt lay perpetually on the trees and shrubs. An industrial entrepreneur who had reconstructed his father's coalmines and steel furnaces into greater productivity, Lord Dudley anticipated the nationalization of all minerals after the nationalization of coalmines. He therefore sold the bulk of the Himley estate in 1947 and moved to Buckinghamshire. Himley Hall then became the National Coal Board's headquarters.[49]

While coalmines were nationalized after the war, land itself was not. Yet the purpose of the 1947 Town and Country Planning Act was to cream off the development value of land for the state. The 1947 Act was based on three wartime reports. The Barlow report of January 1940 had investigated the strategic dangers of the concentration of industries in large conglomerates, the Scott report looked at the impact of the dispersal of new construction on the countryside, and the Uthwatt report dealt with compensation. But, after the war, it was never stated what planning was for. Planning for planning's sake thus became 'the highway to confusion and purposelessness'.[50] With the 1947 Act, there was no inducement for landowners to raise money by selling outlying portions of their estates for development. If permission to develop land was refused, then except in a limited range of cases the landowner would not receive any compensation. But if permission was granted to build on land, then any resulting increase in its value would be subject to a 100 per cent development charge. While land was not actually in public ownership, it was now subject to stricter control by the state.

The administration of the 1947 Town and Country Planning Act was accompanied by tortuous and complicated valuation procedures, reminiscent of Lloyd George's Finance Act of 1910. Yet Lloyd George's Act was straightforward and comprehensible compared with the one in 1947. Since the beginning of the century the control of land had passed from 'an atmosphere of serenity to a state of such intricacy and confusion as had never before faced the professions whose vocation it was to advise upon, deal with and manage it'.[51] The complicated requirements of the Act had largely bypassed landowners, many of whom were unaware of the compensation which they could claim from a £300 million fund. Although the government was only prepared to admit payments where hardship could be shown by the claimant, claims had to be made with every possible development in mind.

In 1949, when the Luttrell family at Dunster Castle in Somerset sold land which had been theirs for 600 years, Geoffrey Luttrell blamed crippling taxation, death duties, and 'the confiscatory and hampering provisions of the Town and Country Planning Act'.[52] Dunster Castle was near Minehead on Somerset's northern coast. Luttrell's grandfather had financed a railway connecting Minehead with the nearby town of Watchet and had also carried out development in Minehead itself, where large sums had been spent by the family since then on the upkeep and maintenance of the harbour. It was hoped that as Minehead developed as a seaside resort land could be sold to recoup much of the family's expenditure. The passing of the Town and Country Planning Act put an end to this.

In the flurry of land sales after the First World War, outlying portions of estates had been sold in order to invest in stocks and securities. After the Second World War, the principal cause of the break-up of estates was the payment of death duties. When the sixth Earl of Harewood died in 1947, his estate was valued at £549,000, on which an interim duty of £182,000 was paid. When a valuation in 1951 of £1.5 million required a duty of £800,000, his heir partially met this by selling just over half of his 22,000-acre estate in Yorkshire. The seventh earl then had to resort to the sale of some of the contents of Harewood House. Just as the sale was going through at Christie's in London, the Chancellor of the Exchequer, Hugh

Dalton, happened to be moving a new clause to be included in the Finance Bill which extended the exemption from estate duty on land given to the National Trust or other public bodies to just the sort of treasures which Lord Harewood was selling.[53]

Land disposed of for death duties was sold with great reluctance as owners saw the vast sums which it yielded immediately handed over to the Exchequer. Yet in 1950, when the total revenue from all taxation was £2,436 million, death duties on agricultural estates contributed £3.3 million, a tiny fraction of the total.[54] In the countryside, these obligatory land sales could cut an estate in half, bringing about far-reaching changes in the pattern of landownership and the demise of numerous landed families. Yet death duties on agricultural land, through pressure from the Central Landowners' Association, had been given a 45 per cent abatement in 1949. Attracting half the normal liability at death, agricultural land slowly came to be viewed as a shrewd investment, and so arrived the new breed of 'death bed purchasers'. Landowners whose capital had long been tied up in land saw the value of farmland increase from an average of £27 an acre in 1938 to £80 an acre in 1950. But this meant that, despite the 45 per cent abatement, the higher rates of estate duty on increasingly valuable land demanded more revenue at death than ever before.

For those landowners who did not have to pay death duties, taxation itself had an equally devastating impact after the war. The Gowers report of 1950, a Treasury report on houses of outstanding historic and architectural interest, stated that because of high taxation no individual, however much his gross income or whatever its source, would have more than £5,000 a year to spend. Many of the large country houses needed very much more than £5,000 a year just to preserve them and their contents from deterioration. But a rent roll of £140,000 a year was reduced to £3,500 a year by income tax, tithe, surtax, and the expense of maintaining the agricultural estate from which it came. Out of this £3,500 the owner might have to maintain two historic houses as well as himself and his family.[55] Moreover, despite the increased value of agricultural land, rents remained stagnant. This had been reinforced by another piece of legislation which affected landowners everywhere, the 1947 Agriculture Act. Rents were usually revised when farms were relet. With security of tenure, tenants could now negotiate rent increases secure against any threats of dislodgement.

The Agriculture Act of 1947 was in many respects a continuation of the food campaign of the war. Such was its success, the campaign had achieved after only eight months what had taken four years during the First World War. Mechanization was the crucial factor behind this and it was this new profitable efficiency which transformed the agricultural landscape of England. Before 1939, farms had fallen buildings where rubble had become overgrown and where the stock of several hundred acres could be some milking cows and a few hens. The food campaign of 1939–45 began to reverse this decline. County war agricultural executive committees were set up and, as in the First World War, efficiency in planning at the local level produced a highly successful farming industry in Britain – by the end of the war it was the most mechanized in the world.[56] After the slowness of the change from horse power to tractors on farms between the wars, tractors could be seen working in fields throughout England. The achievement of six years of war would probably have taken decades in times of peace.

Areas of England which had never even nurtured arable farming, such as swamp and marshland in Cumberland and Cheshire, bracken land in Devon, or acres of forest in Wiltshire, were converted to corn during the war. In East Anglia drainage necessary to cultivate thousands of acres of fenland which had never been ploughed before revealed the remains of a primitive forest.[57] The ploughing campaign had changed the green of England's fields to a landscape chequerboarded with crops. But after 1945, still remembering the 'Great Betrayal' of 1921 when the government had repealed without warning guaranteed prices, farmers were sceptical of continued government support in peacetime. For them, the great advances in farming during the war were seen as temporary measures. They assumed that yet again they would have to fend for themselves. The 1947 Agriculture Act swept away all such fears for here indeed was, according to the Labour Minister for Agriculture, Tom Williams, 'an agricultural charter and a farmers' Bible, which should dispose of any lingering doubt as to our attitude towards agriculture'.[58]

In 1945, an income tax rebate had been given on capital investment in agricultural improvements. This rebate was granted on one-tenth of the cost of the improvement every year for ten years immediately following the execution of the work. This was a crucial concession to landowners and encouraged them to hold on to their

93

estates. Then four years later in 1949 landowners were offered substantial government grants for improvements to water supplies and land drainage, the building of farm cottages, and the rehabilitation of hill farms. Although the grants and concessions were made as part of general government policy to help agriculture, they also helped landed estates, which, with their low rents and high costs, were becoming almost entirely uneconomic.[59]

One of the first results of the numerous legislative changes brought about by the postwar Labour government was a dramatic rise in membership of the Central Landowners' Association. Before the war, the association had been instrumental in securing the exclusion of agricultural property from the general increase in death duties in 1925. Just before the 1945 election the Central Landowners' Association, which changed its name to the Country Landowners' Association in 1949, had secured the concession whereby the full costs of improvements to farmland could be set against taxation in ten equal annual instalments. It was to this association that all landowners turned after the war, its membership increasing from 10,000 in 1945 to 25,000 in 1949. By June of that year the quarterly magazine of the association noted that the role of the landowner had now changed. He had become 'a professional man with a highly complicated job to learn and perform, and has ceased to be, if he ever was, an amateur, an absentee rentier or a spare time agriculturist'.[60]

Landowners who formerly had little interest in the workings of their estate now had an urgent need to keep up with the technological advances of the wartime food campaign, not to mention the changes in their status brought about by so much legislation. In 1946 the centenary celebrations at the Royal Agricultural College in Cirencester were 'symbolic of the strengthened national will to place agriculture on a firm and lasting basis, a basis that the war has taught us must be founded on an ever increasing co-operation between science and practice'.[61]

At the Royal Agricultural College in Cirencester, short courses on farming were organized by the Country Landowners' Association. Above a stifled hum of conversation landowners listened to lectures and were taken on farm walks, where they were asked to inspect crops, livestock, farm buildings, and farm machinery. Just as many of the wives of landowners had become conversant with farming during the war, landowners who returned from the war now took up their turn. After a day of touring, hospitality back at the college was 'princely, from the gargantuan inaugural dinner to the last departing breakfast'.[62] At the course in June 1949 an alfresco banquet on white tablecloths was held in the heart of the Wiltshire Downs. During his speech at the end of the course the president of the Country Landowners' Association observed that such a gathering of sixty landowners was in itself sufficient justification for the association's existence. The course in June 1949 was much more than a conference. The president's address raised it 'almost to the level of a crusade'.[63]

At this meeting of sixty landowners in June 1949 discussions must have taken place of another crusade which, far more than any legislation to do with development values and tenant rights, was aimed at the heart of landed society in England. This was the attempt in Parliament to abolish fox-hunting. It excited the wrath of landed society everywhere, being held up by them as a glorious example of the iniquities of socialism. Fox-hunting had revived after the war, despite the scarcity of fodder for horses, small packs of hounds, and inexperienced hunters. After 1945 there was no longer the inconvenience of the blackout, but full headlights on cars on the return home and stable lights blazing forth when one got there. None the less it was thought that the prewar days of pomp and ceremony, of pink coats, top hats, buttonholes, second horses, luxurious cars, and horse boxes were over. In late 1947 new pink coats required eighteen clothing coupons, 'and the cost may be anything – assuming you can get one at all. . .while hunting silks and bowlers seem to be wholly unobtainable'.[64]

In August 1947 a private parliamentary Bill had been circulated which planned to prohibit fox-hunting and hare-coursing, for which its backers claimed the support of 380 Members of Parliament. It was not until February 1949 that two private members' Bills were balloted for debate in the House of Commons. The first Bill related to hunting and coursing of all animals other than foxes and was ostensibly put forward as a conservation measure. If this Bill went through, then it would be a logical extension to have a second Bill, prohibiting fox-hunting, made law. The prospect of losing votes in rural constituencies where Labour support was anyway weak, and the damage that such bans would do to agriculture, brought about a defeat of the first Bill by a majority of 113. The second Bill was then withdrawn. But the debate brought an impressive array of ministers to the front bench and 'a refreshing glimpse of rural faces to the galleries, while expert evidence on the habits of wild creatures breathed a tang of country air into the debate'.[65] The attitude of landed society to the attempt to ban fox-hunting was summed up in *The Field* which asked: 'what would happen to dog, and horse, and even poultry-breeding without the Hunt? The Hunt balls, the splendid women, the whole fabric of society, the farmers, the charities that benefited'[66] and, as was often mentioned, employment for saddlers.

Fox-hunting, symbolic of the presence of a leisured gentry in the countryside, was saved from threatened abolition, but a great alteration in the countryside after the war was the fate of country houses. Apart from sale, mansions in the country were faced with several alternatives. They could be maintained on a reduced scale. They could be opened to the public. They could be handed over to the National Trust. Or they could be demolished.

The *Architects' Journal* of January 1951 listed examples of houses which were derelict or awaiting demolition. In Wiltshire Draycott House was occupied by the army and badly damaged inside; one of the largest mansions in Suffolk, Redgrave Hall, had been demolished; Wealds Hall in Essex, dating from 1540, was badly damaged during military occupation; Fawsley House in Nottinghamshire was occupied by troops and suffered from pillage by organized thieves soon afterwards. Rufford Abbey in Nottinghamshire awaited demolition; Kiplin Hall in Yorkshire, designed by Inigo Jones for the first Lord Baltimore, was damaged during the war and its future was uncertain. Blatherwyck in Suffolk, owned by the same family since the thirteenth century was destroyed while Rushbrooke Hall in Suffolk awaited its fate.[67]

In Bedfordshire part of Woburn Abbey was demolished. The money needed to restore the damage done by dry rot was just not there. Its altered state was viewed by its new heir, the thirteenth Duke of Bedford, when he revisited his family home. The whole of the east front had been knocked down, together with at least one-third of the north and south wings. The buildings which had housed the indoor riding school and the tennis court had disappeared. Piles of rubble lay everywhere and the courtyard in the centre of the house was full of Nissen huts. The duke recalled:

As the long drive from the lodge gates curved round the last wooded hillock I gasped. The Abbey looked as if a bomb had fallen on it. . . .There were one or two workmen around, but otherwise the place was deserted. A troop of Alsatian dogs, chained to long wires, kept watch at most of the gates, and you could hear them barking and their chains rattling like some eerie scene out of *The Hound of the Baskervilles*.[68]

6

Life after death duties, 1951–63

The return of Winston Churchill as Prime Minister in 1951 coincided with the beginning of a new era of stability and prosperity for landed society in England. His unexpected defeat in the 1945 election after leading the country to victory during the Second World War, was now, six years later, resoundingly reversed. The grand old man of politics, a world statesman now nearing his 80s, Churchill seemed to represent a return to the old school of politics, when Britain had held a commanding position in the world. He set to work by running his Cabinet as if it were still wartime, merging departments and cutting unnecessary bureaucracy, in sharp contrast with the extensive controls of the previous Labour governments. After more than a decade of wartime and socialist restrictions, his rallying cry was to 'Set the People Free'.

A significant manifestation of the postwar return to prewar imperialism occurred soon after Churchill's return as Prime Minister, with the coronation of the young Queen Elizabeth in 1953. Large crowds thronged the London streets and throughout Britain 25 million television viewers watched the lengthy coronation ceremony. It was attended at Westminster Abbey by practically every peer and peeress in the land, who for a few hours were simultaneously on public view. Not long afterwards Evelyn Waugh observed that the revival of the identity of the aristocracy and of the English country house would have been thought impossible during wartime.[1] Shooting parties at country houses were now once more popular and prestigious, the Season made its return, with glittering dances for débutantes in London and the counties. Indeed, the period between the early 1950s and the early 1960s seemed to contain all the elements of a post-Edwardian revival, a return to 'The ice of her Ladyship's manners, The ice of his Lordship's champagne'.[2]

The financial recovery of landed society in the 1950s was partly founded on the increased value of land, which had become an attractive form of investment thanks to the fiscal support given to landowners by the postwar socialist government. As the economy improved, more and more people sought to purchase farms and country estates, whether for sport or for investment. By selling a farm or a few cottages, now in great demand, landowners could supplement their incomes quickly and painlessly.[3] There was also a boom on the Stock Exchange. Landowners began to receive higher returns from their investments in the City than they had for decades. For an estate to have survived the 1920s and 1930s these sources of income had been vital. Well-managed investment portfolios, combined with careful farm and estate management, as well as urban property, financed the revival of country living on landed estates in England. At the same time, 200 country houses were demolished.

Only a country with so rich an architectural heritage could, without public outcry, destroy some of its finest country houses with such speed. Representing an unmanageable way of life, such houses were seen as blots on the landscape, liabilities which simply could not be maintained and unwanted by institutions and schools which already had a wealth of choice before them. As a grim counterpart, then, to the story of postwar revival and survival of the landed classes, the destruction of large country residences throughout England in the 1950s must not be forgotten. Many houses had been abandoned for years before their eventual destruction and were beyond repair. Others were destroyed by fire, but, for a large number, the decision to have them razed to the ground was taken reluctantly by owners who could envisage no alternative.

At the same time, country houses in England opened to the public for the first time after the war became a source of intense fascination for the newly mobile car-owning public. Owners expressed astonishment at the interest of so many people in their homes. For centuries their families had lived in houses hidden by park walls and isolated from inquisitive onlookers. Now they had become big business, as thousands of visitors gazed with unenvying awe at the splendour of treasures acquired over the centuries. Yet for land-owners who died in the 1950s, some of these treasures had to be sold to pay the death duties still demanded from them by the Exchequer. Indeed, when Harold Macmillan was Chancellor of the Exchequer, he had to look on with detached unease as his nephew, the young eleventh Duke of Devonshire, continued to wrestle with death duties brought about by the untimely death of the tenth duke. Land too, as always, was sold off to pay the sums demanded by the government.

Throughout the 1950s the owners of landed estates continued policies of efficient farm management. Thanks to the support given by the 1947 Agriculture Act it was now possible to make money out of farming. Courses in farming and estate management became fashionable. The Royal Agricultural College at Cirencester now joined Eton, Oxford, and Sandhurst on the list of required institutions attended by the landed elite. Here, Professor Bobby Boutflour, who claimed that the college had a former student in every parish in England, taught landowners how to make dairy farming profitable. During the decades of depression in the 1920s and 1930s it had sometimes been impossible to find tenants to take over farms. With the 1948 Agricultural Holdings Act it was very difficult for landlords to give their tenants valid notices to quit. Because of the 1948 restrictions, landowners took land in hand whenever they could and took advantage of the support given to farming.

The lack of domestic servants after the war meant that the traditional country house with its large staff hurrying to perform tasks from early morning until late at night was now a thing of the past, empty and quiet, denuded of such activity. Without its large domestic community, it had become not so much a country house as a house in the country. Some owners adapted to living in a small section of the big house or else moved to a smaller house in the grounds. As many of the stables were magnificent buildings in themselves, even these were sometimes adapted and converted into sumptuously decorated residences.

The disappearance of housemaids and servants, of footmen and butlers who had been an indispensable feature of the country house before the war allowed landed society for the first time to relax, to live like everyone else. Deprived of the burdens of deference, the landed classes discovered that they could live their daily lives in their houses with greater social, if not physical ease. Conversations at meal times no longer had to be monitored to avoid listening maids. Entertaining at weekends could be undertaken with temporary help from the village. The use of modern equipment in the kitchen and throughout the house cut down the need for the numerous pairs of hands necessary to ensure the smooth-running of a house before the war. All that was needed to live comfortably was a cook, someone to clean, and perhaps a butler.

For those families who were able to maintain their houses in the country, the financial recovery in the 1950s seemed to be complemented by the political revival of the old aristocracy. The three successive Conservative governments which held power from 1951 to 1964 and which increased their majority at each election were all led by prime ministers closely associated with landed society. In 1955 Winston Churchill, whose second cousin the tenth Duke of Marlborough resided at Blenheim Palace, handed over the premiership to Sir Anthony Eden who was from an old landowning family in County Durham. Two years later Eden was succeeded as premier by Harold Macmillan, who was married to the daughter of the ninth Duke of Devonshire. Soon after the Suez crisis in 1956, when British and French forces had invaded Egypt to recover the recently nationalized Suez canal, Macmillan managed to resurrect the government. The Suez action, recalling colonial skirmishes of the Victorian era, had been greeted with international diplomatic scorn, bringing home the realization that Britain was no longer a great power.

As the new decade of the 1960s began, the revival of the Conservative Party, apparently controlled by an aristocratic elite, began to lose its edge as events beyond even the control of Macmillan began to take over. In 1963 the new leader of the Labour Party, Harold Wilson, appeared in stark contrast with Macmillan's successor, the fourteenth Earl of Home. No two men could have been more different. The new Prime Minister, owner of estates in Scotland, represented the epitome of the landed classes, with his Eton education, his upper-class accent, and his grouse-moor image. Wilson made the most of this during the run up to the 1964 general election. Indeed, the fact that Home should have been an object of such ridicule seemed to mark the end of the revival of landed society's old aristocratic image in England. Ten years earlier in 1953, in the glory of coronation year, such a bitter attack would have been entirely out of place. By 1963 times had changed.

*   *   *

The coronation of Queen Elizabeth in June 1953 occurred when Britain had not quite recovered from wartime austerity and postwar privations. Yet inside Westminster Abbey rows upon rows of dukes, marquesses, earls, viscounts, and barons, duchesses, marchionesses, countesses, and ladies sat together in sedate splendour, witnessing with confident expectation the dawning of what was then called the new Elizabethan age. The ceremony focused world attention on the unchanging traditions of a postwar Britain where title, rank, and privilege had apparently remained untouched by the upheavals of two world wars. For landed society in England this rainswept June day marked the beginning of a brief and tantalizing return to a time of calm and prosperity.

The Prime Minister, Winston Churchill, had himself witnessed the continuity of the monarchy in Great Britain from the very beginning of the twentieth century. He had been a Member of Parliament at the coronations of King Edward VII in 1902, of King George V in 1911, and of King George VI in 1937. In 1952, on the death of King George VI, Churchill addressed the nation in a speech which evoked Britain still at the centre of the world stage. The death of the king had struck 'a deep and solemn note in our lives which, as it resounded far and wide, stilled the clatter and traffic of twentieth-century life in many lands and made countless millions of human beings pause and look around them'. When Queen Mary died the following year Churchill alluded to the many changes which her long life had encompassed. 'Yet she lived into this atomic age, through the two fearful wars, which cast almost all the thrones of Europe to the ground, and rent but also transformed the world.'[4]

That in the aftermath of war-ravaged Europe a monarchy still survived in Britain was triumphantly displayed in June 1953. London had suffered continuous air raids throughout the war, but now its streets were the setting for a procession of regal splendour. The youth of Queen Elizabeth lent a unique romanticism to the ponderous formality of the occasion. A young life, with a firm yet humble gesture, was embracing with confidence all upon which the landed aristocracy depended, the royal patronage from which for centuries it had derived its prestige and power.

The months before the coronation were a flurry of confused preparation in country houses throughout England, as dukes and marquesses, countesses and barons retrieved coronation robes which had been in storage since before the war. With wearied nonchalance they talked and complained about the effort that it all involved and the decisions that had to be made about coronets, medals, cloaks, and jewels. In this new and uncertain postwar world thoughts turned to the procurement of coaches and tiaras, white gloves and ermine. 'Winnie Portarlington announced at luncheon that she has a harness but no coach; Circe Londonderry has a coach but no horses; Mollie Buccleuch has no postillions – but five tiaras.'[5]

Inside Westminster Abbey the peeresses were able to compare tiaras as they talked while waiting for the young Queen Elizabeth. A gold carpet set off the scarlet uniforms and crimson robes of the peers and the dark velvet cloaks of the Knights of the Garter. Cecil Beaton observed that during the ceremony it was as if the landed aristocratic families had been born to perform their duties, to present a glove, an orb, or a sword to the Queen. As children they had listened to reminiscences of coronations; no one appeared nervous for no one was. 'The ultimate in manners, these people [were] on terms with each other, never surprised or impressed, everything regulated and dignified.'[6] At the moment of the crowning the expression on the Queen's face was one of 'intense expectancy until, with magnificent assurance' the Archbishop of Canterbury placed the crown on her head. At that moment, shouts of 'God Save the Queen' broke out, the peers put on their coronets and caps of State, and the peeresses, with white-gloved arms, placed their coronets on their heads. There was a fanfare of trumpets, a blaze of violins, and the sound of guns fired from the Tower of London further down the Thames.[7]

The Queen's maids of honour at the coronation were all daughters of the landed aristocracy. They were Lady Anne Coke, the daughter of the fifth Earl of Leicester of Holkham Hall in Norfolk; Lady Jane Heathcote-Drummond-Willoughby, daughter of the third Earl of Ancaster of Grimsthorpe Castle in Lincolnshire; Lady Rosemary Spencer-Churchill, the daughter of the ninth Duke of Marlborough of Blenheim Palace in Oxfordshire; Lady Jane Vane-Tempest-Stewart, daughter of the eighth Marquess of Londonderry; and Lady Moyra Hamilton, the granddaughter of the third Duke of Abercorn. All these families lived in magnificent houses surrounded by estates which, along with many others, were all managed with greater efficiency in the increasingly prosperous economy of the 1950s.

Money was still tight in coronation year, but as the country's financial position improved, wartime controls lightened, and the 1947 100 per cent development charges were withdrawn, there began a shift towards a freer market. The year 1954 saw a greater stability in land values than any year since the war, when there was a slight reduction in interest rates and substantial rises in the value of gilt-edged stock, which stabilized investments generally. Although much publicity was given at this time to the break-up of noted estates due to death duties, little publicity was given to the many landowners such as the tenth Duke of Beaufort at Badminton and the sixth Earl of Bradford at Weston Park who added to their estates by shrewd purchasing of adjoining farms.[8] By 1955, many small estates were bought as a whole by new owners who intended to retain them as an investment or for personal occupation.

By the early 1960s the property market in England had 'blossomed in the hothouse climate of the affluent society'.[9] In 1960, the demand for good shooting properties was one of the most important causes in creating high prices. Whereas before the war good shooting or fishing on an estate would have added between 5 and 10 per cent to its market value, in the early 1960s first-class shooting could boost a sale by as much as 25 per cent. At a sale in the west country, one land agent, knowing that there were several substantial buyers for a shooting estate, obtained permission from the owner to increase the price by £10,000. The owner 'nearly succumbed to a heart attack' and the agent confessed to being apprehensive, but the offer was 'snapped up immediately'.[10]

By 1963 there was confidence in the long-term prospects of agricultural investment regardless of a possible change of government, as well as the wish of purchasers to enjoy 'prestige, sporting rights and estate duty concessions'. Some estates had doubled or even trebled in investment value since 1955. In 1963, 'the desire to own land clearly exists as strongly today as it did in the Middle Ages, and nearly always a decision to sell has been reached after long soul-searching'.[11]

Land which had been in the possession of some families since the Middle Ages was among the large acreages put on the market in the 1950s in order to pay death duties. When a landowner died, his trustees had to pay a duty based on the value of his land as well as capital assets such as gilt-edged securities, shares, or cash deposits. The aggregate figure was partially off-set by the 45 per cent abatement given in 1949 to the duty on agricultural land. Death duties could be avoided, however, if the owner handed over all he owned to his successor before he died. In order to avoid duty, he was obliged to make the transfer at least three years before death, which was extended to five years in 1946. The worrying problem involved in handing over everything to the heir was that of ensuring the owner's survival for five years. Indeed, the grim financial consequences of a sudden deterioration in health during this five-year period was on occasion enough to worsen the owner's medical condition.

The most spectacular example of a landowner failing to avoid death duties through premature death was that of the tenth Duke of Devonshire. In November 1950, with only three and a half months to go before he reached the end of the five years, the duke had a heart attack after chopping some wood on his Sussex estate and died.[12] Everything that the family possessed, its investments, houses, land, library, and art collection, were liable for duties of 80 per cent. The value of the Chatsworth Estates Company stood at £6 million of which the Exchequer was owed £5 million, and the amount was payable at once. With interest on the debt at 8 per cent, this mounted up at a rate of £1,000 a day. Although the rising price of land brought prices considerably above the valuations made at the tenth duke's death this was off-set by the eleventh duke's insistence that some of the smaller tenants be allowed to buy their properties at below the current value.[13]

It took seventeen years for the eleventh Duke of Devonshire to pay off the duties, leaving a huge deficit on the trustees' income. This deficit was not cleared until 1974, twenty-four years after the tenth duke's death. Many of the treasures from Chatsworth were sold to pay the death duties. Its nine most important works of art left the house forever: Rembrandt's *Philosopher*, Holbein's cartoon of Henry VII and Henry VIII, Rubens' *Holy Family*, Claude's *Liber Veritatis*, a Greek bronze head of Apollo, the Memling Triptych, the tenth-century manuscript Benedictional of St Aethelswold, Van Dyck's Italian sketchbook, and several fifteenth-century hunting tapestries. In 1953 the eleventh duke decided to offer Hardwick Hall in Derbyshire to the government in further payment of death duties. Land was also sold in Derbyshire and Dumfriesshire, besides town property in Buxton and London and woodlands in Sussex. The ducal estates were reduced from 120,000 acres in 1950 to 72,000 acres.[14]

The eleventh Duke of Devonshire later became Minister for Commonwealth Relations in Macmillan's government. Another close associate of Macmillan was John Wyndham, whose uncle, the third Baron Leconfield, died in 1952. Wyndham had been Macmillan's private secretary but retired when Macmillan became Chancellor in 1955; it was thought somewhat improper for him to have such a close association with the Chancellor of the Exchequer while he paid death duties.[15] It was the first time that the Leconfield family had had to pay death duties since 1901. In the 1880s the family had owned estates in Sussex, Yorkshire, Cumberland, and Ireland, amounting to just over 100,000 acres. In 1952 the trustees of the Leconfield Settled Estates had to pay £2 million in death duties. By December of that year £570,000 had been gained from sales of 11,000 acres in Dumfriesshire and of the 3,000-acre Scarisbrick and Halsall estates near Southport in Lancashire.[16]

The land in Lancashire had changed hands three times in eighteen months, all for death-duty purposes. It was some of the best potato-growing land in that county, and in 1951 had been acquired by the ninth Earl of Hardwicke for £295,000. A few months later he sold it to Lord Leconfield for £350,000, whose trustees sold it to Lord Hillingdon the following year.[17] Meanwhile in Yorkshire one of the original estates belonging to the Leconfield family, the 3,000-acre Wressle estate between York and Hull, was bought as an investment in 1952 by Florence Lady Hesketh for £100,000.[18]

The sale of land back and forth between members of landed society anxious to lessen death duties was an unexpected phenomenon of these postwar years. Lord Leconfield's judicious purchase of land just before his death in order to make the most of the death-duty abatement on land allowed most of the land around Petworth House in West Sussex to be retained, even though the house and its contents, like the Duke of Devonshire's Hardwick Hall, was given to the Treasury, which then sold it to the National Trust. Elsewhere in Sussex 7,000 acres were sold, of which just over 1,000 were bought by the third Viscount Cowdray of nearby Cowdray Park.[19] In Cumberland, two-thirds of the Leconfield estate between Cockermouth Castle and Carlisle were sold. The land here included not only farms let to old-established tenants, but also 6,000 acres which were in hand.[20]

Another landowner who invested in agricultural land shortly before his death was the second Duke of Westminster, who died in 1953. Whereas Lord Leconfield's trustees were faced with the payment of £2 million in death duties, £19 million were demanded from the Duke of Westminster. The second Duke of Westminster was the richest man in England, and on his death a sub-department of the Inland Revenue had to be set up specifically to deal with his tax bill. Sales of silver, carpets, and furniture raised £500,000 and the Westminster tiara was auctioned for a record price of £110,000. Rubens' *Adoration of the Magi* was sold at auction in 1959 for £275,000 and then donated to King's College Chapel, Cambridge.[21] Land which had been bought in anticipation of death duties included 8,000 acres in Norfolk, 6,000 in Shropshire, 3,000 in Surrey, 7,000 in Lincolnshire, 10,000 in Durham, 4,000 in Westmoreland, 22,000 in Denbighshire, and smaller holdings in Wiltshire, Gloucestershire, and Merioneth. In 1950 the entire Grosvenor holdings in Pimlico had been sold in order to help finance the many holdings with which the duke started to diversify his capital.[22]

The diversification of capital meant that by investing in farms which were of low value not only could their worth be disputed for years, but only a half-rate was payable at death. By planting trees and setting up rural industries at a loss, tax liability was lessened. Moreover by employing top advisers, the Grosvenor estate 'was spending thousands to save millions'.[23] The chairman of Sotheby's prepared an inventory of every Grosvenor treasure, and after the second duke died this avalanche of documentation was immediately handed over to the tax inspectors. It took years for the Inland Revenue to wade through the vast and varied assets of the estate. When the Inland Revenue demanded interest from the delay in payment they were justifiably told that as every document had been made available, the Grosvenor estate was not at fault. Negotiations were completed sixteen years after the second duke's death, by which time inflation, rising land values, and the high prices paid for works of art meant that the original tax bill was paid off without too much difficulty.[24]

Yet another duke who died in the early 1950s was the twelfth Duke of Bedford, who accidentally shot himself during a walk on his estate. Like the Duke of Devonshire's, his death in 1953 occurred only months before the expiry of the five-year period. His executors were faced with the payment of nearly £5 million.[25] The 1,000-acre Chenies estate in Buckinghamshire, owned by the family for 460 years, was sold. As well as this the 3,000-acre Great Maytham estate in Kent, purchased in 1951, was sold in 1954. Nine thousand acres of the Tavistock estates in Devon were also put on the market, land which had belonged to the Russells since the dissolution of Tavis-tock Abbey in 1540.[26] In London part of the Bloomsbury estate was sold in 1958. Here three large blocks of property near New Oxford Street, High Holborn, and Southampton Row fetched £3 million.[27]

On the death of his father, the twelfth Duke of Bedford's heir returned from South Africa, having been urged in a letter from Lord Beaverbrook to 'Come back and get on with the job you are supposed to do as Duke of Bedford.' The young duke felt that if Woburn Abbey in Bedfordshire itself was sold 'something would have gone out of the family and indeed the history of England, which could never possibly be replaced'. The duke first saw Woburn in a state of chaos and decay when he returned to his new home, remembering it in its full splendour from visits to his grandparents before the war. He and the duchess set to work in restoring and cleaning the house; it had been decided that 'there must be something in this Duke business after all'.[28]

Inside Woburn Abbey, beautiful but broken Louis XV chairs were found alongside rooms stacked full of paintings and portraits. Among the many priceless treasures littered throughout the enor-mous house the duke discovered a diamond necklace and three or four tiaras. In one of the stable blocks he found a set of Sèvres porcelain lying all over the floor, originally given to the wife of the fourth duke by Louis XV. Within a year the house was opened to visitors. The duke, who once described himself as a national joke,[29] realized that his very presence was a particular source of interest to visitors, a fact of which he made full use in advertising Woburn on television throughout the world. The commercialization of the country house had begun.

While visitors paid to see the splendours of some of the large houses which for centuries had been the homes of the leading members of landed society, there occurred too the unseen destruc-tion of numerous country houses throughout England. The Duke of Bedford had himself witnessed this when he first saw that a wing of Woburn Abbey had been destroyed. The demolition of country houses dated back to the interwar period when landed families had been unable to maintain their houses and estates during the depression in farming. Between 1920 and 1955 thirteen such houses a year were destroyed.[30] 'We had no national pride then and this artistic destruction will long remain a reproach on the English conscience', wrote the art historian John Harris.[31] Many houses destroyed in the 1950s had remained unoccupied for many years. The accumulation of neglect followed by the Second World War put many houses beyond repair.

The history of this demolition of some of the loveliest architecture in England was charted in the early 1970s by a team led by Roy Strong, then director of the Victoria and Albert Museum in London. Of the 700 English country houses destroyed between 1900 and 1975, 200 were destroyed in the 1950s. Some counties in England contributed to this figure more than others. Lancashire lost twenty-one houses in the 1950s, and Herefordshire and Essex both lost twelve, while in Suffolk alone twenty-six country houses were destroyed between the end of the war and the early 1960s. In Suffolk, this meant that almost a quarter of the houses which had been the centre of estates of at least 3,000 acres in the 1880s were demolished between 1946 and 1953. Another sixteen houses centred on smaller estates in Suffolk were also destroyed during this time.

Of the many houses destroyed in Suffolk one was Sudbourne Hall, once centred on a large estate whose owner, Sir Richard Wallace, was the creator of the Wallace Art Collection in London. The house was purchased at the beginning of the century by the Clark family. It was in Sir Richard Wallace's library that the young Kenneth Clark, who later achieved international acclaim through his television series *Civilisation*, first became interested in art. The Clarks left Sudbourne in 1918, and long after the house had been demolished in 1953 the recently ennobled Lord Clark returned to the site of the hall. The scene was that of numerous empty sites in England where country houses had disappeared. Gone were the flights of steps, the brick columns with their stone pilasters, the cupid-ornamented fountain, the roses, and the bay windows. Lord Clark walked towards the middle of the lawn and said, with a wave of his hand, 'That was the view you saw from the front door.'[32] The greenhouses were still there, their glass long shattered. The once cultivated roses spread like brambles among the undergrowth. Down the overgrown path towards the lake, the bridge had long fallen down.

Demolition sales became common in Suffolk, such as the one held at the fourth Earl of Stradbroke's Henham Hall in 1953. Just the shell remained, including eight reception rooms and fifty bedrooms.[33] From some houses, rooms were transferred to museums in America where they were reconstructed; one dealer had 900 rooms transferred across the Atlantic. Three rooms from Sutton Scarsdale in Derbyshire were on view at the Philadelphia Museum of Art in 1961 while the dining room from Kirtlington Park in Oxfordshire, acquired in 1931, and the tapestry room from Croome Court in Worcestershire acquired in 1949 could be viewed at the Metropolitan Museum in New York. A room from Kempshott Park near Basingstoke in Hampshire was in the City Art Museum in St Louis. In California a Yorkshire manor house lay stacked in neatly numbered piles. In New York, the great Long Gallery from Albyns in Essex lay dust-shrouded in a warehouse. 'It is a strange experience to come off helter-skelter Fifth Avenue, plunge into the coolness of a warehouse and find the Palladian grandeurs of Ashley Park, Surrey, propped up against the walls, or William Winde's mellowed gilt and oak room from Combe Abbey, Warwickshire, standing in rickety dust-blown confusion.'[34]

* * *

The demolition of country houses in England was countered by a new movement, slow at first but gaining strength as the economy improved, whereby landed society turned away from their mansions and started to build houses in the country more suitable to postwar life. At first it made little headway. Against 200 demolitions in England, forty houses were reconstructed or built in the 1950s.[35] Yet in Suffolk the decision by the Vernon-Wentworth family, whose origins in the county dated back centuries, to remodel their house was a small yet significant sign of the regeneration of the landed way of life in the twentieth century. Unlike the rest of Europe, whose aristocracy chose to live for most of the year in capital cities, landed society in England still wanted to live in the country.

The majority of these new houses were built or remodelled by families who had owned estates since at least the end of the nineteenth century. This perpetuation of the landed way of life, continued in the 1960s when just over seventy houses were built or remodelled, is a fascinating indication of the determined survival of English landed society in the postwar world. Yet among families who appeared in Burke's 1952 *Landed Gentry*, then a heavy volume containing thousands of ancient names, just four families rebuilt and reconstructed their homes in the 1950s. It was therefore the owners of very large estates in England or the new rich with small estates who decided that they could afford to build a new house in the country.

The architectural style of the new houses was usually Georgian, a simple style of red brick, stone, or stucco. Large sashed windows with rectangular panes enhanced the views of surrounding parkland. Inside were high ceilings with cornices and picture rails, and marble fireplaces flanked by alcoves in which collections of porcelain were displayed behind glass and lit from below. In the drawing rooms, covered sofas and chairs were separated from one another by distances which ensured a loud crossfire of conversation at drinks or at tea. On mahogany tables were stacked piles of hardbound books, alongside more prominent displays of society and country magazines. There were flower arrangements in large bowls, numerous framed photographs of the family with their dogs and horses, large lampshades and plants. Curtains had bright floral designs and some walls were painted in dark reds and greens to set off the colours of the ancestral paintings and portraits. In the 1950s this mixture of comfort and display was created for the first time by professional interior designers, one of the most popular of whom was the seventh Baron Brabourne's brother-in-law, David Hicks. But the postwar country house was still primarily a home, with wellington boots, mackintoshes, shooting-sticks, and umbrellas thrown against parquet floors and mahogany.

Among the old aristocracy, a scheme which summed up the mood of the 1950s was that of the premier earl of England, the sixteenth Duke of Norfolk, who moved out of Arundel Castle in Sussex and into a new house in the park close by. The idea was prompted by the duchess, who found that the opening of the castle to the public had totally destroyed their privacy. For the new house a Palladian style was agreed upon which would incorporate a sense of grandeur with convenience. A central block with a flag pole and walkways was flanked by two wings, separating rooms for domestic staff at one end and the Norfolks' four daughters at the other. The front door was taken from Norfolk House in St James's Square in London, which had been demolished in 1938. Inside, the house provided a much more appropriate setting than the castle for the eighteenth-century furniture.[36]

The decision to live in a smaller residence was taken with somewhat more drastic consequences by the eighth Marquess of Lansdowne in Wiltshire. He had inherited the house and estate after the death in the war of his cousin, the seventh marquess, in 1944. In 1951 the eighth marquess began to realize that the family could live in part of Bowood again. Bowood House itself, first built in 1755 and decorated by Robert Adam, was demolished exactly 200 years later in 1955. Two large stable courts and the so-called Little House were retained, which still provided a substantial residence. The greenhouse designed by Adam was adapted as a picture gallery for the Lansdowne collections from three other houses and the principal library was repaired. The new house could be adapted according to the numbers staying, and the Adam picture gallery could be used as a more formal approach to the main rooms.[37] Houses such as Bowood, along with every other country house still inhabited by landowning families, became the settings for formal entertaining once more during the 1950s and early 1960s.

On the arrival of the guests at a country house by car on Friday evening, their luggage was taken away to their rooms and unpacked. In houses where owners still dressed for dinner, a dinner jacket might be tactfully supplied by a valet. After an early night, there was a large breakfast the next morning attended by the men only, who helped themselves from silver dishes on the sideboard in the dining room. The meal was eaten in silence, interrupted only by the rustle of newspapers, while the ladies had breakfast in their rooms upstairs. If the morning was spent shooting, then the ladies viewed the last drive before luncheon from a Land Rover. At tea, the hosts' children joined the party, to be 'admired by the ladies, ignored by the gentlemen and soon removed by a hovering nurse'.[38] At six o'clock, drinks were served, and the highlight of the weekend was dinner. At the end of the meal the ladies moved into the drawing room and the men might then discuss 'the merits of the day's sport, the Prime Minister. . .the demerits of the day's sport and Mr Harold Wilson'. It was then time to join the ladies for bridge or canasta in the drawing room. On Sunday morning breakfast would be a longer and later meal, not a word being spoken until midday when three things happened: the ladies descended from upstairs, the Catholics in the house party came back from Mass, and drinks were offered. After lunch, guests were taken to see the stables, a garden, a house nearby, or the rest of the house in which they were staying. After supper in the evening, guests departed, leaving tips for the members of staff.[39]

Although after the war smaller numbers of guests were entertained at weekends, there were occasions when the prewar splendour reappeared. Parties for débutantes were held in the country rather than in London when, if only for one weekend, the big house came into its own again, hostesses striving to rehabilitate and display the 'style and beauty, grace and elegance, which in so many instances had been for long obscured by dustsheets and shutters'.[40] Among the memorable dances of the 1955 Season was the one held for Lady Diana Herbert, daughter of the sixteenth Earl of Pembroke, at Wilton House. It was at Wilton that the D-Day landings had been planned, but now in the Double-Cube room the glint of tiaras was enhanced by the painted ceiling lit by obelisks of shells in white and gold. In London, the Duchess of Argyll gave a party at Claridge's for her daughter, later the Duchess of Rutland, which was preceded by a dinner for a hundred.[41] Lady Glenconner held a dance in a marquee lined with white and gold wallpaper for her daughter the Hon. Emma Tennant, 'who has emerged as the best-dressed, best-mannered débutante of the year', and at Lady Irene Astor's dance in the country, the Queen stayed 'till the birds were singing in the Sussex dawn'.[42] At Stonor Park in Oxfordshire in 1956 the Hon. Mrs Sherman Stonor undertook all the catering for a dance which was in a marquee, leaving room in the house for eating, sitting out, and games of bridge and canasta.[43]

These years were remembered for the emergence of the 'Margaret Set'. At parties in the country and in nightclubs in London the heirs to some of the oldest titles and largest estates in England whiled away their time with the attractive sister of the Queen, Princess Margaret. The princess's admirers included the Hon. Colin Tennant, heir to the second Baron Glenconner; Lord Porchester, the heir to the sixth Earl of Carnarvon of Highclere Castle in Hampshire; the seventh Baron Plunket, who owned estates in Ireland; Lord Brooke, heir to Warwick Castle; the Hon. Peter Ward who was the son of the third Earl of Dudley; and Billy Wallace, the son of Captain Euan Wallace who owned an estate in Sussex. The group was fond of jazz and expert at the new dances of the time.[44]

The revival of large dances, which demanded considerable skills of planning and a great deal of work on the part of hostesses, grew throughout the 1950s and into the early 1960s. Yet after 1958 débutantes were no longer presented at court, which had been the ritual start of the Season. Presentations at court had become less formal after the war, being held in the afternoon rather than in the evening. Until 1958, the great gates of Buckingham Palace used to swing open and a procession of limousines, 'a string of polished jet', formed up in the Mall. The first débutantes made 'their breathless curtsies to the Queen', then walked out onto the lawns behind Buckingham Palace 'to take tea and chocolate cake, to the accompaniment of a splendidly accoutred band playing selections from the newest American musical'.[45]

Without its traditional royal send-off, brought to an end by the Queen, who considered presentations at court to be out of date, the Season lost some of its formality. As more and more people could afford to join it so the social scene became blurred. Yet the old families, whose income, title, and position had been derived initially from the land, maintained their exclusive solidarity, however much they appeared to welcome the new rich. With the introduction of life peerages in 1958, whose titles to the uninitiated might signal landed status, there could be a world of difference between a baron who was a life peer and an eighteenth earl.

The division between the old rich and the new rich was publicized in 1956 by the second Baron Redesdale's daughter, the Hon. Nancy Mitford, editor of *Noblesse Oblige. An Enquiry into the Identifiable Characteristics of the English Aristocracy*. The book set out to describe in detail the differences between being upper class, or 'U', and not upper class, or 'Non-U', and how the two classes could be linguistically separated. With the mass prosperity of the 1950s, the landed classes were staking their claim to their intransigent superiority by drawing attention to the correct enunciation of the way they spoke. The opening chapter, by Professor Alan Ross of Birmingham University, was a paper originally printed in 1954 for the *Bulletin de la Société Néo-philologique de Helsinki*.[46] In it Professor Ross attempted to describe the pronunciation and vocabulary of upper-class speech in England. Just one slip by a 'Non-U' speaker attempting to describe himself as 'U' would give the game away. Numerous examples were given in this 'essay in sociological linguistics' of the clipped speech of the upper classes and the phrasing they used, such as 'having a bath' rather than 'taking a bath', and asking 'Have some more tea?' and not 'How is your cup?' A 'U' response to the greeting 'How do you do?' would be to say 'How do you do?' The 'Non-U' response would be 'Pleased to meet you'. A midday meal for the 'U' class would be lunch, which for the 'Non-U' would be dinner. It was pointed out that in addressing a gardener or a groom a 'U' speaker would say 'You'd better finish that job after you've had your dinner.' To have said 'after lunch' would have implied equal social status.[47] Soon after the *Noblesse Oblige* book appeared *The Field* gave examples of what the 'U' class and the 'Non-U' class would say in the shooting field. It would have been 'Non-U' to say 'The partridges came with great rapidity on the wind in the last drive, and I had difficulty in shooting them.' U-usage would be 'They came like stink that time, didn't they? I got off 13 squibs and only connected twice.'[48]

During Cabinet meetings Harold Macmillan sometimes used analogies from the shooting field, starting sentences with the phrase, 'Of course, if you brown into a covey of partridges. . .', eliciting a perplexed reaction from some of his colleagues.[49] Yet the majority of Macmillan's Cabinet ministers were well versed in such terms. Macmillan's Cabinets were notable also for the degree to which their members were related to each other by marriage. It was calculated at the time that of the eighty-five members of Macmillan's first government, thirty were related to him by marriage, including seven of the nineteen members of his Cabinet.[50] Long-forgotten names from the House of Lords were given political office. The numerous connections within landed society, particularly among old Etonians, meant that every landed family in England could claim some connection with a member of the government. There had been 'nothing like it in England since the eighteenth century Duke of Newcastle. . . .Mr Macmillan has more cousins and less opposition than any Prime Minister in our history.'[51]

The connections between members of the government were studied in 1959 by two sociologists from Manchester University. Illustrating their findings with diagrams, they expressed academic surprise that so many of the ruling class should share a common background and the degree of trust and familiarity this engendered.

The sociologists had been prompted to investigate these links between what they called the 'Top Decision Makers' after studying the proceedings of a tribunal which had inquired into allegations that information about the raising of the bank rate was improperly disclosed in 1957. During the tribunal, they noted that Lord Kindersley had said to Lord Bicester, of Morgan Grenfell bank, 'Look here, Rufie, is it too late to stop this business or not?'[52] Such easy familiarity was characteristic of the relationships which existed in the governments of the 1950s when land, business, and politics were associated so closely. In the 1962 edition of his *Anatomy of Britain* Anthony Sampson set out what some of these connections were.[53]

The sister of the first Baron Bicester, of Tusmore Park in Oxfordshire, was married to Lord Rennell, also of Morgan Grenfell bank. Lord Rennell's son, the Hon. Peter Rodd, was married to the Hon. Nancy Mitford. Nancy Mitford's younger sister Deborah was married to the eleventh Duke of Devonshire. The eleventh Duke of Devonshire's aunt was married to Harold Macmillan. From 1960 to 1962 the Duke of Devonshire was Under-Secretary of State for Commonwealth Relations and from 1962 to 1964 Minister of State at the Commonwealth Relations Office. Having been appointed to the posts by his uncle the prime minister, accusations of nepotism became somewhat difficult to refute.

The prime minister's son, Maurice Macmillan, was a Member of Parliament and married to the sister of the Hon. David Ormsby-Gore, heir to the fourth Baron Harlech, owner of large estates in Shropshire and Wales. The Hon. David Ormsby-Gore was an old friend of President Kennedy, whom he had met in the 1930s in London, when Kennedy's father had been ambassador to the Court of St James.[54] Kennedy's sister Kathleen, a close friend of David Ormsby-Gore's Roman Catholic wife Sylvia, had married the Marquess of Hartington, heir to the tenth Duke of Devonshire, and later killed in France in 1944. Harold Macmillan recalled that on his first meeting with Kennedy as president, the president had asked him who was to be the next British ambassador in Washington. Macmillan asked him who he would like to have. When Kennedy suggested his old friend David Ormsby-Gore, Macmillan's reply was 'Well, that's all right, that is the best reason I know for appointing an ambassador and I will arrange it.'[55]

When President Kennedy made an official tour of Europe in the summer of 1963, he stayed with Macmillan at the premier's home in Sussex. Kathleen, Marchioness of Hartington, had been killed in an air crash in 1948; President Kennedy's arrival in Sussex was delayed after visiting his sister's grave in the churchyard not far from the Duke of Devonshire's Chatsworth. In Sussex, although Macmillan's house and his son's were made available, they were not enough to accommodate the vast entourage of 'Secretaries of State, Ambassadors, members of the Foreign Office and State Department, secretaries, typists and all the protective apparatus which constituted his immense court'.[56] Hotels and inns nearby were commandeered and Macmillan invited neighbours, children from local schools, tenants, servants, and estate staff to greet Kennedy on his arrival. Because of the close relationship between the president of the United States and Britain's prime minister, there was none of the solemnity which usually accompanied such grave international conferences. As Macmillan recalled, 'After all, we were all friends and many of us intimate friends; and the whole atmosphere was that of a country house party.'[57]

At the time of Kennedy's visit in the summer of 1963 the Minister of State for Colonial Affairs was the eighth Marquess of Lansdowne. There were more connections. Lansdowne's aunt, who had married the ninth Duke of Devonshire, had been Macmillan's mother-in-law. And the Marquess of Lansdowne's mother had married as her second husband the first Baron Astor of Hever. Lord Astor of Hever was the uncle of another Lord Astor, the third Viscount Astor, owner of Cliveden in Buckinghamshire. It was by a swimming pool at Cliveden, at a country weekend in 1961, that the War Minister, John Profumo, first saw Christine Keeler. The mass of publicity given in 1963 to the scandal that ensued contributed to the fall of Macmillan's government.

Successive events in 1963 emphasized that the postwar country-house party in England had come to an end. Landed society stopped looking back to the beginning of the century, when their Edwardian fathers and grandfathers had remained detached and aloof from the rest of society, and began to realize that perhaps they were now just one rather obscure and out-dated part of high society, increasingly detached from the modern world. As with royalty, their activities began to be publicized and satirized by the media. Particular events in 1963 confirmed this new trend.

In May, the outcome of the divorce action against the Duchess of Argyll was widely reported, the conclusion of a legal battle which had lasted for four years. The judgement was a particularly cruel one, which 'constituted nothing less than a savage character assassination. I could scarcely believe that any man – let alone a judge – could be so merciless or capable of inflicting such unnecessary pain on another human being' wrote the duchess.[58] Although she had no connection with politics, in the public mind titled people at that time were by implication associated with Macmillan's government.[59] Then as the summer of 1963 progressed, the relentless details of the Profumo affair, with its persistent allegations of corruption in high places, seemed never to go away.

In July 1963 peers were for the first time allowed to renounce their titles if they wished to stand for Parliament. During the debate in the House of Lords the second Baron Milford said that the hereditary principle belonged to the Divine Right of Kings, 'entirely out of place in this age of automation, space flights, sweeping technological changes; the age of the advance of socialism, the democratic rights of the common people and the national liberation of the colonial people'.[60] It was this incongruity of technological progress with a Britain still in the hands of the country-house set which was seized upon by the new leader of the Labour Party, Harold Wilson. The issue was heightened when, after the leadership crisis at the Conservative Party conference in October 1963, a new prime minister 'emerged'. The fourteenth Earl of Home took on the post with genuine reluctance after much in-fighting as to who should succeed Macmillan. When the former Viscount Hailsham, who had renounced his title thanks to the recently passed Peerage Act, openly advertised his desire to take over the premiership, this was considered 'bad form'. Disapproval of his blatantly competitive stance seemed to sum up Britain's weakened position in the modern world. When the fourteenth Earl of Home was eventually appointed prime minister, Harold Wilson said that 'whatever happens in the age of change Britain will still be governed from the grouse moors'.[61]

The symbolic occasion on which the power and influence of Macmillan's aristocratic government reached its apogee was when President Kennedy was entertained for a weekend in the Sussex countryside, when affairs of international importance had been discussed at Macmillan's country home. The older English statesman and the young president had become close friends. On his departure, Kennedy, 'combining that indescribable look of a schoolboy on holiday with the dignity of a President and Commander-in-Chief', walked briskly across the lawn at Birch Grove House to his helicopter. Macmillan recalled:

I can see the helicopter now, sailing down the valley above the heavily laden, lush foliage of oaks and beech at the end of June. He was gone. Alas, I was never to see my friend again. Before those leaves had turned and fallen he was snatched by an assassin's bullet from the service of his own country and the whole world.[62]

7

'Little else but a title and a dying empire', 1964–79

When Lord Home took over as prime minister in October 1963 the leader of the Labour Party, Harold Wilson, asked: 'How can a scion of an effete establishment appreciate and understand, let alone read, the scientific revolution, the mobilization of the skill and talents of all our people in the struggle to restore Britain's position in the world?'[1] Following the Labour Party's general election victory of 1964, it was Harold Wilson himself who took his seat as prime minister in the House of Commons. Like President Kennedy, he was elected with a very narrow majority. Had 900 voters not voted the victory would have been a Conservative one. For Wilson, the results were referred to by him as his Cook County, the district of Illinois which had swung the election for Kennedy.[2]

At about this time there were emerging in England the beginnings of unprecedented social changes. This universal questioning of old values had been anticipated in 1960 by Macmillan's allusion to the 'wind of change' when he had initiated the final dismantling of the British empire. Quietly and unobserved, the steady departure from the colonial past had been replaced by an uncertain present of high technology and greater prosperity, of classlessness and new freedom. Wilson's cynical contrasting of the old world and the new in 1963 had been quite correct. It was the precarious interplay of these two worlds in the decades to come which was, for English landed society in the twentieth century, to pose the most powerful challenges of peacetime.

In the 1960s and 1970s English landed society was assailed by forces which touched every aspect of their lives. The social explosion of the mid-1960s pushed the old aristocracy firmly into the background, replacing it with the youth culture which drew its talent from large cities, and making Britain the focus of world attention. Younger members of landed society embraced these changes with enthusiasm. The rebellion of youth brought numerous conflicts within landed families as the generation gap assumed a greater significance than ever before. The ordered world of deference in villages dominated by landed estates was hard to reconcile with the abandonment of such values by the heirs to such properties. Up until now the economics of running houses and estates had been the prime preoccupation of their owners. With the possibility of the young generation showing little interest in such things, worries about handing on properties were now centred on the attitude and behaviour of those closest to the owner, of the interests of the heirs themselves.

The aristocratic dropouts who went in search of eastern culture emphasized that the old traditions of their fathers and grandfathers, of military careers and field sports, could not have been more incongruous. At the same time, the Labour governments of 1964–70 continued the attack on the landed interest initiated by their socialist predecessors elected in 1945. A capital gains tax of 30 per cent, a tax on employers, the attempt once again to reap for the state the unearned increment in land values, the extension of the five-year rule to seven years to avoid death duties, all contributed still more problems for landowners running their estates.

A brief respite occurred in the early 1970s when many of these measures were modified by the Conservative government and when there was a sudden property boom. But the oil crisis which hit the western economy in 1973 was followed by a Labour budget in 1974 which was aimed quite clearly at the redistribution of wealth. The combination of high inflation and an avalanche of legislation in the rest of the 1970s brought about the greatest difficulties for landed society in England since the immediate postwar period. It was this combination of unprecedented social changes, unprecedented political attacks, and what seemed to be unprecedented financial difficulties that was to be the lot of landowners in England throughout the 1960s and 1970s, all of which occurred with startling speed.

Seldom before the general election campaign of 1964 had a prime minister received less media attention. Lord Home had renounced his title so that he could lead the country from the House of

Commons. After winning a hastily arranged by-election, he took his seat on the front bench as Sir Alec Douglas-Home. As he toured the country in the autumn of 1964, he never quite mastered television interviews, press conferences, or set platform speeches.[3] The loud heckling which greeted him everywhere, which he tried to counter with polite sarcasm, seemed to pinpoint the new mood of the mid-1960s when every aspect of authority would be challenged.

Sir Alec Douglas-Home was closely connected with England's landed aristocracy. One brother had married Lady Margaret Spencer, the daughter of the sixth Earl Spencer of Althorp Park in Northamptonshire; another was married to the daughter of the fourth Viscount Hampden, while his sister was married to Lord William Montagu Douglas Scott, son of one of Britain's largest landowners, the seventh Duke of Buccleuch. Douglas-Home himself owned large estates in Scotland, comprising hill farms, forests, and grouse moors in Lanarkshire and Berwickshire. His principal residence was 'an elegant eighteenth-century pile. . .and up a long drive' where the telephone number was simply Coldstream 1.[4] On shooting holidays with the family at another of his houses in Scotland, Douglas-Home used to wander about 'arranging the flowers, working with his feet up on the sofa and endlessly looking for his spectacles'.[5] But the seemingly vague demeanour of Sir Alec was the disguise of a shrewd political negotiator, who had for many years held high office in government. In 1965, wearied by a lengthy political career at the top, Douglas-Home opted to hand over the leadership of the party to someone more able to cope with the parliamentary battering to which he was subjected by the quick and energetic prime minister Harold Wilson. He chose an analogy from the cricket field to explain his decision to stand down:

> At the wicket, at least until one's eye is in, it is wise to wait for the half-volley or the long hop. That is the way to build up a score. Blind slogging at every ball soon receives its deserts. I did not like the game any better because the slick knockabout was something at which Mr Wilson excelled.[6]

Sir Alec's replacement by Edward Heath in 1965 coincided with a unique change in London society, in which the prestige and influence of the landed aristocracy was quite suddenly submerged. In January of that year, the last farewell to the Edwardian era occurred with the funeral of Winston Churchill. Such was Church-ill's world standing that there was 'an expression of grief and commemoration which, in its intensity, its scope and the breadth of its international incidence, had almost certainly never been equal-led before in the entire history of the world'.[7] After a funeral service in St Paul's Cathedral attended by leaders of almost every indepen-dent state in the world, the coffin was put on a launch on the River Thames, where the cranes lining the docks dipped in salute. The coffin was then taken by train to Bladon where, by the church tower which could be seen through the windows of Churchill's birthplace, Blenheim Palace, it was put alongside other graves of the Duke of Marlborough's family. From then on, this quiet Oxfordshire village became a source of pilgrimage for visitors from all over the world.

In the summer of 1965 London was the object of world attention for quite different reasons. It had now become the leader of fashion in the arts, in music, in the theatre, in photography, and in interior design. The new aristocracy were now talented young playwrights, photographers and fashion designers, pop musicians, models, and artists, most of whom had grown up in the London suburbs. These entertainers, satirists, designers, and architects led an extra-ordinary explosion of revolt against the class-ridden world of the 1950s. Music, fashion, restaurants, and nightclubs were now all aimed at the young. New dances such as the twist had been given royal approval in April 1963 when it was included in the pro-gramme at the dance in Windsor Castle given by the Queen on the engagement of her cousin Princess Alexandra.[8] By the spring of 1965 the twist was already out of date, but at dances in London and in the country less floor space was now needed; for the first time men and women separated to adopt a new form of competitive dancing.

Several talented figures from the upper-class world submerged their identity in the exciting classlessness of London in 1965.[9] They included the wealthy journalist Jocelyn Stevens, editor of *Queen* magazine, through which he proclaimed the death of the old aristocracy. The seventh Baron Brabourne's brother-in-law David Hicks continued to design new interiors for houses in London and in the country. Alexander Plunket Greene was husband and busi-ness partner of Mary Quant, one of the most internationally successful designers in London at the time. The fifth Earl of

Lichfield, the owner of a large estate in Staffordshire, where he lived in an apartment in his ancestral home of Shugborough Hall, became a widely acclaimed photographer.

Another photographer working in London at about that time was the young Anthony Armstrong-Jones. His mother had married as her second husband the sixth Earl of Rosse, the owner of two large country residences. When in 1960 the Queen's sister, Princess Margaret, married Anthony Armstrong-Jones, this anticipated the beginning of the merging of royalty with the modern world. Historians observed that it was the first time for more than 450 years that a prince or princess had married outside the peerage.[10]

After their marriage Princess Margaret and her husband resided in Kensington Palace, making occasional forays into swinging Kensington High Street on a motorbike, he dressed in leather, and she wearing dark glasses and a scarf on her head. Later the princess's husband, created Earl of Snowdon on his marriage, took over a cottage on his mother's Sussex estate as a retreat from London. At a mock-ceremonial opening of his new abode, the Queen Mother cut a ribbon while the Queen looked on applauding.[11] That a young photographer, who had lived in a studio flat converted from an ironmonger's shop in Pimlico Road, was now part of the royal set, anticipated the rebellious and classless decade of the 1960s, a decade which the landed aristocracy was to embrace with fervour.

The release from staid entertainments and high ceremonial, from unnecessary snobbishness and remote country living, hailed an unprecedented era of freedom for England's landed elite. A young couple who were part of this revolt was the ninth Marquess and Marchioness of Londonderry, who managed to achieve a fusion of 'trad and beat'. Both 'sharp dressers', they were as much involved in the world of arts as in the traditional activities of running their large estate centred on Wynyard Park in County Durham. The marquess, at 27, was 'a 1964 dandy and fashion setter'. The marchioness entertained and opened fêtes in the way that was expected of her, but at the same time promoted a pop group called The Scorpions. In Gloucestershire, the young Lady Bathurst was a director of the home farm and organized charity work at Apsley Park, but she also ran a boutique in the town of Gloucester.[12]

At Cowes in the summer of 1967, a boutique was opened for the traditional end-of-Season sailing regatta. The shop was run by the lead guitarist of the Band of Angels pop group who also set up a discotheque in this quiet town on the Isle of Wight. In 1967 mini skirts were allowed for the first time by the Royal Yacht Squadron, which for years had banned women in trousers, and the Band of Angels provided the music in the annexe in the evening.[13] Viewers of the regatta from the lawn in front of the exclusive building could through binoculars see one or two psychedelic sails. Even in the most traditional pastimes, the new decade of the 1960s was making its mark.

In the same year people carrying a banner proclaiming 'Stop the murder in Vietnam' ran in front of the oncoming horses at Ascot. Cecil Beaton, who had designed the striking black and white scene of Edwardian Ascot for the film *My Fair Lady*, commented that the colours in the crowd in 1967 were predominantly 'magenta, orange and viridian'. For Beaton the plastic and nylon of the ladies' dresses 'looked crummy in the outdoors; the crocheted shift, the mini skirts and little-girl fashions were hardly right'. Loelia Duchess of West-minster greeted Beaton with a despairing look. He was later lifted from depression by the sight of the elegant French ambassadress wearing an art nouveau picture-hat adorned with water lilies.[14] In 1968 lounge suits instead of the traditional morning suits were allowed in the Royal Enclosure at Ascot, a significant relaxation of the sartorial rules during a year of unrest and rebellion throughout the world. More significant perhaps was that hardly anyone chose to take advantage of this new rule.

Aristocratic hippies who took part in the drug culture of the late 1960s and early 1970s came from some of the richest landed families in England. Large trust funds allowed them to acquire all the essential needs of this expensive return to nature. A sombre indication of this new experimentation occurred in the summer of 1966 when Laura Canfield, a cousin of the twelfth Earl of Wemyss and formerly married to the third Earl of Dudley, entertained guests for a weekend in her house in Buckinghamshire. Her husband appeared at the door of her room and told her that one of their guests had brought with him some LSD capsules. 'Ivan and I have already swallowed ours and of course Roger has probably taken even more. . . .There is one for you and another for Kate.' Declining this offer from her husband, Laura was left to observe her guests' behaviour. While her husband remarked to the gardener that the Mercedes were growing well, she found another guest lying in the orchard in the pouring rain. 'He was quite unlike himself, almost rude when I told him he would catch a dreadful cold and he must come inside and eat.' He then rushed through the house and upstairs to lock himself in his bedroom, only to emerge at the end of the day to say that he had thought he had been trapped in a red marble ball. Lunch was a dreary silent occasion, and those on a trip ate nothing. Laura observed that the servants seemed somewhat bewildered.[15]

The estate employees at Longleat in Wiltshire were somewhat bewildered two years later when before leaving for his honeymoon in Majorca the sixth Marquess of Bath's younger son, Lord Christopher Thynne, was arrested at London airport for having thirty-seven amphetamine 'pep pills' in his camera case. Compassionate authorities however let him proceed with the honeymoon, saying that police would charge him on his return.[16] Lord Christopher, sipping tomato juice in the lounge while waiting for his rebooked flight, told reporters, 'It's a damned unfortunate thing.'[17]

Lord Christopher Thynne's wedding, when he married Antonia Palmer in the ornate Queen's Chapel in St James's Palace, saw a colourful gathering of hippies from landed society and Mick Jagger among the guests. The bride was the daughter of a lady-in-waiting to the Queen and the Queen attended the wedding reception. Lord Christopher Thynne's hair hung thickly to his shoulders and both he and his bride were dressed in the latest 'gear' from Chelsea boutiques. The bride's brother Sir Mark Palmer wore a flowered kaftan and orange velvet trousers. 'I'm sure nobody was embarrassed', said the Hon. Catherine Tennant, the daughter of the second Baron Glenconner. 'Maybe we even did some good by subverting a few of the "straights" through the force of example. We felt a little messianic.'[18]

At another wedding in London two years later in 1970 the fifth Earl of Liverpool, who played the drums in the Black Sheep pop group, married the daughter of the fifth Earl of Gainsborough, Lady Juliana Noel, who gave her name to the mobile discotheque, Juliana's. A reception for 700 was held at Claridge's and the couple started married life in a mews house in Kensington designed by another member of the Black Sheep.[19] A few months previously in Paris the former sister-in-law of the sixth Marquess of Bute married as her second husband the Aga Khan. Unlike the weddings of her aristocratic contemporaries in London, at this wedding pearls were thrown instead of confetti. The couple sat demurely on two silk-draped chairs, side by side, heads bowed, while among the guests could be seen gold turbans, embroidered cloaks, and saris, 'all very different from the day the bride-model girl Sally Stuart married the Marquess of Bute's brother ten years ago'.[20]

Fascination with the east was a pervading theme of late-1960s social life in England among aristocratic youth, who felt that they had inherited 'little else but a title and a dying empire'.[21] In the late 1960s and early 1970s, following the footsteps of their parents and grandparents, the sons and daughters of landed society went to India and Africa on an entirely different mission, this time to absorb the indigenous cultures over which their families had ruled as governors and as aides-de-camp. At Longleat, however, Africa came to England, when the Marquess of Bath opened a safari park in the grounds surrounding his large Elizabethan mansion in Wiltshire. Mulling over the idea after a strong drink, the marquess, whose family motto was 'I have good reason', eventually decided that the venture would make commercial sense and help bolster the failing fortunes of Longleat. In April 1966 the British public in their thousands came to see lions basking in the sun in the English countryside.[22] As another attempt to raise revenue, the marquess had staged a pop festival in the grounds of Longleat, where the Rolling Stones had attracted a crowd of 24,000. In Cornwall in 1970 Lord Eliot, heir to the ninth Earl of St Germans, planned to stage a pop festival in the grounds of his home which he hoped would rival the one held in the Isle of Wight. In the same year Lady Egremont of Petworth House made her fourth visit to Vietnam to help a mission of nuns look after 2,000 patients, of which many were children rescued from burnt-out villages.[23]

The new mood of the 1960s, with its confused searching for a better alternative to the staid conventions of upper-class society, was encapsulated by Sir Mark Palmer. For him, Eton was 'not my scene' and Magdalen College, Oxford, 'very uncool'. One day in 1962, while writing an examination paper, he noticed that 'it was a beautiful day outside – so I split'. He started to grow a reddish beard and shoulder-length hair, wore goatskin jackets, and wanted to start a commune along the lines of Sir Thomas More's *Utopia*.[24] The winter of 1969 found Sir Mark in a converted farm-cart in the grounds of Mick Jagger's home in Berkshire. The walls and floor were covered with fur rugs, there was a portable record player with a burning candle beside it, and a postcard of the Madonna and Child. 'Down here, life is much easier, much more balanced', said Sir Mark.[25]

In Wiltshire the Marquess of Bath's heir, Viscount Weymouth, attempted to start a commune at Longleat. A twelve-man team of young artists whose talents ranged from silverwork to pottery and woodcarving was set up near the house in the late 1960s. A mill on the estate was converted into a studio while the community lived with their wives and children rent-free in cottages on the Longleat estate. Lord Weymouth redecorated some of the walls of his ancestral home with pornographic murals, while the community took on the redecoration of a local restaurant. Lord Weymouth attended its opening with his hair tied back, characteristically dressed in turquoise trousers, an orange shirt, and a multi-coloured embroidered waistcoat.[26]

At about this time at Tor Hill in Gloucestershire, Sir Mark Palmer and his friends camped out to await the second coming of Christ. The Hon. Catherine Tennant said that when it happened the 'first thing we shall do is renounce our titles and give away all our money. In the meantime though, Mark just pulls out a cheque book whenever we need to buy something.'[27] Yet when in early 1970 the Hon. Catherine Tennant flew out to Malta, the authorities there refused her entry on the grounds of her being unable to support herself. She said, 'Really, it was the straight anti-hippy bit. I am quite rich you know. If the officials had let me stay they could have checked with my Maltese bank when it opened.'[28]

The Hon. Catherine Tennant was visiting the fifth Baron Harlech's daughter the Hon. Jane Rainey and her husband Michael, who had decided to spend three years of contemplation on the island. At a gathering in Glastonbury, Jane had been widely criticized for allowing her son, Saffron Neon Gabriel Mao, to sleep on a pile of hay. 'Jane knows what she is doing', said her father. But Lord Harlech, formerly British ambassador in Washington, was relieved when his daughter and son-in-law, having failed to find contentment in Malta, returned to the Harlech estate. Here they devoted their lives to farming and Michael Rainey helped with the harvesting on his father-in-law's fields.[29]

* * *

By the time Michael Rainey had started work on the harvest on Lord Harlech's estates in the summer of 1970, there had occurred a complete reversal on the national political scene. Quite unexpectedly, in the general election of 1970, the Conservative Party led by

Edward Heath was returned to power with a majority which confounded all the polls and predictions. Early editions of one newspaper showed a cartoon of the outline of Harold Wilson as he hurled himself back through the door of 10 Downing Street. With the unexpected return of Heath, an entirely different story was headline news.

The new government of 1970 set out to reduce the controls which had been introduced by Labour governments between 1964 and 1970. Landowners had been affected by five particular aspects of socialist legislation in five successive years. These had been the introduction of a 30 per cent capital gains tax in 1965, a selective employment tax introduced in 1966, the setting up of a Land Commission in 1967, the extension of the five-year rule with regard to death duties to seven years in 1968, and in 1969 the plugging of tax loopholes regarding works of art. Under the Conservatives, selective employment tax was cut by half and the Land Commission abolished. Landowners who sold land at development prices for housing and industrial use could avoid capital gains tax provided the money was invested in agriculture within three years.

Landowners who sold farms had large sums to invest quickly. During 1971, as a result of this and the sheer amount of money that was now available, the value of land with planning permission doubled. In 1972, when interest rates were at their lowest for ten years, the value of farmland doubled in only five months, between April and September. Between the autumn of 1971 and the end of 1972 farms had trebled in value. Choice estates in a good location and with sporting attractions had probably exceeded even this rate of increase.[30] Overnight, it seemed, every landed estate in England had become a goldmine. '1972 was like an Indian Summer', recalled Lord Shelburne. The stock market was at an all-time high, there was a Conservative government in power, and the OPEC countries had not yet shattered the economies of the free world. Lord Shelburne remembered, 'We moved confidently into Bowood. What an illusion it was.'[31]

What seemed to be the apogee of landed estates in twentieth-century postwar England, which occurred for a brief moment during the great property boom, coincided with the Conservative government's partial undoing of the legislation of the Labour governments of the 1960s. A capital gains tax at 30 per cent was accepted without too much difficulty during the boom in share prices. The selective employment tax, a tax levy paid by employers, was designed both to raise revenue and to encourage the movement of labour from service to manufacturing industries. For landowners who still managed to keep domestic staff, this could prove the straw that broke the camel's back. The requirement of handing over property at least seven years before death rather than five was another burden. But for landowners who were on the fringe of urban development, it was the Land Commission which caused most concern.

The initial purpose of the Land Commission when Wilson's government came to power in 1964 had been to buy up land when planning permission was granted for its development or redevelopment as an attempt to end the competitive scramble for building land. In a White Paper in 1965, the impracticality of these hopes were acknowledged, and an entirely new proposition was introduced. Concern for reduced land prices had given way to preoccupation once more with the unearned increment in land values. As the value attached to land by the right to develop it had been substantially created by the community it was thought that it should be returned to the community.[32]

When the Land Commission came into effect in 1967 it could acquire land compulsorily for any purpose whatever, and was required only to give reasons for its action. Property owners were deprived of the right to demand a public enquiry or a private hearing. It was only a late amendment which shielded families who owned their houses from this. A leading exponent of the economics of large landholdings in England in the twentieth century wrote of the commission that

> the reformers saw a promised land, the happy band of reapers and the sickles among the rigs garnering unearned increments in land values, fruit of the people's toil, into the people's barns. On the flats, where the mists of dreams condense into the realities of life, the reaping process has become 112 pages of the Parliamentary draftsman's art, a toil so intricate and complex that none but a few can comprehend the true gist of the text, let alone resolve its numerous ambiguities.[33]

One landowner voiced the sentiments of many in 1965. 'Land Commission? Land Commission?' barked the owner of an estate

129

which reached from his pillared porch to the next range of hills. 'These people don't even know what land is.'[34]

When in 1970 the Land Commission was abolished by the Conservatives, the Country Landowners' Association declared that the 'Hydra's teeth had been withdrawn'. For three years owners had had 'to feed this gross creature with fourfold tithes'.[35] From now on, if a landowner changed the use of his land from agriculture to land for recreation, gains would no longer have to be paid to the 'monster'. It was only when he disposed of his land that capital gains tax would still bite, unless the money was invested in agriculture.

The 'roll-over' relief from capital gains tax introduced by the Conservatives was one of the many factors which prompted the sudden land boom of the early 1970s. Apart from the boom in the economy there was the anticipated prosperity of farming when Britain would finally join the European Economic Community in 1973; there was a fear of inflation, the desire of newly-rich businessmen to own and reside on a farm, the influence of low land prices in the rest of Europe, the advantages still given to death duties on agricultural land, and the continuing demand for land for purposes other than agriculture. During this time, many City institutions entered the market to reap the fixed advantages of landownership and the anticipated continued increase in land values.[36]

In 1972 there was a 'feeling of disbelief' at the prices fetched for land. The eighteenth Viscount Hereford sold his 2,000-acre Hampton Court estate at Leominster in Herefordshire for £750,000 in early 1972. Had he waited another six months he would have got considerably more. At the end of 1972 the third Viscount Wimborne in Dorset sold 542 acres of land at South Canford Heath to Poole Corporation for £7.6 million. And when eighteen acres of land belonging to Canford School was sold at auction for £590,000, planning permission for sixty-five houses commanded as much as £33,000 an acre. The land here had once been a floral farm, the orchard once belonging to Canford Manor, sold by Lord Wimborne's family in 1920. Other hereditary landowners who disposed of their holdings at this time were the trustees of the Grosvenor Estate, who sold 7,000 acres of land that once formed the estate of the fourth Duke of Westminster. The sale yielded £3.5 million, which the trustees intended to reinvest in farms. In Somerset the eighth Duke of Wellington gained £231,000 for the 500-acre Wellington estate near Taunton and just over £1 million for the 1,000-acre Silchester estate in Hampshire.[37]

With the boom in the economy, the arrival of the many newly rich property developers in the early 1970s revitalized the London Season. Titled members of landed society who had for generations taken the Season for granted found themselves the object of veneration among the millionaires who took part in the traditional round of racegoing and dances. Such was the increased popularity of the Season, which since the war had been opened up to a much wider public, that events which had been tranquil and exclusive gatherings were now the scenes of large crowds. The 'private view' at the Chelsea Flower Show was always crowded and at Royal Ascot the journey from the grandstand to the paddock was hazardous and slow. There was difficulty in getting a view at Wimbledon, while at Goodwood the Earl of March announced in 1970 that the racecourse was now 'in the entertainment industry'. The Private Stand was renamed The Richmond Stand. Just five members opposed this 'revolution', one complaining that it would mean 'letting in all the riff-raff instead of some of them'.[38]

Goodwood was still followed by Cowes and Scotland, but for those who could afford it the jet had widened the Season to racing at Dublin in the first week of August, Monte Carlo for the second week, and Deauville for the end of the month. Then, for some, there was Venice in September, New York in November, St Moritz after Christmas, and the Bahamas and the West Indies in January and February. Back in England millionaires with luxurious country houses who could provide a first-class shoot, boxes at the York or Cheltenham races, tickets for the opera at Glyndebourne in Sussex, or access to the Stewards' Enclosure at Henley were particularly popular among business colleagues and friends. The counties rather than London became scenes for large gatherings in the summer. In the 1930s there had been about thirty large dances a year, mostly held in London. In the summer of 1971 there were more than 250 private dances, all held out of London, most with between 400 and 800 guests and some with over a thousand.[39] Yet these years of optimism and high living, of yachts and international travel were soon to be transformed by the economic crisis which hit the western world in 1973 and from which it was to take many years to recover.

* * *

In the autumn of 1973, following the Yom Kippur war between Israel and the Arab states, higher oil prices were introduced by the Arabs, aimed specifically at crippling the western economy. New militant nationalist regimes had gained power in Algeria, Libya, and Iraq, and they soon changed their relations with the multi-national oil companies. The price of oil was now used as a political weapon. As two-thirds of Britain's oil came from the Middle East this had a disastrous effect on the economy.[40] Yet worse was to come. When in February 1974 the Labour Party was narrowly returned to power, the Chancellor of the Exchequer cleverly diverted the nation's attention from the economic crisis by producing a budget which aimed to 'soak the rich'.

It was the first time in the twentieth century that landed society in England was faced with policies aimed specifically at the redistribution of wealth. As far as the Labour government was concerned, their tax proposals were not primarily a means of gaining revenue. In 1974 they were part of a bitter political crusade. The only country which reshapes its tax laws every year, Britain in 1974 had no less than three budgets, in March, July, and November. The first two were specifically aimed at bringing the rich to their knees.

Since the introduction of death duties in 1894 taxation at death had over the years come to be known as 'the voluntary tax'. Despite the occasional glaring examples, when owners had not outlived the five- and the seven-year-rules, death duties could largely be avoided by setting up trusts and through gifts. Realizing the disconcerting success with which the rich had managed to sidestep the taxes, the Chancellor of the Exchequer, Denis Healey, tried to reverse this trend. He stated quite clearly that he wanted to reverse 'the unfair advantages enjoyed by generation after generation of the heirs and relatives of wealthy men'.[41] He rallied his parliamentary colleagues by saying that he could not believe that they could reasonably complain if he now took steps to see that 'a tax that has been on the statute book for nearly 80 years is at last made effective'.[42]

Estate duty payable at death was abolished and in its place was created capital transfer tax. This meant that any transfer of wealth, except between a husband and wife, was subject to tax. It was no longer possible to set up trust funds to avoid paying tax. Yet all was not gloom. For farmers, gradually and grudgingly, there were tax reliefs. Similarly, tax relief was given to the owners of historic houses and their surrounding parkland and contents if they were opened to the public for at least thirty days a year. Once again, by careful management and reorganization, it was possible for landowners to avoid the worst of the new tax.

Immediately after 1974 the price of land fell. Yet with concessions given to farmers and the effect of membership of the European Economic Community land revived as an attractive investment. But still more legislative measures were aimed at landowners. These included the 1975 Community Land Act, reminiscent of Lloyd George's Finance Act of 1910. In 1976, close relatives of tenant farmers could succeed to tenancies for three generations and farm workers in estate cottages were given security of tenure. Agricultural landlords were also placed at a fiscal disadvantage compared with owner-occupiers in that the letting and management of land was not treated as a business for income-tax purposes and rents were subject to an investment-income surcharge. After taxation, the amounts available for reinvestment were negligible.

By 1977, the legislative programme which since 1974 had been 'heavy with menace' was quieter than at any time since Labour took office.[43] But the previous three years had involved the Country Landowners' Association in the 'most intense and prolonged bout of Parliamentary activity in its history', when 'irrational Government outbursts about abolishing the relics of feudalism had made sensible dialogue difficult'.[44] It was the initial budget proposals of 1974, made law with some concessions in 1975, which had caused the most difficulties for landowners. By looking at a fictitious estate in 1975, it is possible to see what some of these problems were.

A typical estate might consist of a country house, a dower house, a leisure company, some land with development potential, some woodland, a trust fund based abroad, and a home farm.[45] If after the war the country house had been donated to the National Trust, the house and gardens might be open from Easter to October on one afternoon a week. After 1975, historic houses would have to have much more public access to property and treasures. The valuable dower house might have been handed over to the present owner on his marriage by his father, thus avoiding death duties under the marriage gifts exemption clause; such avoidance would no longer be possible after 1975. A leisure company run by the son and heir might have let sporting rights on the estate, the income being sent abroad free of tax. Again, this would no longer be possible after 1975. In the 1950s planning permission could have been acquired to schedule farming land for building purposes, but after 1975 the increased value of such land would be taxed. As far as the woodland was concerned, the death-bed transfer of woodland had always been valuable in delaying payment on some death duties; growing timber was not counted as a taxable asset until it was felled and sold, allowing postponement of tax for fifteen years or more. On this, some relief was still available.

A discretionary trust set up abroad might have controlled all the owner's property apart from the house, the home farm, the development land, and the dower house. This would have prevented the British tax authorities from touching any assets; after 1975 this loophole was likely to be blocked for British residents. Finally, the ownership of the home farm might have been transferred to the oldest son in anticipation of death duties. He and his wife would then draw salaries as directors of the farm, which would be taxable as earned income. The family's cars would appear on farm accounts and the twelve 'farm hands' could also act for the family as butler, chauffeur and gamekeeper. Both the owner and his son derived incomes from the farm and therefore qualified as 'working farmers'.[46] Continued government support to farming in peacetime, thirty years after this initial guarantee had been introduced after the Second World War, meant that if landowners became farmers, considerable relief could be derived from capital transfer tax.

The continued support given to farmers in the form of tax concessions and the benefits of membership of the European Economic Community meant that, once again, if professionally advised, landowners could reorganize their finances to reap substantial advantages. Yet landed society was still being pulled in two directions. In European Architectural Heritage Year in 1975 attention was drawn to the urgent need to preserve the unique English contribution of the country house. In the same year, a wealth tax was threatened and inflation was getting higher and higher. The need to save the nation's architectural heritage became the overriding objective of the rest of the 1970s, one in which owners of historic houses were compelled to play a part during years of economic recession.

The most imponderable problem facing landowners with historic houses in the 1970s was inflation. Between March 1972 and March 1974 repair costs had risen by about 60 per cent.[47] Moreover, a landowner now had to adopt a number of roles when dealing with the numerous bureaucratic demands of being a custodian of an estate. He had to deal with local authorities and with tax authorities not only as a landowner, but as a farmer, a company director, a landlord, and an individual. Given the tax changes and increased legislation of the 1974–9 Labour government, running an estate during a time of high inflation demanded more and more of his energy and time.[48]

From 1974, the Department of the Environment's Historic Buildings Bureau quarterly list of buildings increased rapidly as a result of the Chancellor of the Exchequer's measures and threats against the owners of large houses. The list included some of the most beautiful houses in England.[49] Since the Second World War, grants from the Historic Buildings Council had helped to save many houses, but often needed much prompting. Burdened by the weight of their dealings with local and central government, some owners were unwilling to apply for a grant from the Historic Buildings Council for fear of entering into yet another series of encounters with bureaucracy. Much now depended on the personality of the landowner, on whether he was capable of dealing with these problems, and, more importantly, on whether or not he wanted to.[50] Considerable enterprise was shown by the eighth Marquess of Hertford at Ragley Hall in Warwickshire. After no answer for a year from the Historic Buildings Council, he managed successfully to advertise his need to save his historic home where the roof was leaking, the front steps crumbling, and where there were blue flashes when the lights were switched on and off. The marquess had been invited to give a lecture to the Council for the Protection of Rural England, and he saw to it that newspapers, radio, and television were all invited. He then announced that unless he got a grant, he would demolish his house and build a smaller one. It was then that the Historic Buildings Council took action.[51]

The preservation of a historic house required skilled workers, whether they were gardeners, masons, bricklayers, carpenters, roofers, joiners, decorators, restorers, or textile repairers. Yet because of skilled craftsmen's rates and the high cost of special materials, between mid-1978 and mid-1979 the cost of repairs to existing buildings rose one-third more than the cost of new construction. On top of this, value added tax at 15 per cent was charged on all building work described as repair and maintenance. Construction, demolition, and alterations required no payment of value added tax.

An owner could alter or extend his house, but was charged for trying to keep it standing.[52]

Following the sudden rise in oil prices in 1973, the cost of keeping houses warm was an urgent problem. The Marquess of Hertford paid just over £2,000 a year to heat and light Ragley Hall in 1975, but this increased to just over £6,000 in 1977. Garden and maintenance costs had risen from £1,700 in 1975 to £3,600 in 1977.[53] The problems of life in a country house in the 1970s were summed up by Charles Clive-Ponsonby-Fane, who in 1974 made the bold decision to return to live in his family home of Brympton d'Evercy in Dorset. He wondered 'how many more generations would be willing to accept a home life with no privacy and appalling discomfort along with the steady deprivation of their most treasured possessions?'[54]

* * *

In the midst of recession and inflation, the announcement in August 1976 of the engagement of the sister of the future sixth Duke of Westminster to one of the richest landowners in Scotland, the tenth Duke of Roxburghe, seemed to be a gesture of defiant solidarity in the face of economic difficulties by the landed super-rich. By marrying the young Duke of Roxburghe, Lady Jane Grosvenor was connecting two of the wealthiest landowning families in Britain. Only a year before, in 1975, Lady Jane's sister Lady Leonora had married the photographer, the Earl of Lichfield. And the Earl of Lichfield, along with several other members of English landed society, regularly spent holidays on the island of Mustique in the West Indies during these recession-hit times, an island which offered a welcome respite from the hostile political and economic climate at home.

The 1,400-acre island of Mustique had been bought by the Hon. Colin Tennant, heir to the second Baron Glenconner, in 1959. He had spent much money since then on its development as a holiday resort, to which he had attracted many of his friends. Colin Tennant was married to the daughter of the fifth Earl of Leicester of Holkham Hall in Norfolk, and had been an original member of the 'Margaret Set'. This sub-tropical outpost of English landed society in the twentieth century was the scene of happy times during these years. On the island in April 1976 was Viscountess Royston whose late husband had been heir to the ninth Earl of Hardwicke. The Earl of Lichfield had purchased some land on the island close to Princess

Margaret's house, which had been a present from Colin Tennant. Here the second son of a Welsh landed family, Roddy Llewellyn, son of Sir Harry 'Foxhunter' Llewellyn, had created a garden. So too could be found the ubiquitous Mick Jagger, playing the island's version of cricket. But a poignant sign of the times was the presence off the island of the Saudi Arabian Oil Minister's 500-ton yacht, lent to him by the arms dealer Adnam Khashoggi. In the employment of Sheikh Ahmed Yamani as a bodyguard was Lord Patrick Beresford, brother of the eighth Marquess of Waterford. The polo-playing Lord Pat, formerly a member of the Special Air Service, led a five-man detachment which guarded the Sheikh twenty-four hours a day.[55]

A young landowner who was noticeably hit by rising costs during this time was the third Baron Hesketh. High inflation in 1975 forced him to wield the economy axe. 'Entertainments are being cut to a minimum and yachts are out – all the money available will be spent on the car.'[56] In 1974 the motor-racing Lord Hesketh, owner of the 9,000-acre Towcester estate in Northamptonshire, had entered the Monaco Grand Prix. In that year he had chartered a 200-foot yacht for his stay, with a swimming pool and a helicopter and with a Rolls-Royce close by on the quayside. In 1975 Hesketh was reduced to staying in a hotel in Monte Carlo. Times were also hard for the third Viscount Cowdray's son, the Hon. Michael Pearson. In May 1975 he put up his yacht *Hedonist* for sale. For Pearson there was 'a limit to how long one can go on cruising around the Med. I want to do other things and see other places now.'[57]

Tax exile in France was the fate of at least three prominent members of landed society during these straitened times. Lord Brooke, heir to Warwick Castle, followed his father the seventh Earl of Warwick who had gone into tax exile fifteen years earlier. Lord Brooke lived in a small apartment in Paris and took French lessons in the morning, going to the Travellers' Club for lunch, where he spent the afternoon. A friend said 'He's rather miserable; although he is invited out by a lot of French hostesses who want to marry their daughters off.'[58] In England, not far from Lord Brooke's Warwick Castle, the third Viscount Wimborne's Ashby St Ledgers estate was put on the market in 1975. His father had invested in farmland, but Lord Wimborne had made almost £10 million in land sales and planned to spend April in Paris as a start to his tax exile.[59] Another aristocratic expatriate in the French capital at this time was the thirteenth Duke of Bedford. Having transformed Woburn into a commercial concern immediately after the war, he made the sudden decision to leave for Paris in April 1974, leaving his young heir, the Marquess of Tavistock and his wife, to cope with the problems of running a large country house. Indications of a desire to withdraw to a leisurely retirement had been apparent in 1971, when the duke said 'Who the hell wants to have 32 sitting rooms anymore? I don't have time to sit in them anyhow.'[60]

Families such as the Heskeths, the Cowdrays, the Bedfords, the Lichfields, the Westminsters, and the Wimbornes had survived the twentieth century relatively unscathed, although few of them would probably agree. During the 1960s and 1970s surveys were undertaken to establish just how unusual these families were. In his book *The Aristocrats*, published in 1968, Roy Perrott showed that members of the aristocracy were still the biggest individual landowners and that each county contained between six and twelve large landowners. He estimated that there were 350 titled families who owned enough land to make it an important part of their life and income and a further 1,500 families with estates of several thousand acres. But since 1873, when the first survey of landownership was published, the number of landed lords had declined by just over a third and untitled landowners had declined by two-thirds. Many of these smaller families had moved out of the old hall to a small house, where they had turned to farming themselves.[61] Some of these ancient families found that they no longer appeared in Burke's *Landed Gentry* in 1965. In the 1952 edition, the qualification for inclusion in the 4,500 entries had been a family seat and at least 300 acres. In the next edition in 1965 there was more interest in the history of 'socially significant' families who might not own any land at all.

Soon after the original 1873 survey of landownership had been put in a more accessible way by a landowning squire called Bateman, the *Spectator* had commented on the results. A hundred years later the *Spectator* published a contemporary version. To establish the degree to which the fifty-four landowners who in 1873 had owned estates of at least 20,000 acres were still there, the *Spectator* managed to trace the high number of thirty-three. But trying to establish the whereabouts of the landed aristocrats and how much land they owned was, and still is, a more elusive problem. Once contacted, one landowner could not quite remember how much land he did own.

'I do find it so difficult to remember what an acre looks like when I drive across the estate.'[62]

During the property boom of the early 1970s, when the value of estates had sometimes doubled or even tripled, there had been concern at the number of City institutions buying up land. There was concern too at the number of Arabs who appeared to be taking over land after the rapid increase in oil prices after 1973. Yet these fears were exaggerated. 'There appears to be a widespread though mistaken belief that the estate market has become some sort of *souk* in which there are hundreds of Arabs longing to spend their oil-gotten gains on anything they can find', noted Michael Hanson of *Country Life*.[63] Many such purchases could all be attributed to one man, Mohammed Mahdi Al-Tajir, the United Arab Emirates' ambassador to Britain. In Kent he had purchased Mereworth Castle, an eighteenth-century Palladian house along with 400 acres of woods and parkland, a stud farm, and a hundred acres of paddocks. He also bought three other mansions in the country as well as a large house in Kensington.[64] Yet it was the appearance on the market of Arabs, Dutchmen, other foreigners, and City institutions which caused a government committee to be set up in 1977 to investigate the 'Acquisition and Occupancy of Agricultural Land'.

The results of the committee headed by Lord Northfield showed that, after all, only 1 per cent of the agricultural land in Great Britain was owned by financial institutions. Ninety per cent was privately owned,[65] and the rest was held by public and semi-public bodies such as the Forestry Commission, government departments, local authorities, county councils, nationalized industries, Crown Estates, the National Trust, Church Commissioners, and Oxford and Cambridge colleges. In 1979, 6 million acres in England and Wales, compared with 12 million acres in 1873, were held in private hands in estates of at least 5,000 acres – some 1,200 landowners.[66] Included among these estates were those which belonged to the fifth Baron Tollemache. Back in 1965 he had summed up his attitude to landownership, which would have been echoed by other landowners when the Northfield report was published in 1979, and will be carried through the twentieth century and beyond.

My friends all have much the same interests as me – they own estates and work in London, and they have enough initiative and guts to enjoy themselves. I don't see why country estates shouldn't go on as they are, provided they are well run and the tenants are happy and have a better deal than they would if they were independent. There is no doubt about it, it can be great fun and you get on jolly well together.[67]

8

Embarrassment of riches

The general election of May 1979 saw the Conservative Party returned to power once more. The five years of socialist government from 1974 to 1979 coupled with economic recession had caused more problems for landowners than at any time since the immediate postwar period. Despite the prevailing economic problems, the outcome of the 1979 election provided new hope for English landed society. It was now represented at all levels of government by Cabinet ministers, ministers of state, and under-secretaries of state who had close links with the land and with the farming interest. In 1979, a third of the new government's members were farmers or landowners. Almost half of the Cabinet, by happy coincidence, were farmers or landowners.[1] Members of Mrs Thatcher's first government had their closest link with the one area of the economy which had the highest subsidies. When during the Conservative administration of 1979–83 officers of the Country Landowners' Association entertained members of the Cabinet in their London clubs, there was no need to explain to them the problems which concerned farmers and landowners.

It was perhaps a sign of the new prime minister's strength that in attempting to reverse the economic policies of all postwar Conservative governments since Churchill, she chose to surround herself in her Cabinet with many of her opponents. Her dedication to free-market economics and her determination to cut government spending was questioned by, among many others, Churchill's son-in-law Lord Soames, who was at the Privy Council Office.

The Foreign Secretary was the sixth Baron Carrington. The owner of a large country house centred on an estate in Buckinghamshire, his family had first taken their seat in the House of Lords at the end of the eighteenth century. Lord Carrington's first mission was to oversee a settlement for Rhodesia, the last African country in the old British empire to be given independence. At this he achieved a great diplomatic success, sending the fifth Baron Harlech to bring back a first-hand account of what needed to be done and sending Lord Soames as Rhodesia's last Governor. Later on Lord Carrington resigned as a matter of honour when an old colonial outpost near Argentina, the Falkland Islands, were invaded. During his time at the Foreign Office from May 1979 to April 1982, Carrington had working under him Nicholas Ridley, younger brother of the fourth Viscount Ridley of Blagdon Park in Northumberland.

William Whitelaw, who had inherited from his grandfather estates on rich coal seams in Dumbartonshire was Home Secretary.[2] Whitelaw's Under-Secretary of State at the Home Office in 1979 was a Deputy Lieutenant for Suffolk, the second Baron Belstead. Sir Ian Gilmour, brother-in-law of one of the largest landowners in Great Britain, the ninth Duke of Buccleuch, was Lord Privy Seal. George Younger, son of the third Viscount Younger of Leckie who owned land in Stirlingshire, had in 1963 stepped down from his seat so that Sir Alec Douglas-Home could fight a by-election in order to lead the party from the House of Commons. He was rewarded in 1979 with the Scottish Office. Younger's Minister of State at the Scottish Office was the eighth Earl of Mansfield, who resided at Scone Palace in Perthshire, where he owned some 30,000 acres. Other Scottish landowning connections in the 1979 government included the Hon. Peter Morrison, the son of the first Baron Margadale, who owned land on the island of Islay off the south coast of Mull as well as land in Hampshire. Lord John Douglas-Hamilton, the brother of the fifteenth Duke of Hamilton, was also a Lord Commissioner. Lord Thorneycroft, owner of 44,000 acres in Scotland, was chairman of the Conservative Party.

Francis Pym, whose ancestors had a long association with Parliament, was Defence Secretary from 1979 to 1981. The owner of a 500-acre estate in Bedfordshire centred on Hazell's Hall, Pym was appointed Foreign Secretary after Lord Carrington's resignation in 1982. His place at Defence was taken in 1981 by John Nott, owner of a farm in Cornwall. The Environment Secretary, Michael Heseltine, modestly described himself in the *Register of Members' Interests* in 1980 as the 'owner occupier of houses in London and Northamptonshire'.[3] Having made his money in publishing in the early 1970s, he lived at Thenford House, an eighteenth-century mansion set among 400 acres in Northamptonshire where his wife was a member of the Bicester Hunt. Whereas few members of landed society could now afford a house in Belgravia, Heseltine could himself lay claim to such a privilege.

Another businessman in the 1979 Cabinet who had invested in land was the Employment Secretary, James Prior. From 1970 to 1972 he had been the Minister of Agriculture in Edward Heath's government. His successor in 1979 was Peter Walker, a self-made millionaire who then owned 400 acres in Shropshire. Peter Walker's ministers at Agriculture were the thirteenth Earl Ferrers of Hedenham Hall in Suffolk and Alick Buchanan-Smith, owner of land in Scotland. Walker's decision to give a massive injection of support to farmers during a time of government cutbacks saw the spirit of the Heath administration, with its high government spending, 'resuscitated out of time, like Lord Palmerston as the last relic of the Regency surviving into the high Victorian era'.[4]

When James Prior was Minister of Agriculture, he had given farmers in 1971 the biggest financial award ever.[5] A year before, protesting farmers had disrupted Whitehall traffic. After Prior's intervention it was soon recognized that they were more likely to be 'jamming the market towns with their new Jaguars than Whitehall with their tractors'.[6] In 1979 farmers were encouraged by Peter Walker to push up production once more. Higher levels of production had been called for by Ministers of Agriculture each year since 1947 when the system of price support had first been introduced, but in 1979 Peter Walker 'pushed agriculture into overdrive and roared the engine'.[7] Maximum production was the target. Right up to the general election of 1983, farmers were urged to produce more. 'Then the gear was slammed into reverse.'[8]

The result of this postwar demand for increased food production was seen throughout the English countryside in the destruction of many of its most picturesque features. Conservation of the countryside now became a political issue. A book which appeared in 1980, called quite simply *The Theft of the Countryside*, outlined what this destruction was. The blame was put quite emphatically on the farmers themselves. The price-support system meant that farmers were the only group of producers who were guaranteed an acceptable price for whatever they produced in whatever quantity regardless of demand. Every 'unfelled wood or undrained wetland [represented] forfeited profit'.[9] Between 1945 and 1974, 4,500 miles of hedgerow had been removed every year and nearly one-third of ancient woodland had been destroyed.[10] Yet what emerged from Marion Shoard's book of 1980 was that landowners with long associations with their local communities wanted to keep their land as they remembered it. Not wishing to antagonize the local people among whom their families had lived for generations, and with the prospect of handing on an estate to future generations, long-term benefits were as important for landed society as they had been for centuries.[11] Field sports often took precedence over the maximization of profits. In the choice between high production from farmland and hunting or shooting on estates, it was these traditional sports which always won, allowing the natural habitat of wildlife to be saved on landed estates throughout England.

The sixth Earl of Carnarvon's Highclere estate in Hampshire showed the role that the rearing of pheasants played in conserving the countryside. Seven thousand pheasants were reared every year to provide sport for Lord Carnarvon and his guests. Much of the land was left unfarmed, or was maintained as woodland, where beech trees interspersed with conifers surrounded two fishing lakes. The central part of the estate was parkland and in the southern third wild flowers and beech woods flourished on the chalk hills. Even where the estate was devoted to intensive agriculture, the thick hedgerows provided extra cover for the birds. Farmed by financial institutions, the woods and the open downland would have been transformed into blank fields of corn.[12] The beech trees on Lord Carnarvon's Highclere estate had taken more than a century to reach maturity. Conifers, however, took sixty years. For members of landed society with large taxable incomes, the planting of conifers could be particularly lucrative. The tax advantages that accrued to landowners were often the main incentive for those engaged in forestry.[13]

With the passing of the 1981 Wildlife and Countryside Act by the farming and landowning Conservative government, some landowners could benefit from another potential source of revenue. With their detailed knowledge of all aspects of wildlife in the countryside, peers in the House of Lords spent eighty-two hours debating this Bill. The result of the 1981 Act was that if landowners possessed on their estates Sites of Special Scientific Interest, of which there were 4,000 in Britain, and if they did not farm these sites, they would be compensated by a grant. Lord Bruce-Gardyne later observed that such compensation meant that landowners could benefit by 'not undertaking schemes which they had no intention of carrying out anyway'.[14] The seventh Earl of Onslow had noted that the third Earl Peel, who owned land in the Yorkshire Dales national park, 'had only to come up with a scheme to lime, slag and re-seed his acres – a scheme which would certainly be turned down by the Act – and he would pick up anything from £75,000 to £300,000 a year'.[15]

Conservation won the day in another important ruling by the new Conservative government. In April 1982 the Environment Secretary, Michael Heseltine, after a lengthy public inquiry refused permission for the National Coal Board to dig up one of the most beautiful tracts of farmland in England, the Vale of Belvoir. Another brave decision by the Environment Secretary in the cause of conservation was when he refused his Cabinet colleague, the Defence Secretary Francis Pym, permission to demolish his seventeenth-century mansion of Hazell's Hall. One of 'the hundred best houses of its type in the country', it had been letting in the rain for several years. The beautiful Adam plaster ceilings had begun to fall in and vandals had smashed the glass in the windows.[16] It was later bought by the architect Kit Martin, and its repair and adaptation as twelve self-contained residences was a scheme by which many country houses were saved from demolition.[17]

Not only conservation of the countryside but the heritage had become an important political issue. In the Queen's Speech of November 1979 'the heritage' was mentioned for the first time. Members of landed society whose houses were part of the nation's heritage were represented by the Historic Houses Association, formed in 1973. Thanks to the work of Commander Michael Saunders Watson of Rockingham Castle in Northamptonshire, owners of historic houses could set up maintenance funds which would be free from party political tampering at every budget. In the budget of 1980 new measures allowed such maintenance funds to be set up to maintain not only historic buildings and their surrounding land, but also land of outstanding scenic, historic, or scientific interest. Moreover, works of art accepted in lieu of tax were allowed to remain on the walls of privately owned historic houses. One landowner who benefited from this important legislation was the seventeenth Duke of Norfolk. In the House of Lords he summed up his attitude to the heritage, to which English country houses made a vital contribution, by saying 'We have not had the ravages of wars such as they have had on the continent. We have not had those awful revolutions they have had. What we have is absolutely unique.'[18] At the duke's Arundel Castle in Sussex, portraits, including one of Cardinal Newman by Sir John Millais, were given to the National Portrait Gallery on condition that they stayed in the castle.

Another portrait of Cardinal Newman hung in the office of the Arts Minister, Norman St John-Stevas. He and Michael Heseltine were responsible for heritage issues, in which St John-Stevas found his colleague 'sympathetic and helpful in the battle against the philistines'.[19] As Leader of the House of Commons St John-Stevas was able to give priority to the Bill which set up the National Heritage Memorial Fund, later to save the property of some of England's richest landowners. Responsibility for administering the old Land Fund was taken from the Treasury and given to trustees, all chosen by the Prime Minister. The chairman of the trustees was Lord Charteris, a brother of the twelfth Earl of Wemyss. At Cecil Beaton's memorial service in St Martin-in-the-Fields in London, St John-Stevas found himself standing next to Lord Charteris, to whom he was able to indicate that he would be appointed chairman.[20]

The original Land Fund had been set up in 1946 by the Old Etonian Labour Chancellor of the Exchequer Hugh Dalton. Dalton had served on the Italian front during the First World War. Deeply regretting the deaths of so many of his friends in that war and of his younger friends in the Second World War, he was determined to seize the opportunity which being Chancellor of the Exchequer gave him of establishing a memorial worthy of all the people who had died in the two world wars. This memorial was to be the preservation and enhancement of the beauty of the countryside.[21] Through the sale of surplus war stores, Dalton set up a fund of £50 million to reimburse the Inland Revenue for land offered by executors to pay death duties. But the difference between high market values and low probate valuations discouraged the kind of transactions which Dalton envisaged. After 1951 Conservative governments raided the fund for other purposes. In 1957 the

Chancellor of the Exchequer Peter Thorneycroft, later Lord Thorneycroft, reduced the capital in the fund to £10 million.[22]

The renamed National Heritage Memorial Fund was founded partly as a result of the public outcry in 1977 when the seventh Earl of Rosebery decided to dispose of his vast Victorian mansion in Buckinghamshire, Mentmore Towers. Offered to the government for a mere £2 million to pay death duties, it had been turned down because of the heavy repair and maintenance costs. Lord Rosebery, therefore, whose grandfather had in 1894 been Prime Minister when Sir William Harcourt had introduced his death duties, sold much of the contents of Mentmore to Sotheby's for £5 million.[23] Mentmore was then bought by an oriental mystic sect and became the headquarters of the 'World Government of the Age of Enlightenment'. But the inability of even the Labour government to save Mentmore had posed important questions concerning the fate of any other such offer by private owners.

One of the first purchases by the trustees of the National Heritage Memorial Fund was the painting 'Christ taking leave of his Mother' by the German artist Altdorfer, from the Wernher family. The trustees contributed £850,000 of the purchase price paid by the National Gallery for the picture. From the proceeds of the sale the Wernher family were able to maintain their country house, Luton Hoo in Bedfordshire, in excellent condition and accessible to the public.[24] Other important achievements of the Fund were a grant of £8 million in 1983 for Belton Park in Lincolnshire and a contribution to save Calke Abbey in Derbyshire in 1984. In 1985 the government gave an extra £25 million to the Fund to preserve three houses; Weston Park in Shropshire, where the sixth Earl of Bradford had died suddenly and unexpectedly in 1981 leaving a large tax bill, Kedleston in Derbyshire, and Nostell Priory in Yorkshire.

Kedleston was unique in that the Palladian house, its contents, its gardens, and its park were a magnificent Georgian ensemble. The second Viscount Scarsdale had died in 1977 and his family had been faced with a tax bill of £2 million. The third Viscount Scarsdale was a nephew of Lord Curzon, the Viceroy of India. Since 1969 Viscount Scarsdale had been the estate manager at Kedleston. 'When I succeeded my cousin in 1977, I sacked myself', he said, 'but immediately took myself on again because there was no one else to do the job.'[25]

In 1986 the trustees of the National Heritage Memorial Fund completed the purchase of the 'finest collection of documented Chippendale furniture in the world' at Nostell Priory in Yorkshire.[26] The collection faced the threat of dispersal after the death of the fourth Baron St Oswald in 1984, when liabilities of £4 million had to be met. The fifth Baron St Oswald set up a new charitable trust, the income of which would be devoted to the maintenance and management of Nostell Priory itself and several thousand acres of parkland. If the National Heritage Memorial Fund had not bought the Chippendale collection, it could have been dispersed by the St Oswalds and could have fetched as much as £40 million. Lady St Oswald said 'It was sorely tempting at times to take the money, especially in the winter when the house is cold. . . .Or you could be somewhere else in the sunshine or somewhere else in England and be absolutely comfortable.' But Lord and Lady St Oswald were determined to keep the collection together because of the strong family connections. Lord Charteris pronounced it 'a triumph of good sense in the pursuit of what is best for the nation or, a little more informally, it is a damned good show'.[27]

The unique collection of Chippendale furniture was saved for the nation when the St Oswalds decided to stay on at Nostell. Yet the consequences of giving in to temptation, and to take the money and run, were seen in the 1978 sale by Lord Brooke of the entire contents of Warwick Castle. Lord Brooke, the heir to the seventh Earl of Warwick, whose family motto was 'I scarcely call these things our own', sold not only the contents of Warwick Castle but also its archives, which were the written source of much of the history of Warwickshire.[28] The castle was bought by Madame Tussauds, who set up a waxwork reconstruction of a house party in 1898 in twelve rooms in the castle.

The decision to sell unique treasures from a country house collection was taken with a good deal more soul-searching when much of the contents of Holkham Hall in Norfolk had to be sold after the fifth Earl of Leicester died in 1976. Here, seven manuscripts were given to the nation in lieu of tax at a valuation of nearly £250,000. On the open market they probably would have fetched more than £1 million.[29] The sale of the Codex Leicester, Leonardo Da Vinci's mostly illegible treatise on the nature, weight, and movement of water, which had been of fundamental importance when he created the landscape in the *Mona Lisa*, brought the

Leicester family £2 million.[30] The last Leonardo manuscript in private hands, it was purchased by the wealthy American, Armand Hammer. Norman St John-Stevas was faced with the problem of whether the Codex should be given an export licence and therefore allowed to leave the country. In the middle of some Christmas shopping on the Portobello Road, St John-Stevas had an idea and rang Claridge's where Hammer was staying. He said that he would agree to give an export licence on condition that the manuscript be exhibited in Britain for three months each year. In this way, more people would have a chance to see the Codex which, when it was exhibited in Washington during President Reagan's inaugural celebrations in January 1981, was described in the catalogue as Codex Hammer.[31]

* * *

The election of President Reagan in 1980, eighteen months after the election of Mrs Thatcher in 1979, saw the beginning of a unique partnership between Britain and America. When President Reagan visited Britain in 1982 he was the first American president to stay at Windsor Castle. When the Queen visited America in 1983, the President and Mrs Reagan celebrated their wedding anniversary with a dinner on board the Royal Yacht in the harbour at San Francisco. Two years later in November 1985 members of landed families flew to America to be present at the opening of the 'Treasure Houses of Britain' exhibition, an exhibition which further consolidated the Anglo-American alliance. Held in the modern East Building of the National Gallery of Art in Washington it was the most successful exhibition ever held in America. Between its opening in November to its extension to the middle of April 1986, the exhibition was seen by almost a million people.

The idea of the exhibition had been that of the Director of the National Gallery in Washington, J. Carter Brown. An Anglophile, Carter Brown had in 1976 married his second wife in Westminster Abbey. He recalled:

> I made a courtesy call on the Dean of Westminster Abbey, and he said he wouldn't *hear* of our being married anywhere *else* but the Henry the Seventh *Chapel*, which is one of the most beautiful architectural *jewels* that exist, that *incredible* ceiling that it has. . . .[32]

Such enthusiasm for English architecture was politely welcomed by his hosts when Carter Brown visited country houses in England in preparation for the exhibition in Washington. His enthusiasm went back further however, to childhood stays at Stonor Park in Oxfordshire, home of Lord Camoys. J. Carter Brown retained his links with this unspoilt, unchanged country house set in a sheltered valley, being godfather to the son and heir of Lord Camoys. During his travels around England, Carter Brown almost lost his life in a car accident on the way to Castle Howard, having inspected Chippendale furniture at Harewood House in Yorkshire. But November 1985 found him well able to cope with the sudden aristocratic whirl of lenders of treasures from Britain who arrived to be entertained in Washington for the opening of the exhibition.[33]

'A motorcade of double-decker red buses, full of historic house owners, roaring through downtown Washington flanked by a police escort with sirens blaring' was a somewhat unusual spectacle for observers of English landed society in the twentieth century.[34] Entertainments for lenders of the treasures saw a unique gathering in America of the owners of some of the most beautiful and most visited houses in England: the Duke and Duchess of Marlborough from Blenheim Palace; the third Baron Montagu from Beaulieu Abbey in Hampshire; the young Marquess and Marchioness of Tavistock from Woburn Abbey; the young Lord and Lady Romsey from Broadlands in Hampshire, and the even younger Hon. Simon Howard, who had inherited Castle Howard at the age of 28 in 1984. Along with many other members of English landed society, these lenders of treasures enjoyed the series of dinners and parties and luncheons held throughout this extravagant week in Washington.

At the exhibition were specially constructed rooms which included a Jacobean Gallery, a Sculpture Rotunda, and an Edwardian room containing Sargent's large portrait of the ninth Duke of Marlborough and his Duchess, Consuelo Vanderbilt. At the exhibition, some of the lenders of the exhibits gave the impression of 'not having looked seriously at things' for quite a long time.[35] It had always been considered not good manners to notice what other people owned and many lenders were 'genuinely bewildered by the scale of socialising'. While Henry Harpur-Crewe asked if he could sleep in the reconstructed bed from his Derbyshire home of Calke Abbey, the fifth Baron Leigh arrived at one reception dressed in his coronation robes as a flamboyant gesture to please his American hosts.[36] Hostesses in Washington were somewhat more impressed however by the arrival of the Prince and Princess of Wales to open the exhibition. They stayed at the British Embassy and were entertained at the White House by President and Mrs Reagan.

Had the Prince of Wales, Prince Charles, attended the 'Treasure Houses of Britain' exhibition without the princess, it would not have had quite the same glamour. In July 1981 their wedding had perpetuated another distinctive feature of English landed society in the twentieth century, that of the unchanging traditions of suitable marriages.

*   *   *

The glittering, joyous ceremonial of the royal wedding, after which the Prince and Princess of Wales were drawn in a carriage from St Paul's Cathedral to Buckingham Palace, saw large crowds in London. The scenes were reminiscent of the coronation in 1953, while television viewers gazed at the occasion from all over the world. The choice of an English bride, a young girl from a landed aristocratic family with long connections with royalty, gave added romance to the occasion.

Royal weddings were traditionally held in Westminster Abbey, but to accommodate the many guests the wedding was held at St Paul's. For the first time at a royal wedding since the Reformation, a Roman Catholic Cardinal, formerly Abbot of the Benedictine monastery of Ampleforth in Yorkshire, was invited to give his blessing. The wedding was notable not only for the significant relaxation of centuries of division between the Church of England, of which the Queen was the Supreme Governor, and the Roman Catholic Church; on this occasion, it was 'a mark of the new Elizabethan era that divorce [had] been allowed to encroach closer to the Throne than at any time since the reign of Henry VIII'.[37] The parents of the young bride were divorced and both her father and her mother had remarried. When wedding guests were allowed to bring with them their second husbands or second wives in 1981, this marked an unprecedented break with tradition as far as the royal family was concerned. Divorce had become socially acceptable in the royal circle with some speed.

In 1955 the sister of the Queen, Princess Margaret, after a meeting with the Archbishop of Canterbury, had announced her decision after years of speculation not to marry the divorced Group

Captain Peter Townsend, who had been an equerry of her father, King George VI. Five years later in 1960 Princess Margaret married Anthony Armstrong-Jones, himself the son of divorced parents. In 1967 the Queen's cousin, the seventh Earl of Harewood of Harewood House in Yorkshire, was sued for divorce by his wife, the Countess of Harewood. As Lord Harewood wanted to marry again, this posed a problem for the Queen, as her consent for his remarriage was needed by the conditions of the Royal Marriages Act. The Queen would have been willing to grant it had it not looked as though she, as Supreme Governor of the Church, were condoning divorce.[38] A solution was provided by her Prime Minister, Harold Wilson. He would put the matter to the Cabinet and they would advise the Queen to grant permission for her cousin's marriage. As constitutional monarch she was obliged to take their advice. In 1967, the divorced Lord Harewood married his divorced second wife and a royal precedent was set.[39]

The Earl of Harewood did not attend the funeral of his uncle the Duke of Windsor in 1972, nor the wedding of the Queen's daughter, Princess Anne, in 1973. In 1976, Princess Margaret and her husband separated. In 1978 they were divorced and the Princess's husband, the first Earl of Snowdon, married a divorcée. By 1981 therefore it would have been somewhat inappropriate to exclude any royal guest from the wedding list for reason of their being divorced or remarried. Inside St Paul's Prince Charles's uncle, Lord Snowdon, was placed in the tenth row of the nave and the bride's stepmother, Lady Spencer, in the fourth row.[40] In 1955 Princess Margaret had announced that 'mindful of the church's teaching that Christian marriage is indissoluble' she would not marry a man who was divorced.[41] Had such a statement been publicly made in the 1980s, it would have appeared somewhat incongruous.

Like many from broken homes, the Princess of Wales' childhood had been a mobile one. For her and for many others, her parents' second marriages had produced still more connections between landed families; she now had links with the Earls of Dartmouth and with the Shand Kydd family, who owned land in Scotland. Her mother was the daughter of the fourth Baron Fermoy, who had been a close friend of George V. Born at Park House on the Sandringham estate in Norfolk, Frances Fermoy had in 1954 married, at the age of 18, Viscount Althorp, heir to the seventh Earl Spencer, in Westminster Abbey. The couple lived at first in Gloucestershire, where the viscount attended the Royal Agricultural College in Cirencester. They then moved back to Park House in Norfolk where Viscount Althorp farmed. The young Frances Althorp had two daughters, a son who died, and then a third daughter, Diana. The death of their first son caused great sadness, and the couple began to drift apart.[42] The birth of another son in 1964 ensured the direct succession of the Spencer title. In 1967 Frances left her husband and four young children, obtained a divorce from Viscount Althorp two years later, and then married the recently divorced Peter Shand Kydd.

Lady Diana Spencer, along with her two sisters and young brother, spent her childhood moving between her mother's homes in London, Sussex, and Scotland and her home in Norfolk. Then in 1975 her grandfather, the seventh Earl Spencer, died and Althorp Park in Northamptonshire, with its paintings by Reynolds, Gainsborough, Rubens, Van Dyck, and Lely, became Lady Diana's new home. In that year, Lady Diana's father had collaborated on a book called *What is Our Heritage?* with the Countess of Dartmouth.

The Countess of Dartmouth was the daughter of Barbara Cartland. She had in 1954 married the Hon. Gerald Legge, nephew of the seventh Earl of Dartmouth. On the death of his uncle in 1958, Gerald Legge became Viscount Lewisham and then on the death of his father in 1962 he became ninth Earl of Dartmouth. The couple had three sons and a daughter and Lady Dartmouth was energetically involved in local government. As Lady Lewisham, she had stood for Lewisham West as a Conservative candidate in 1958. In 1976 she obtained a divorce from the Earl of Dartmouth and married Earl Spencer. They had been married for two years when Earl Spencer collapsed with a brain haemorrhage at Althorp and spent months in a coma. The new Lady Spencer devotedly looked after her new husband. Hearing of a drug that was available in Germany, she 'got hold of a supply of it through her friend Bill Bentinck', later ninth Duke of Portland. The doctors agreed to try it. The eighth Earl Spencer 'opened his eyes and was back'.[43]

Had Earl Spencer died during this critical time, the title and estate would have passed to his son, Charles. But the effects of divorce and remarriage among landed society could be considerably more complicated. If there were only daughters by a first marriage, then a son by the second or third or fourth marriage would become the heir. Such was the case with the Hampshire landowner Ronald Ferguson, a great-grandson of the sixth Duke of Buccleuch. By his

153

first marriage to the niece of the ninth Viscount Powerscourt he had two daughters. Two years after his divorce Ferguson married again and by his second wife he had another family. The oldest son of this new generation was then in line to inherit the 800-acre Hampshire estate. The age gap between Ferguson's children was considerable. When in 1986 his 26-year-old daughter Sarah married the Queen's second son, the newly created Duke of York, her youngest half-sister was aged nine months. The complicated implications, therefore, of divorce settlements and custody of the children, of remarriage and of inheritance, of torn lives, broken homes, stepmothers and half-sisters, brought their toll on landed society as on so many families where divorce had become so widespread.

The disturbing consequences of remarriage among English landed society seemed to be shown by the heir to Blenheim Palace in Oxfordshire, Jamie Spencer-Churchill. His father, who was the Marquess of Blandford before he became eleventh Duke of Marlborough in 1972, had married Susan Hornby in 1951. Jamie Spencer-Churchill was born in 1955 and his sister in 1958. In 1960 the Marquess and Marchioness of Blandford were divorced. Two years later the Marchioness of Blandford married Alan Heber-Percy. A year before that, in 1961, the Marquess of Blandford married as his second wife Athina Onassis. A Greek heiress in her own right, Athina Onassis was recently divorced from the Greek shipping tycoon Aristotle Onassis. She married the Marquess of Blandford in the Greek Orthodox Church in Paris.[44] Their marriage lasted for ten years and they were divorced in 1971, when Jamie Spencer-Churchill was sixteen. His Greek stepmother then married another wealthy Greek tycoon, Stavros Niarchos. The following year the tenth Duke of Marlborough, Jamie's grandfather, died. In the same year his father married for the third time, this time a Swedish countess. His new stepmother, now Duchess of Marlborough, had three children by the Duke of Marlborough, a son who died after a few months, another son born in 1974, and a daughter in 1977. The heir to Blenheim, now with the title Marquess of Blandford, had a half-brother and half-sister who were some twenty years younger than him. Eight years after his father's third marriage, the Marquess of Blandford's mother was divorced in 1980 from her second husband, Alan Heber-Percy. His stepfather then married the twice-married daughter of Sir Cyril Kleinwort. Three years later in 1983 the marquess's mother married for the third time, when her son was

28. It was at about this time that press reports of Blandford's involvement with drugs began to attract the public's attention. After escaping from several drug rehabilitation centres and after spending some time in Wormwood Scrubs, the marquess, destined one day to be a member of the House of Lords, was eventually given a two-year suspended sentence in 1986 for possessing cocaine. When the defence counsel appealed to the judge for a merciful sentence, 'the Duke of Marlborough dabbed at his tears with a handkerchief and his first wife started to weep'.[45]

Perhaps it was the massive military memorial of Blenheim that was getting everyone down. In her autobiography, *Laughter from a Cloud*, the Dowager Duchess of Marlborough, who had married the tenth duke just before he died in 1972, recalled that through her the duke had come to refer to the palace as 'The Dump'.[46] Choosing a dress for what was her fourth wedding, the duchess had decided on one that would also be suitable to wear when she made her first speech in the old riding school at Blenheim, where the annual party for the estate staff was held. Like her husband's mother, Consuelo Vanderbilt, before her, the duchess knew that she had to take on 'the onerous task of improving many things and all the other duties entailed in helping the people who worked on an estate of this size'. The tenth Duke of Marlborough died not long afterwards, the duchess having spent weeks at his bedside. Asked by the duke's family to hand back the wedding gifts that he had given her, she was left with little.[47]

The family motto of the Dukes of Marlborough was 'Faithful, though unfortunate'. While the complicated upbringing of the heir to Blenheim was unusual among ducal families resident in England, the divorce rate among marquesses closely approximated to the national average. Of the thirty-six marquesses in 1986, twelve had been divorced at least once. The financial and legal difficulties which divorce and remarriage could bring about was shown by the family of the sixth Marquess of Exeter, who owned Burghley House in Northamptonshire. The marquess died in 1982 and his widow died eight months later. The direct heir to the title was a brother of the late marquess, who lived on a ranch in British Columbia where he headed a religious sect called 'Emissaries of Divine Light' and who had no interest in Burghley House.

The Marquess of Exeter had been married twice. By his first marriage he had three daughters. His eldest daughter was married to the eleventh Baron Barnard of Raby Castle in Durham. The marquess had hoped that his second daughter's son would live at Burghley and run the estate with his father, who had looked after the property for twenty-five years. However, because the marquess's widow had not changed her will, the estate was left to his children and grandchildren, rather than reverting to the trustees for the benefit of the family as a whole. A further complication was that the second Marchioness of Exeter had two children by a previous marriage. Her daughter was married to Robin Leigh-Pemberton, later Governor of the Bank of England and himself owner of an estate in Kent, while her son had also been regarded as a son by the late marquess.[48] The problem was eventually solved amicably when the marquess's only daughter by his second marriage, Lady Victoria Leatham, took over the running of Burghley. Having worked for Sotheby's and being a trained art expert, her talents were put to full use while rummaging through the assorted neglected treasures in the Elizabethan house. Priceless pieces of porcelain had been used as door stops. It was later discovered that these and other odd pieces throughout the house were the finest and first recorded private collection of Japanese porcelain outside the Orient.[49]

* * *

The reported divorce settlements demanded by the ex-wives of landed society tended to belie the successful camouflaging of wealth constructed by them since 1974, when the Labour government had launched its political attack on the rich. Even their vocabulary had become 'full of prevarications, designed to gloss over incriminating and taxable evidence of wealth and status'. Thus, a party for sixty was 'having a few neighbours in'. To talk of 'Charles, who turns a few bob in the City', meant that he was a millionaire.[50] When seen by the public, members of landed society tended to draw attention to their apparently impoverished status by appearing in clothes which suggested long days of hard work spent out of doors. Wearing old and messy clothes, shoes that had been chewed by dogs, khaki jackets, and blue jeans, they liked to slam the doors of their expensive cars which were kept permanently mud-spattered. Colours were chosen to merge with the countryside, to which women might add an expensive silk headscarf as their concession to femininity. At the annual gathering at the horse trials at Badminton, where the royal family mingled with the crowds, they and other titled onlookers deliberately dressed down, not only as a practical measure as they walked near the muddy course, but as an indication, it seemed, of their equal status among the crowds when in the presence of horses. Yet for landed society, despite spending long days getting wet and cold at the Badminton horse trials or while hunting or shooting or walking on their estates, there were occasions in the evening when 'they're in black tie and eating off this fabulous china, wonderful tables with the silver gleaming in the candlelight, and it's just a total transformation', observed J. Carter Brown.[51]

With extravagant high living at parties and dances in the 1980s, women took to wearing romantic ball gowns once more, encouraged by the sight of the magnificent evening dresses worn by the young Princess of Wales. Lady Silvy Thynne, 'swathed in a dress of phosphorescent gold', greeted each guest as they moved up the imperial staircase at her 21st birthday at Longleat.[52] 'Through Heaven's Gate a glittering 500 swept down the icy valley to a floodlit Longleat topped with turrets of fluorescent blue.' Inside, there was a profusion of exotic flowers, candlelight, and roaring fires in the red and gold tapestried hall. Through the mullioned windows the floodlighting illuminated the ceiling copied from St Mark's library in Venice.[53] At Belvoir Castle, 800 guests attended a party given by the Duke and Duchess of Rutland for their son the Marquess of Granby and their daughter Lady Teresa Manners. The Duchess of Buccleuch 'waltzed with Colin Tennant; the Duchess of Bedford danced with her husband', Lady Diana Cooper 'watched nostalgically from a table next to the band', and the Marquess of Blandford 'looked rather worried'.[54] The demands of the discotheque being too much for the castle's wiring, the evening was intermittently plunged into darkness. 'Perhaps they should switch to coal' suggested one guest, which, at a time when the Vale of Belvoir was still threatened by the Coal Board's intention to turn it into a mining conglomeration, was considered somewhat unfeeling. Yet the next morning the band and the discotheque were still playing at eleven o'clock, when the last guests left by motor-cycle, 'their white ties covered by leather jackets'.[55]

While some of the castles and houses in England were occasionally the settings for crowded and exuberant entertaining, their owners often lived in just a few rooms, or in a house in the grounds. At Chatsworth, the Duchess of Devonshire, who with her husband the eleventh duke had made the decision to move back into the house in the 1950s, lamented that she lived surrounded by things which would never belong to her.[56] Always aware that if she became a widow then she would have to move out of the house to allow her son, the Marquess of Hartington and his family to take over, a life spent as a custodian of treasures was quietly accepted by women such as the duchess. In her bedroom overlooking the landscaped gardens surrounding the house, the Duchess of Devonshire lived surrounded by her dogs, where the bright colours of the electric kettle and toaster seemed somewhat out of place among the lovely furniture. Yet such was its size, she could be unaware of a thousand people visiting Chatsworth; 'the faintest murmur, like a distant sea, is all you hear'.[57]

At Badminton in Gloucestershire the eleventh Duke of Beaufort's mother-in-law, formerly married to the sixth Marquess of Bath, lived in the converted laundry close to the house. The brick niches once used for heating flat-irons were now used as alcoves for ornaments by the former chatelaine of Longleat. The view through the windows was of the orchard, where the linen was once hung out to dry. The old horse pond was now a duck pond.[58] Meanwhile at Longleat her son, Viscount Weymouth, continued the life with which he had been identified in the 1960s. In the morning, after his butler, Bob, rang the bell, the viscount did twenty minutes of meditation 'and I plait my own hair, although its always much better when someone else does it'.[59]

Chatsworth and Badminton and Longleat were still centred on large estates despite their reduction throughout the twentieth century when land had been sold to pay death duties. At Badminton the old tenth duke noticed everything that went on on his 50,000-acre estate. It would have been 'unthinkable to cut down a tree without him noticing'.[60] But at Arundel Castle in West Sussex the seventeenth Duke of Norfolk spent relatively little time on his 14,000-acre estate. He already owned houses in Yorkshire and Buckinghamshire when in 1975 he succeeded his cousin, who had been duke for nearly sixty years. At Arundel the seventeenth duke had ten tenant farmers. The largest holding was farmed by a family partnership formed by the duke, who had taken the unusual step of purchasing the farm from the previous duke's executors.[61]

The wealth of landowners such as the Dukes of Norfolk and Beaufort and the Marquess of Bath was tied up in the treasures they owned, in houses which they would never sell and of which they were custodians for the next generation. But the survival of their estates in the 1980s was complemented by an increase in the number of millionaires in Britain, from 4,000 in 1981 to 19,000 in 1986.[62] And among these millionaires there was still the desire to buy a country house and some land. In 1986 the Chancellor of the Exchequer, Nigel Lawson, replaced capital transfer tax with inheritance tax. This meant the abolition of tax charges on lifetime gifts, provided the donor survived seven years. In the historic budget of 1988, top rates of tax were lowered to 40 per cent. The opportunity to pass on land to another generation free of inheritance tax meant that landed families, both new and old, began to feel that at last the fiscal climate was beginning to come more in line with their interests. Moreover, the successful legal manipulation of tax laws in the twentieth century, laws which for many ill-advised landed families had been their downfall, was spectacularly demonstrated by the wealthy Vestey family. Their continued fortune was second only to those of the Queen and the sixth Duke of Westminster. The Vestey case, a tax case in the House of Lords publicized in October 1980, was just one trust of one family. But it showed how with professional advice tax loopholes, in this case off-shore trusts, could be successfully and legally used.[63]

The Vesteys were the owners of companies which made up the biggest privately-owned multinational in the world. It had started as a cold storage firm in Liverpool at the end of the nineteenth century and had eventually grown not only through their pioneering of refrigeration techniques, but through the family's policy of owning the ranches in Argentina on which they raised beef cattle, of owning the packing plants that slaughtered the cattle and that processed the meat, of owning the refrigerated ships in which the products were sent abroad, the insurance companies that insured the cargo, the docks where the cargo was unloaded, the cold store where the meat was stored, and the wholesale and retail shops that eventually sold the meat.[64] From meat packing in Argentina, the firm turned its attention to China, from where they imported eggs. This was done by breaking the eggs in China, freezing the beaten eggs, and shipping them to Liverpool for sale to the catering trade. When in 1922 the Vesteys were given a barony, they chose for their coat of arms a motif which incorporated three eggs supported by an iceberg.[65] Yet when the first Baron Vestey took his seat in the House of Lords it was not only as a businessman but also as a landowner.

Apart from land in Gloucestershire, the Vesteys owned land in Norfolk and some 100,000 acres in Scotland.

Gloucestershire was the home not only of the Vesteys at Stowell Park but also of several members of the royal family. Gatcombe Park and its surrounding 700 acres had been bought by the Queen in 1973 from Harold Macmillan's former Chancellor of the Exchequer, R. A. Butler, for her daughter, Princess Anne. Here the princess lived with her husband Captain Mark Philips who had attended the Royal Agricultural College in Cirencester not far away. The president of the college was the Prince of Wales, who lived at Highgrove House near Tetbury, six miles from Gatcombe and who purchased Highgrove from Harold Macmillan's son Maurice Macmillan in 1980. On this 300-acre estate, somewhat modest compared with the 128,000 acres owned by the Prince of Wales as Duke of Cornwall, the prince turned stables into workshops and planted English wild flowers. Hunting with one of the most prestigious hunts in England, the Beaufort, was another attraction for living in Gloucestershire for the prince and for other members of landed families in that county. At Badminton, where the royal family were guests every year of the Duke of Beaufort, the toast at the end of the dinner in the evening was 'To foxhunting!' ('Foxhunting, foxhunting, foxhunting'). 'To the hounds!' ('The hounds, the hounds').[66]

Badminton was the only large country house in England which was not open to the public. Practically every other such house centred on a large estate was open to visitors at certain times; some 700 houses in England. Many had joined the list after the 1975 tax exemption clause. Exemption from capital transfer tax had been given to houses of historic interest provided the property was properly maintained, preserved, and repaired, objects with an association with the building were kept there, and reasonable public access of at least thirty days a year was given. But the cost of opening houses to the public was not covered by admission charges. Of the 700 houses open to the public in England, ninety-six were owned by the National Trust. Of these houses just under half were still lived in by the family.[67]

Families who lived in houses which had been handed over to the National Trust did not have the worry of maintenance. In these houses, professional experts were called in to arrange, clean, and preserve the art treasures. Yet families living in such houses still had to pay local government taxes, a share of the wage bill, heating costs, and be responsible for some interior decoration. Expenses which seemed small when the house had first been given to the Trust had mounted up to high levels with inflation.[68] There was no longer the same pride of ownership after their houses had been transformed from homes into professional showcases by the Trust. For the seventh Baron Brownlow at Belton Park in Lincolnshire, handing the house over to the National Trust in 1983 was preceded by several attempts to open it on a private commercial basis. In 1978 Lord Brownlow had engaged a manager to run the house and had opened it for seven days a week. He launched an advertising campaign, had special events arranged every weekend, and employed seventy people.[69] But after two years the costs had made the whole venture unprofitable. Before leaving his family's beautiful ancestral home Lord Brownlow said: 'Well, we tried the big time. . . .I feel I have now proved at least I have convinced myself – that it doesn't work.'[70]

Belton Park's location away from any large town was a major disadvantage in regularly attracting the public. But in Shropshire, the seventh Earl of Bradford's Weston Park was situated near enough to Birmingham for it to be a successful venue for gourmet dinners run by the earl himself, who already owned restaurants in London. Up to thirty-five guests could stay in Weston Park, savouring for an evening life in an English country house. It was the young Lord Bradford's determination to run the home in which his family had lived for 300 years as a commercial concern which was vital to the success of the enterprise. Another successful aristocratic entrepreneur, the Earl of March, publicly urged owners of historic houses to think commercially, saying that they 'had got to learn to become businessmen'.[71] There were several options. Apart from opening hotels, such as the Earl of March's Goodwood Park Hotel at Goodwood in West Sussex, or entertaining paying guests in their houses, other sources of revenue could be the conversion of old farm buildings or stables into premises for small businesses, the setting up of nature trails and garden centres, or hiring out houses for films or television.

The Secretary of State for the Environment in Mrs Thatcher's Cabinet from October 1986 was Nicholas Ridley, whose brother, the fourth Viscount Ridley, lived at Blagdon Park in Northumberland. Here Viscount Ridley converted farm buildings which could not be adapted for modern farm machinery into offices and workshops for small businesses. Most of the building work was done by estate craftsmen. Viscount Ridley said, 'This is a scheme in which everyone wins. The estate has an asset, firms have premises and people have jobs.'[72]

At Chatsworth in Derbyshire, the Chatsworth Carpenters were set up as an important sideline to the house. The nightclub owner John Aspinall placed an order for furniture from the Chatsworth Carpenters for his new gaming club in London, Curzon House. For those members of landed society who gambled at Aspinall's club, 'it must either be a comfort or cause for chagrin to know that the timber which they sit upon comes from an estate determined to remain intact', observed the Duchess of Devonshire.[73]

On Captain Jeremy Elwes' estate in Lincolnshire the conversion of farm buildings into a restaurant and education centre won an award from the Council for the Protection of Rural England. Other attractions included the Elsham country park. There was an arboretum, butterfly and bird gardens, rare breeds of livestock and poultry, pony trekking and nature trails, a crafts centre, working forge, and an art gallery in the stables. Visiting Elsham, Hugh Montgomery-Massingberd observed that

> watching Jeremy Elwes prostrate himself unselfconsciously beside some children examining the carp, it strikes one that few can have done more to increase the townee's understanding of the country, or to illustrate the value of private landownership and field sports to the countryside.[74]

Where houses were used for films or television serials, this too could attract more visitors. At Rainthorpe Hall in Norfolk George Hastings said, 'You've got to be prepared to be totally disrupted and they have to pay you enough to make you feel it's worth it'; but at Castle Howard in Yorkshire, the filming of the televised version of Evelyn Waugh's *Brideshead Revisited* increased the number of visitors to the house by more than a third.[75]

The owner of Castle Howard at the time, George Howard, was the grandson of the ninth Earl of Carlisle. In 1940 the cupola and lantern of the dome and part of the south front of the house had burned down after a fire started by a schoolgirl housed there during the war. George Howard was in hospital in India in 1944 when he heard that his two brothers had both been killed in action and that the trustees of the estate had already sold off the Canaletto paintings. Howard immediately sent a telegram telling the trustees not to sell anything more. After his return, he had the house restored and opened to the public.[76] Howard later became president of the Country Landowners' Association, president of the Historic Houses Association, and eventually chairman of the governors of the British Broadcasting Corporation. His expertise helped fellow members of the Historic Houses Association in drawing up television contract guidelines. Throughout his career, George Howard, created Lord Howard of Henderskelfe in 1983, was remembered as a flamboyant figure. 'It was the grandee in him that sometimes gave the impression that the whole world was an extension of Castle Howard.'[77]

That the determination to survive in an increasingly competitive world hinged on the personalities of owners was shown at Holkham Hall in Norfolk. The fifth Earl of Leicester had died in 1976. When his nephew moved into Holkham and a fire was lit in one of the rooms for a cocktail party, it was for the first time since 1949, when the fifth earl's eldest daughter, Lady Anne Coke, had her coming-out party. Four years after succeeding to the title the new heir, Eddie Coke, had turned the home farms into a profit as well as working out a plan to revive the 1,800 acres of woodland. The Dowager Lady Leicester said that not a day passed 'when we don't say, thank God for Eddie Coke'.[78]

At Holkham the fourth Earl of Leicester, who died in 1944, was remembered for his lifelong enjoyment of shooting on the marshes not far from the sea. After hours spent wet to the skin and in the bitter North Sea wind, the earl had been 'the despair and admiration of tenant farmers, London guests, village sportsmen, country parsons, keepers and others who went with him'.[79] Yet, forty years after the fourth earl's death, shooting rights were an important source of income on many estates such as Holkham. Even if a small estate was planted with trees on its less productive areas, its rental income could be increased between five and ten times. Eight in ten landowners who had planted small woods on their estates gave game shooting as their reason.[80] The richest landowner in England, the sixth Duke of Westminster, had spent much time and money on improving the 15,000-acre grouse moor in Cheshire which he bought in 1980. Increasing the number of keepers, he went back 'to Victorian standards', making sure that any vermin were soon killed and that the heather grew well'.[81] At the same time on the Duke of Rutland's Belvoir estate, the Belvoir Hunt was looked after by a large hunt staff, and still run on the old lines. On Wednesdays and Saturdays the Belvoir Hunt could number as many as 200. 'Dashing young army officers – for they still exist – rich men from the city and powdered ladies will be among those who swell the numbers.'[82]

While big estates such as the Duke of Rutland's and the Duke of Westminster's were still run on the old lines, among the smaller landed families who had quietly sold their houses and estates throughout the twentieth century a significant number had just as quietly stayed on. They were discovered by the intrepid observer of English landed society in the late twentieth century, Hugh Montgomery-Massingberd. In a weekly series in *The Field* called 'Family Seats', he had by 1987 described more than a hundred small country houses centred on small estates and still lived in by their owners. On 24 May 1986 he announced that the death of the country house had been greatly exaggerated. Of the 10,000 country estates in the British Isles a hundred years before, he estimated that one-fifth remained in private occupation.[83] During his tours of country houses after the Second World War, James Lees-Milne had discovered the 75-year-old Lady Montgomery-Massingberd scrubbing the stairs at Gunby Hall. As he visited country houses forty years later her great-nephew observed: 'Today, as one peregrinates about the place recording the passing show, the evidence of one's eyes – and I fear, one's stomach – tells quite a different story.'[84]

The many families visited by Hugh Montgomery-Massingberd included the Mounsey-Heyshams and the Fryer-Speddings in Cumbria, the Baker-Cresswells in Northumberland, the Lancelyn Greens in Cheshire, the Sheepshanks family in West Yorkshire, and in Staffordshire the Pipe Wolferstans and the Inges-Innes-Lillingstons.[85] He visited the Jenner-Fusts in Gloucestershire, the Bagges in Norfolk, and the Capel Cures in Essex.[86] Hugh Montgomery-Massingberd also visited Orleton Hall in Shropshire. On this estate, the North Shropshire Hunt would occasionally meet in front of the house, and there was archery, fishing, and cricket. Two cricket grounds not far from the house were supported by the owner of Orleton Hall, Vesey Holt, who was president of the Shropshire county cricket club. The cousin of the sixth Earl of Powis, who was the largest landowner in Shropshire and who lived at Powis Castle, Vesey Holt had taken over the running of the Orleton estate in 1968. Since then he had been chairman of Shropshire county council, High Sheriff of the county and Deputy Lieutenant.[87] His wife

Elizabeth also served on many committees. In the general election of
October 1974 she had stood as a Conservative candidate. Impecca-
bly dressed, smoking Gitanes cigarettes and with a pilot's licence to
her name, she also combined all the timeless qualities of a chatelaine
of a country house. Such dedicated service to local government by
the Holts, in a county where many old families still survived in
country houses hidden far away from the public gaze, was a sign of
the continued contribution to county life by landed society in
England in the late twentieth century.

On the other side of England, country houses in Yorkshire had
not only survived but had sometimes been lavishly refurbished by
their owners. At Newby Hall near Ripon the Adam house was
redecorated and the gardens restored. At Burton Constable east of
Hull the house was carefully returned to its former state. At
Sledmere between Newby and Burton Constable, Sir Tatton Sykes
was noted for his 'irrepressible urge to put into action impossibly
grandiose-sounding plans'.[88] Such plans included having a 100-foot-
high jet of water issue forth from the ornamental pond in front of the
house as well as re-erecting a Regency Gothic orangery nearby. Sir
Tatton's scheme to have the plasterwork ceiling of the library gilded
where before it had been painted yellow took two years. 'Early
morning sun streaming across the park and through the windows
now makes the ceiling dance in its 24 carat brilliance.'[89]

Another house in Yorkshire was Carlton Towers, home of the
Duke of Norfolk before he inherited his cousin's estate and title in
1975. The duke's son, the Earl of Arundel, spent more time on his
father's estate in Sussex, where he ran the woodlands as a going
concern. Here he entertained friends for shooting parties. In Arundel Cathedral, built by the fifteenth duke as a replica of a fourteenth-
century French cathedral, on the morning of Sunday 28 December
1986 the heir to the seventeenth Duke of Norfolk sat with his guests
in the family pew at the front of the cathedral, separated from the
rest of the congregation by a purple rope. But at a country weekend
far away in the north-west of England only three months before
there had been no such separation. In the tiny church of the Holy
Family in Kirkby Stephen in the heart of the Pennine hills, on the
morning of Sunday 21 September, standing right at the back of the
church, was the heir to the throne, Prince Charles, Prince of Wales.[90]

Prince Charles was staying with Hugh Van Cutsem and his
family, whose son had been a page at the royal wedding in 1981.

Hugh Van Cutsem's sister had married the ninth Earl of Arran. In November 1986 the Countess of Arran and other members of English landed society attended the annual general meeting of the Historic Houses Association, the first to follow the success of the 'Treasure Houses of Britain' exhibition in Washington. With some of the richest landowners in England wearing a label bearing their name and title, the meeting seemed to show that landowners had indeed become businessmen.

* * *

The life and fortunes of landed society do not primarily depend on the land which they own – a theme difficult to trace through the fortunes and misfortunes of this century. When a house, its contents, and some land have to be sold, the event to some degree exposes the ownership. But the wealth either of the vendor or the purchaser, invested in industrial equities, town property, or in marriage settlements, remains hidden. The facts are not made public. Why should they be?

On the other hand it is possible to look at the trends of what went on in agriculture on the land which landed society owned. After the repeal of the Corn Laws in 1846 it took thirty years or more before farming felt the effects of imported corn. Thus it was not until the 1880s that farming suffered its great depression. The First World War saw a general return to prosperity in farming. The 'betrayal' of farming by the government through the repeal of wartime legislation in 1921 plunged farming into a depression once more. The Second World War brought prosperity once again to farmers. This time the unexpected continuation of profitable high efficiency following the success of the wartime food campaign went on for forty years, so that the huge surpluses, added to those of the European Economic Community surpluses, are now leading to the gradual withdrawal of subsidies. For the many landowners who had turned to farming, from which they had supported their houses, this reversal may mean grave difficulties.

There is no simple alteration of fortune and misfortune in the case of landowners who have in general only been partially dependent on agriculture. Their fortunes have been more at the mercy of social legislation. This legislation, with its political objectives, appears to have been only partially successful. What has been done has been merely vindictive, and with even less benefit to 'the people'.

However imbued with a 'social conscience' were the ministers responsible for the legislation during this century, they seemed, like some of the owners they wished to dispossess, to know little about country life. That they have failed so far to dispossess the great names in the land does not mean that many smaller landowners were not dispossessed as effectively as landowners evicted tenants in centuries past. But whom did it help?

Taxation which deprived some owners of centuries-old connections with a locality, or who 'lost' a fortune by dying a month too early, added only a minuscule percentage to the national exchequer. The big fish seemed as always to find convenient loopholes in the taxation net.

And the grass blows in the wind where once stood the 700 English country houses demolished by their owners in the twentieth century.

Notes and references

1 'THE DIMINISHING VISTAS OF THAT OTHER ENGLAND'

1 O. Sitwell, *The Scarlet Tree*, London, Macmillan, 1946, p. 161.
2 ibid., p. 277.
3 O. Lyttleton, *The Memoirs of Lord Chandos*, London, Bodley Head, 1962, p. 9.
4 K. Rose, *Superior Person. A Portrait of Curzon and His Circle in Late Victorian England*, London, Weidenfeld & Nicolson, 1969, p. 185.
5 S. Jackson, *The Sassoons*, London, Heinemann, 1968, p. 130.
6 K. Simpson, 'The officers', in I.F.W. Beckett and K. Simpson (eds), *A Nation in Arms. A Social Study of the British Army in the First World War*, Manchester, Manchester University Press, 1985, p. 65.
7 O. Sitwell, *Great Morning*, London, Macmillan, 1948, p. 123.
8 ibid., pp. 118–19, 128.
9 W. S. Churchill, *My Early Life*, London, Thornton Butterworth, 1930, p. 78.
10 ibid., p. 122.
11 Rose, op. cit., p. 6.
12 J. Morris and S. Winchester, *Stones of Empire. The Buildings of the Raj*, Oxford, Oxford University Press, 1983, p. 76.
13 Rose, op. cit., p. 7.
14 J. Morris, *Pax Britannica. The Climax of an Empire*, London, Faber & Faber, 1968, p. 285.
15 ibid., p. 286.
16 Sitwell, *Great Morning*, p. 143.
17 Earl Winterton, *Pre-War*, London, Macmillan, 1932, p. 35.
18 A. H. Brodrick, *Near to Greatness; a Life of the Sixth Earl Winterton*, London, Hutchinson, 1965, p. 82.
19 O. F. Christie, *The Transition to Democracy 1867–1914*, London, Routledge, 1934, p. 167.

20 J. P. Cornford, 'The parliamentary foundations of the Hotel Cecil', in R. Robson (ed.), *Ideas and Institutions of Victorian Britain*, London, Bell, 1967, p. 310.
21 Lord F. Hamilton, *The Days Before Yesterday*, London, Hodder & Stoughton, 1920, p. 215.
22 ibid.
23 Sitwell, *Great Morning*, p. 218.
24 P. Magnus, *King Edward the Seventh*, London, Murray, 1964, pp. 274–5.
25 D. Hunn, *Goodwood*, London, Davis Poynter, 1975, p. 164.
26 Jackson, op. cit., pp. 19, 85.
27 ibid., pp. 67–8.
28 A. Lejeune, *The Gentlemen's Clubs*, London, Macdonald & Jane's, 1979, p. 295.
29 ibid., pp. 59, 65.
30 A. G. Gardiner, *The Life of Sir William Harcourt*, Vol. II, *1886–1904*, London, Constable, 1923, p. 573.
31 ibid., p. 569.
32 M. A. Havinden, *Estate Villages*, London, Lund Humphries, 1966, p. 77.
33 ibid.
34 Christie, op. cit., p. 165.
35 Among the owners of estates of at least 10,000 acres, who between them owned almost a quarter of England, one-fifth of their gross rents came from acres hardest hit by falling grain prices: R. J. Farrelly, 'The large landowners of England and Wales 1870–1939: an elite in transition', unpublished PhD thesis, University of Toronto, 1980, p. 126.
36 F. M. L. Thompson, 'Free trade and the land', in G. D. Mingay (ed.), *The Victorian Countryside*, Vol. I, London, Routledge & Kegan Paul, 1981, p. 105.
37 R. Perren, 'The landlord and agricultural transformation', in P. J. Perry (ed.), *British Agriculture 1875–1914*, London, Methuen, 1973, p. 126.
38 F. M. L. Thompson, *English Landed Society in the Nineteenth Century*, London, Routledge & Kegan Paul, 1963, p. 312.
39 F. H. W. Sheppard (ed.), *Survey of London. The Parish of St Paul Covent Garden*, London, Athlone, 1970, p. 49.
40 *Parliamentary Papers*, 1895, XVI, R.C. on Agriculture, p. 176.
41 Thompson, op. cit., pp. 306–7; Farrelly, op. cit., p. 97.
42 Marchioness of Londonderry, *Henry Chaplin. A Memoir*, London, Macmillan, 1926, p. 229.
43 *Hansard*, House of Commons, 4th ser., 8 May 1894, col. 684.
44 R. G. Heape, *Buxton under the Dukes of Devonshire*, London, Robert Hale, 1948, p. 121.
45 *Parliamentary Papers*, 1895, XVI, R.C. on Agriculture, p. 230.
46 A. Eden, *Another World 1897–1917*, London, Allen Lane, 1976, p. 40.
47 'Wire and hunting', *Country Life*, 5 December 1908, p. cxxx.

48 B. B. Gilbert, 'David Lloyd George: land, the budget and social reform', *American Historical Review*, vol. 81, no. 5 (1976), p. 1,064.

49 N. Blewett, *The Peers, the Parties and the People*, London, Macmillan, 1972, p. 69.

50 W. S. Churchill, *Liberalism and the Social Problem*, London, Hodder & Stoughton, 1909, pp. 329–30.

51 Lord Willoughby de Broke, *The Passing Years*, London, Constable, 1924, p. 249.

52 John, Duke of Bedford, *A Silver-plated Spoon*, London, Cassell, 1959, p. 8.

53 Sheppard, op. cit., p. 50.

54 D. Cannadine, *Lords and Landlords: the Aristocracy and the Towns, 1774–1967*, Leicester, Leicester University Press, 1980, p. 421.

55 ibid.

56 *Parliamentary Papers*, 1919, XII, Coal Industry Commission, Reports, pp. 596, 626.

57 B. Masters, *The Dukes. The Origins, Ennoblement and History of Twenty-six Families*, London, Blond & Briggs, 1975, p. 244.

58 C. Vanderbilt Balsan, *The Glitter and the Gold*, London, Heinemann, 1953, p. 56.

59 Sitwell, *Scarlet Tree*, pp. 170, 173.

60 Lord E. Hamilton, *Forty Years On*, London, Hodder & Stoughton, 1922, p. 293.

61 Earl of Birkenhead, *Halifax. The Life of Lord Halifax*, London, Hamish Hamilton, 1965, pp. 30–1.

62 ibid., p. 27.

63 ibid., pp. 27–8.

64 M. Davie (ed.), *The Diaries of Evelyn Waugh*, London, Weidenfeld & Nicolson, 1976, p. 434.

65 V. Sackville-West, *English Country Houses*, London, Collins, 1941, p. 9.

66 Frances, Countess of Warwick, *Afterthoughts*, London, Cassell, 1931, p. 250.

67 Lord E. Hamilton, op. cit., p. 133; Rose, op. cit., p. 3.

68 H. Prince, 'Parkland in the English landscape', *Amateur Historian*, vol. 3, no. 8, 1958.

69 L. Fleming and A. Gore, *The English Garden*, London, Michael Joseph, 1979, p. 98.

70 Sitwell, *Scarlet Tree*, pp. 252–3.

71 J. Cowper Powys, *Autobiography*, London, Bodley Head, 1934, p. 318.

72 Balsan, op. cit., pp. 83–4.

73 ibid., p. 93.

74 'Shooting at Glevering Hall', *Country Life*, 9 January 1904, p. 64.

75 J. Amherst, *Wandering Abroad*, London, Secker & Warburg, 1976, p. 5.

76 ibid.

77 Sitwell, *Scarlet Tree*, p. 178.

78 'Glorious stirring sight', *Country Life*, 20 October 1983, p. 1,052; Sitwell, *Scarlet Tree*, p. 64.

79 Sitwell, *Scarlet Tree*, p. 172.
80 D. Sutherland, *The Yellow Earl. The Life of Hugh Lowther, 5th Earl of Lonsdale, K.G., G.C.V.O., 1857–1944*, London, Cassell, 1965, p. 153.
81 D. Cooper, *The Rainbow Comes and Goes*, London, Rupert Hart-Davis, 1958, p. 35.
82 ibid.
83 'Spacious living', *Harpers' and Queen*, November 1979, p. 253.
84 D. Burnett, *Longleat. The Story of an English Country House*, London, Collins, 1978, p. 144.
85 L. Stone and J. C. Fawtier Stone, *An Open Elite? England 1540–1880*, Oxford, Clarendon, 1984, p. 145.
86 Amherst, op. cit., p. 19.
87 Viscount Churchill, *All My Sins Remembered*, London, Heinemann, 1964, p. 29.
88 Hon. E. Cadogan, *Before the Deluge. Memories and Reflections 1880–1914*, London, Murray, 1961, p. 159.
89 'The colonies and the younger son', *Country Life*, 19 February 1910, p. 254.
90 E. Trzebinski, *Silence Will Speak. A Study of the Life of Denys Finch Hatton and his Relationship with Karen Blixen*, London, Heinemann, 1977, p. 41.
91 Lord Cranworth, *Kenya Chronicles*, London, Macmillan, 1939, pp. 1, 3–4, 19–20.
92 D. K. Kennedy, 'A tale of two colonies: the social origins and cultural consequences of white settlement in Kenya and Rhodesia 1890–1939', unpublished PhD thesis, University of California, Berkeley, 1981, p. 64.
93 Cranworth, op. cit., p. 108; E. Huxley, *White Man's Country. Lord Delamere and the Making of Kenya*, Vol. I, *1870–1914*, London, Chatto & Windus, 1953, p. 250.
94 Huxley, op. cit.
95 ibid., pp. 251, 256.
96 ibid., p. 257.
97 Sitwell, *Scarlet Tree*, pp. 175, 176.
98 Marchioness of Londonderry, op. cit., p. 121.
99 Viscount Churchill, op. cit., p. 18.
100 Duke of Beaufort, *Fox-hunting*, Newton Abbot, David & Charles, 1980, p. 11.
101 S. Sassoon, *Memoirs of a Fox-hunting Man*, London, Faber & Gwyer, 1928, p. 203.
102 S. Kaye-Smith, *Little England*, London, Cassell, 1918, p. 4.

2 THE DARK COLOURS OF MOURNING, 1914–18

1 E. Olivier, *Without Knowing Mr Walkley. Personal Memories*, London, Faber & Faber, 1938, p. 198.
2 Olivier, op. cit., p. 204.

3   H. T. Moore (ed.), *The Collected Letters of D. H. Lawrence*, Vol. I, London, Heinemann, 1962, p. 378.

4   J. Terraine, *Impacts of War 1914 & 1918*, London, Hutchinson, 1970, p. 3.

5   B. Tuchman, *The Proud Tower. A Portrait of the World Before the War, 1890 to 1914*, London, Hamish Hamilton, 1966, p. xiii.

6   Olivier, op. cit., p. 199.

7   E. Weber, *Peasants into Frenchmen. The Modernisation of Rural France 1870–1914*, Stanford, Stanford University Press, 1976, p. 475.

8   G. Dangerfield, *The Strange Death of Liberal England*, London, MacGibbon & Kee, 1966, p. 354.

9   J. M. Winter, 'Some aspects of the demographic consequences of the First World War in Britain', *Population Studies*, vol. 30, no. 3 (1976); J. M. Winter, 'Britain's "Lost Generation" of the First World War', *Population Studies*, vol. 31, no. 3 (1977), pp. 450, 458, 464.

10 *Debrett's Peerage and Baronetage 1919*, pp. xviii–lix; J. Bateman, *The Great Landowners of Great Britain and Ireland*, Leicester and New York, Leicester University Press and Humanities Press, 1971, *passim*; H. Clemenson, *English Country Houses and Landed Estates*, London and New York, Croom Helm and St Martin's Press, 1982, pp. 20, 24, 27. Of 331 owners of at least 10,000 acres in 1883, 228 were titled. Of the 1,032 owners of between 3,000 and 9,999 acres, 330 were titled. Thus there were 558 titled landowners of English estates of at least 3,000 acres, of whom approximately fifty lost a direct heir in the conflict.

11 They were the barony of Ribblesdale, and the baronetcies of Compton-Thornhill and Graves-Sawle.

12 'Lord Powis's heir', *The Times*, 14 October 1916, p. 8.

13 'Funeral of Lord Wendover', *The Times*, 24 May 1915, p. 9.

14 N. Mitford (ed.), *Noblesse Oblige. An Enquiry into the Identifiable Characteristics of the English Aristocracy*, London, Hamish Hamilton, 1956, p. 39.

15 'Captain Reginald Wyndham', *The Times*, 14 November 1914, p. 6.

16 Lionel, Lord Tennyson, *From Verse to Worse*, London, Cassell, 1933, pp. 126–7.

17 Hastings, Duke of Bedford, *The Years of Transition*, London, Andrew Dukers, 1949, pp. 83–4.

18 ibid., pp. 84–5.

19 P. Ziegler, *Diana Cooper*, London, Hamish Hamilton, 1981, p. 62.

20 ibid., p. 47.

21 Charlotte, Viscountess Barrington, *Through Eighty Years (1855–1935)*, London, Murray, 1936, p. 199.

22 J. Gore (ed.), *Mary Maxse (1870–1944). A Record Compiled by her Family and Friends*, London, Rolls House Publishing Company, 1939, p. 64.

23 'Fittleworth', *West Sussex Gazette*, 10 September 1914, p. 3; P. Horn, *Rural Life in England in the First World War*, Dublin and New York, Gill & Macmillan and St Martin's Press, 1984, p. 28; G. Blakiston, *Woburn and the Russells*, London, Constable, 1980, p. 225.

24 'Recruiting meeting at Arundel', *West Sussex Gazette*, 12 November 1914, p. 2.
25 'Women's emergency corps at Cowdray park', *West Sussex Gazette*, 29 July 1915, p. 7; A. Marwick, *Women at War 1914–1918*, London, Croom Helm, 1977, p. 40.
26 M. Beard, 'The impact of the First World War on agricultural society in West Sussex', unpublished MLitt thesis, University of Cambridge, 1984, p. 79; Blakiston, op. cit., p. 225; 'Engaged in women's work. On behalf of the maimed and wounded sufferers in the cause of liberty', *Tatler*, 5 April 1916, p. 15; 'The camera in society', *Tatler*, 3 January 1917, p. 5.
27 D. Burnett, *Longleat. The Story of an English Country House*, London, Collins, 1978, p. 167; 'Whose privilege it is – to have suffered irreparable loss for his country and for freedom', *Tatler*, 5 July 1916, p. 25.
28 R. Graves, *Goodbye To All That. An Autobiography*, London, Jonathan Cape, 1929, p. 310.
29 Tennyson, op. cit., p. 173.
30 '700 wounded soldiers at Arundel Castle', *West Sussex Gazette*, 3 August 1916, p. 4.
31 'A day with the recruits in Belton Camp', *Country Life*, 26 September 1914, p. 411.
32 Ziegler, op. cit., p. 51.
33 D. Cooper, *The Rainbow Comes and Goes*, London, Rupert Hart-Davis, 1958, p. 143.
34 Tennyson, op. cit., p. 174.
35 'On short leave from the front', *Country Life*, 16 January 1915, pp. 69–70.
36 'Shooting in the third year of war', *Country Life*, 15 July 1916, p. 6.
37 Horn, op. cit., p. 42.
38 Hon. G. Lambton, *Men and Horses I Have Known*; London, Thornton Butterworth, 1924, p. 15.
39 Horn, op. cit., p. 41.
40 A. H. Brodrick, *Near to Greatness: A Life of the Sixth Earl of Winterton*, London, Hutchinson, 1965, p. 165.
41 N. Mosley, *Julian Grenfell. His Life and the Times of his Death 1888–1915*, London, Weidenfeld & Nicolson, 1976, p. 259.
42 ibid., p. 249.
43 'Marriage of Miss Cotterell', *West Sussex Gazette*, 23 November 1916, p. 2; 'The two great wedding functions of last week', *Tatler*, 25 July 1917, pp. 108–9.
44 Ziegler, op. cit., p. 77.
45 O. Mosley, *My Life*, London, Nelson, 1968, p. 13.
46 Mosley, op. cit., p. 262.
47 Lord Ribblesdale, *Charles Lister. Letters and Recollections with a Memoir by his Father, Lord Ribblesdale*, London, T. Fisher Unwin, 1917, p. 188.
48 ibid., p. 154.

49 P. Fussell, *The Great War and Modern Memory*, London and New York, Oxford University Press, 1975, pp. 169–74, 181–7.
50 'Life in the trenches', *The Times*, 11 November 1914, p. 5.
51 'Life in the trenches', *Chichester Observer*, 5 May 1915, p. 8.
52 S. Cloete, *A Victorian Son. An Autobiography 1897–1922*, London, Collins, 1972, p. 237.
53 F. M. Ford, *Parade's End*, London, Penguin, 1982, p. 569.
54 'Arundel's peace celebrations', *West Sussex Gazette*, 31 July 1919, p. 4.
55 'Goodwood's revival', *West Sussex Gazette*, 31 July 1919, p. 4.

3 THE BURDENS OF ESTATE OWNERSHIP

1   *Dictionary of National Biography, 1931–40*, p. 722.
2   'Relations with Lloyd George', *The Times*, 14 May 1925, p. 18.
3   P. Horn, *Rural Life in England in the First World War*, Dublin and New York, Gill & Macmillan and St Martin's Press, 1984, p. 57.
4   'The Duke of Leeds' Yorkshire land', *Country Life*, 7 February 1920, p. 182.
5   S. G. Sturmey, 'Owner-farming in England and Wales 1900 to 1950', *Manchester School of Economic and Social Studies*, vol. 23, no. 3 (1955), pp. 253–5.
6   F. M. L. Thompson, *English Landed Society in the Nineteenth Century*, London, Routledge & Kegan Paul, 1963, pp. 332–3.
7   H. Clemenson, 'Diminishing Derbyshire estates', *Geographical Magazine*, vol. 53, no. 2 (1980), p. 118.
8   Thompson, op. cit., pp. 329, 330.
9   'Review of the year 1919', *Estates Gazette*, 3 January 1920, pp. 12, 13.
10 'The Duke of Sutherland decides to sell Lilleshall', *Shrewsbury Chronicle*, 26 January 1917, p. 3; 'Review of the year 1919', *Estates Gazette*, 3 January 1920, p. 13; 'Lilleshall and other transactions', *Country Life*, 14 June 1919, p. 730.
11 Duke of Sutherland, *Looking Back*, London, Odhams, 1957, p. 86.
12 'Review of the year 1919', *Estates Gazette*, 3 January 1920, p. 13; Thompson, op. cit., p. 332.
13 'The sale of Bakewell', *Country Life*, 12 June 1920, p. 843; 'Review of the year 1920', *Estates Gazette*, 1 January 1921, p. 12; 'Ilkeston under the hammer', *Country Life*, 28 Auguust 1920, p. 284.
14 Sir Oswald Mosley, *My Life*, London, Nelson, 1968, p. 17.
15 'Review of the year 1920', op. cit., p. 12.
16 B. Falk, *The Bridgewater Millions. A Candid Family History*, London, Hutchinson, 1942, p. 234; 'Review of the year 1920', op. cit., p. 12.
17 'Lord Brownlow's £190,000 sale', *Country Life*, 21 February 1920, p. 246.
18 Earl of Warwick and Brooke, *Memories of Sixty Years*, London, Cassell, 1917, pp. 131–2.
19 *Parliamentary Papers*, 1919, IX, Wages and Conditions of Employment in Agriculture, Reports, p. 550.
20 ibid.

21 H. Belloc, *The County of Sussex*, London, Cassell, 1936, p. 12.
22 M. Girouard, *The Victorian Country House*, London and New Haven, Yale University Press, 1979, pp. 399–400.
23 P. Brandon, 'The diffusion of designed landscapes in south-east England', in H. S. A. Fox and R. A. Butlin (eds), *Change in the Countryside. Essays on Rural England, 1500–1900*, London, Institute of British Geographers, 1979, p. 174.
24 W. D. Rubinstein, 'New men of wealth and the purchase of land in nineteenth-century Britain', *Past and Present*, no. 92 (1981), p. 146.
25 For the career of Sir Weetman Pearson see: J. A. Spender, *Weetman Pearson, First Lord Cowdray, 1856–1927*, London, Cassell, 1930; K. Middlemas, *The Master Builders*, London, Hutchinson, 1963; D. Young, *Member for Mexico*, London, Cassell, 1965.
26 Science Museum, London, Historical archives of S. Pearson & Son Ltd, Box A/9.
27 A. H. Brodrick, *Near to Greatness; a Life of the Sixth Earl Winterton*, London, Hutchinson, 1965, p. 96.
28 W. D. Rubinstein, *Men of Property. The Very Wealthy in Britain since the Industrial Revolution*, London, Croom Helm, 1981, p. 131.
29 'Sudbourn Hall and Torridon', *Country Life*, 1 July 1922, p. 903.
30 'Parham Park revisited', *Country Life*, 6 and 13 June 1985, pp. 1,566–70, 1,658–62.
31 'Broad acres purchased', *Aberdeen Press and Journal*, 2 May 1927, p. 5.
32 Figures taken from J. Bateman, *The Great Landowners of Great Britain and Ireland*, Leicester and New York, Leicester University Press and Humanities Press, 1971, *passim*.
33 'Lord Leconfield's Yorkshire estates', *Country Life*, 6 March 1920, p. 312.
34 'Private transactions', *Country Life*, 25 November 1922, p. 692.
35 West Sussex Record Office, Sales Particulars, 61, 62.
36 'Duke of Norfolk's Sheffield land', *Country Life*, 3 April 1920, p. 455.
37 'Derwent Hall: momentous decision', *Country Life*, 19 June 1920, p. 888.
38 '60,000 acre Scottish sale', *Country Life*, 27 May 1922, p. 720.
39 Viscount Mersey, *A Picture of Life 1872–1940*, London, Murray, 1941, p. 333.
40 West Sussex Record Office, Sales Particulars, 7.
41 D. Cannadine, *Lords and Landlords: the Aristocracy and the Towns, 1774–1967*, Leicester, Leicester University Press, 1980, p. 421.
42 ibid., p. 422.
43 Thompson, op. cit., p. 336.
44 F. H. W. Sheppard (ed.), *Survey of London. The Grosvenor Estate in Mayfair*, Pt I, London, Athlone, 1977, p. 67.
45 ibid., pp. 72–3.
46 'The estate market', *Country Life*, 15 February 1919, p. 180.
47 'Sale of twenty acres at Berkeley Square', *Country Life*, 31 May 1919, p. 630.
48 'Review of the year 1919', op. cit., p. 13.

49 E. B. Chancellor, *The Private Palaces of London*, London, Kegan Paul, Trench, Trübner, 1908, p. ix.

50 M. C. Borer, *Mayfair. The Years of Grandeur*, London, W. H. Allen, 1975, pp. 190–1.

51 R. Colby, *Mayfair. A Town Within London*, London, Country Life, 1966, p. 110.

52 'Dorchester House, Park Lane', *Country Life*, 4 December 1926, p. cxvi.

53 Colby, op. cit., p. 43; C. S. Sykes, *Private Palaces. Life in the Great London Houses*, London, Chatto & Windus, 1985, p. 330.

54 Sheppard, op. cit., p. 101.

55 Borer, op. cit., p. 37.

56 'The passing of Devonshire House', *The Nineteenth Century and After*, vol. 100 (July–December 1926), p. 312.

57 ibid., p. 319.

58 'The passing of the private palace', *Quarterly Review*, vol. 255, no. 505 (July 1930), p. 154.

59 Viscount Churchill, *All My Sins Remembered*, London, Heinemann, 1964, p. 44.

4 FAST LIVING AND FEUDALISM, 1919–39

1 Loelia, Duchess of Westminster, *Grace and Favour*, London, Weidenfeld & Nicolson, 1961, p. 84.

2 P. Balfour, *Society Racket. A Critical Survey of Modern Social Life*, London, John Long, 1933, pp. 72–3.

3 J. Fairfax-Blakeborough, *Country Life and Sport*, London, Philip Allan, 1926, pp. 29–30.

4 F. Donaldson, *Child of the Twenties*, London, Rupert Hart-Davis, 1959, p. 145.

5 *Parliamentary Papers*, 1941–2, IX, Committee on Land Utilisation in Rural Areas, Report, p. 441.

6 A. Harris, 'Agricultural change on a Yorkshire estate: Birdsall 1920–1940', *Journal of Regional and Local Studies*, vol. 3, no. 1 (1983), pp. 40–1.

7 ibid., pp. 41, 43.

8 E. H. Whetham, 'The mechanisation of British farming 1910–1945', *Journal of Agricultural Economics*, vol. 21, no. 3 (1970), p. 320.

9 ibid., pp. 319, 327.

10 Balfour, op. cit., p. 218.

11 C. Hall (ed.), *The Twenties in Vogue*, London, Octopus, 1983, p. 108.

12 O. Sitwell, *The Scarlet Tree*, London, Macmillan, 1946, p. 195.

13 H. Macmillan, *Winds of Change 1914–1939*, London, Macmillan, 1966, p. 182.

14 Lord E. Hamilton, *The Halcyon Era. A Rambling Reverie of Now and Then*, London, Murray, 1933, p. 21.

15 S. Jackson, *The Sassoons*, London, Heinemann, 1968, p. 220.

16 'West Sussex Farmers' Union: the annual luncheon', *West Sussex Gazette*, 3 March 1921, p. 3.
17 P. Horn, *Rural Life in England in the First World War*, Dublin and New York, Gill & Macmillan and St Martin's Press, 1984, p. 210.
18 Balfour, op. cit., p. 56.
19 'Landed proprietors and properties', *Burke's Landed Gentry*, Vol. I, 1965, p. xx.
20 A. Bell, *The Cherry Tree*, London, Bodley Head, 1932, p. 139.
21 ibid., p. 143.
22 R. Strong (ed.), *The Destruction of the Country House 1875–1975*, London, Thames & Hudson, 1974, pp. 188–91; Balfour, op. cit., p. 259.
23 C. L. Mowat, *Britain Between the Wars 1918–1940*, London, Methuen, 1955, p. 204.
24 'The country house of today', *The Field. Country House and Estate Supplement*, 28 March 1931, p. 1.
25 Balfour, op. cit., p. 260.
26 '1930: "Nil nisi bonum"', *Country Life*, 3 January 1931, p. 25.
27 P. Gibbs, *England Speaks*, London, Heinemann, 1935, p. 104.
28 'The old county class', *The Field*, 4 January 1930, p. 2; Fairfax-Blakeborough, op. cit., p. 37.
29 'Mr Lloyd George's land policy', *Fortnightly Review*, vol. 122 (1927), p. 99.
30 'Record of an agricultural estate sold in 1920', *The Nation and Athenaeum*, 5 May 1928, p. 134.
31 *Parliamentary Papers*, 1941–2, IV, Committee on Land Utilisation in Rural Areas, Report, p. 441.
32 E. H. Whetham, *The Agrarian History of England and Wales 1914–39*, Vol. VIII, Cambridge, Cambridge University Press, 1978, pp. 235–6.
33 Bell, op. cit., p. 37.
34 Westminster, op. cit., p. 124.
35 C. Cross, *Philip Snowden*, London, Barrie & Rockliff, 1966, p. 270.
36 'Farming in Kent', *Country Life*, 10 January 1931, p. xxviii.
37 'Death duties on country house property', *The Field*, 28 May 1932, p. 795.
38 'Goodwood beeches', *Country Life*, 18 January 1930, p. 70.
39 R. Fedden, *The National Trust. Past and Present*, London, Jonathan Cape, 1968, p. 43.
40 J. R. M. Butler, *Lord Lothian (Philip Kerr) 1882–1940*, London, Macmillan, 1960, p. 151.
41 Margaret, Duchess of Argyll, *Forget Not. The Autobiography of Margaret, Duchess of Argyll*, London, W. H. Allen, 1975, p. 68.
42 'A study of home farm finance', *Journal of the Land Agents' Society*, January 1931, p. 13.
43 'Empire farmers' tour', *West Sussex Gazette*, 21 June 1928, p. 1.
44 M. Waterson, *The Country House Remembered. Recollections of Life Between the Wars*, London, Routledge & Kegan Paul, 1985, p. 106.

45 J. Ramsden, *The Age of Balfour and Baldwin 1902–1940*, London, Longman, 1978, p. 360.
46 P. E. Wright, *Portraits and Criticisms*, London, Eveleigh, Nash & Grayson, 1925, pp. 36–7.
47 S. Baldwin, *On England and Other Addresses*, London, Philip Allan, 1933, pp. 5–6.
48 K. O. Morgan, *Consensus and Disunity. The Lloyd George Coalition Government 1918–1922*, Oxford, Clarendon, 1979, p. 160.
49 Bell, op. cit., p. 64.
50 D. Fielding, *Mercury Presides*, London, Eyre & Spottiswoode, 1954, p. 110.
51 'In the shires', *Vogue*, 6 February 1935, p. 57.
52 'Coming of age of the Duke of Norfolk', *West Sussex Gazette*, 6 June 1929, p. 5.
53 Historical Archives of S. Pearson & Son, Ltd, Box A/24, Memorial press notices.
54 L. McTaggart, *Kathleen Kennedy. The Untold Story of Jack Kennedy's Favourite Sister*, London, Weidenfeld & Nicolson, 1983, pp. 210–11.
55 'The Duke and Duchess of Norfolk', *West Sussex Gazette*, 25 February 1937, p. 3.
56 Macmillan, op. cit., p. 60.
57 Balfour, op. cit., p. 107.
58 Westminster, op. cit., p. 107.
59 Hall, op. cit., p. 38.
60 F. Marshall, *London West*, London and New York, The Studio, 1944, p. 30.
61 'Our lives from day to day', *Vogue*, 23 July 1930, p. 45.
62 'The north-bound exodus', *Country Life*, 14 August 1926, p. xlvii.
63 Waterson, op. cit., p. 233.
64 Fielding, op. cit., p. 112.
65 John, Duke of Bedford, *A Silver-plated Spoon*, London, Cassell, 1959, p. 64.
66 P. Purser, *Where Is He Now? The Extraordinary Worlds of Edward James*, London, Quartet, 1978, p. 70.
67 I. Nairn and N. Pevsner, *The Buildings of England. Sussex*, London, Penguin, 1977, p. 274.
68 M. Young, *The Elmhirsts of Dartington. The Creation of an Utopian Community*, London, Routledge & Kegan Paul, 1982, p. 98.
69 ibid., p. 107.
70 ibid., pp. 116, 118, 119, 121.
71 'The story of Dartington', *The Countryman*, January 1953, p. 43.
72 *A Dartington Anthology 1925–1975*, Dartington, Dartington Press, 1975, pp. 3, 54.
73 V. Glendinning, *Vita. The Life of Vita Sackville-West*, London, Weidenfeld & Nicolson, 1983, p. 224.
74 N. Nicolson, *Portrait of a Marriage*, London, Weidenfeld & Nicolson, 1973, p. 220.

75 R. Rhodes James (ed.), *Chips. The Diaries of Sir Henry Channon*, London, Weidenfeld & Nicolson, 1967, p. 68.
76 H. Acton, *Memoirs of an Aesthete*, London, Methuen, 1948, p. 206.
77 N. Nicolson (ed.), *Harold Nicolson. Diaries and Letters 1930–1939*, London, Collins, 1966, p. 60.
78 Hall, op. cit., p. 131.
79 ibid.
80 Duchess of Windsor, *The Heart Has Its Reasons*, London, Michael Joseph, 1956, p. 166.
81 Rhodes James, op. cit., p. 101.
82 J. Guinness and C. Guinness, *The House of Mitford*, London, Hutchinson, 1984, p. 418.
83 D. Cooper, *Old Men Forget*, London, Rupert Hart-Davis, 1953, p. 200.
84 K. H. Abshagen, *Kings, Lords and Gentlemen. Influence and Power of the English Upper Classes*, London, Heinemann, 1939, p. 72.
85 Fielding, op. cit., p. 187.
86 W. S. Churchill, *The Second World War*, Vol. I, *The Gathering Storm*, London, Cassell, 1949, p. 231.
87 Bell, op. cit., p. 41.

5 DARK DAYS OF WAR AND PEACE, 1939–51

1 C. Sykes, *Evelyn Waugh. A Biography*, London, Collins, 1975, p. 210.
2 D. Fielding, *Mercury Presides*, London, Eyre & Spottiswoode, 1954, p. 191.
3 ibid., p. 196.
4 'The other side of the picture', *Vogue*, July 1944, p. 23.
5 E. Waugh, *Brideshead Revisited*, London, Chapman and Hall, 1960, p. 376.
6 J. Lees-Milne, *Ancestral Voices*, London, Chatto & Windus, 1975, p. 5.
7 J. Wake, *The Brudenells of Deene*, London, Cassell, 1953, p. 473.
8 D. Cecil, *The Cecils of Hatfield House*, London, Constable, 1973, p. 285.
9 J. Colville, *The Fringes of Power. Downing Street Diaries 1939–1955*, London, Hodder & Stoughton, 1985, p. 27.
10 'Malvern at Blenheim', *Country Life*, 3 February 1940, p. 120.
11 Fielding, op. cit., p. 191.
12 M. Amory (ed.), *The Letters of Evelyn Waugh*, London, Weidenfeld & Nicolson, 1980, p. 163.
13 Lees-Milne, op. cit., p. 111.
14 O. Sitwell, *Queen Mary and Others*, London, Michael Joseph, 1974, p. 35.
15 'Doubling up', *The Sketch*, 20 September 1939, p. 526.
16 'I'm just back from the country', *Vogue*, July 1941, p. 44.
17 E. Waugh, *The Life of the Right Reverend Ronald Knox*, London, Chapman and Hall, 1959, p. 282.

18 C. Beaton, *The Years Between. Diaries 1939–1944*, London, Weidenfeld & Nicolson, 1965, p. 49.

19 D. Cooper, *Trumpets from the Steep*, London, Rupert Hart-Davis, 1960, p. 83.

20 ibid.

21 'Country change', *Vogue*, July 1941, p. 21.

22 'The way things are', *Vogue*, January 1941, p. 16.

23 'I'm just back from town', *Vogue*, July 1941, p. 45.

24 'Débutantes dancing', *Tatler*, 19 March 1941, p. 424.

25 'Death of Duke of Northumberland', *The Times*, 3 June 1940, p. 6.

26 'A friend's tribute', *The Times*, 21 May 1941, p. 7.

27 'Lord Alington', *The Times*, 25 September 1940, p. 7.

28 'Lieut.-Colonel Lord Apsley, M.P.', *The Times*, 22 September 1942, p. 6.

29 'Personal tributes', *The Times*, 10 June 1940, p. 9.

30 'Personal tribute', *The Times*, 31 March 1943, p. 7.

31 'Memorial services', *The Times*, 20 February 1945, p. 6.

32 'Major Lord Hartington', *The Times*, 20 September 1944, p. 7.

33 'By-election in West Derbyshire', *Derbyshire Advertiser*, 29 January 1944, p. 4.

34 'Innocence of the marquis', *Daily Mirror*, 14 February 1944, p. 1.

35 'West Derbyshire by-election', *Derbyshire Advertiser*, 18 February 1944, p. 4.

36 Colville, op. cit., p. 474.

37 ibid.

38 Earl of Kilmuir, *Political Adventure*, London, Weidenfeld & Nicolson, 1964, p. 138.

39 K. O. Morgan, *Labour in Power 1945–1951*, Oxford, Clarendon, 1984, p. 305.

40 This and the following paragraph J. Lees-Milne, *Caves of Ice*, London, Chatto & Windus, 1983, pp. 7, 13, 14, 64, 174.

41 R. B. McCallum and A. Readman, *The British General Election of 1945*, London, Oxford University Press, 1947, pp. 44, 51.

42 'Wentworth Woodhouse', *The Field*, 4 May 1946, p. 495.

43 'Stately is as stately does', *Time*, 29 April 1946, p. 19.

44 Lees-Milne, op. cit., p. 53.

45 'Offer to National Trust', *The Times*, 8 April 1946, p. 2.

46 Lees-Milne, op. cit., p. 63.

47 'Breach of National Trust', *The Field*, 18 October 1947, p. 427.

48 M. Waterson, *The Servants' Hall. A Domestic History of Erdigg*, London, Routledge & Kegan Paul, 1980, p. 200.

49 T. J. Raybould, *The Economic Emergence of the Black Country. A Study of the Dudley Estate*, Newton Abbot, David & Charles, 1973, pp. 127–8, 242–3.

50 D. Denman, *Land in a Free Society*, London, Centre for Policy Studies, 1980, p. 49.

51 'The control of land', *Country Life*, 22 July 1949, p. 279.

52 'A Planning Act Sale', *Country Life*, 26 August 1949, p. 635.
53 'Harewood estate cut by three-fifths', *Country Life*, 6 July 1951, p. 59.
54 W. Walker Watson, *Agricultural Death Duties. A Handbook for Landowners*, London, Country Gentlemen's Association, 1952, p. 7.
55 H. M. Treasury, *Report of the Committee on Houses of Outstanding Historic and Architectural Interest*, London, HMSO, 1950, p. 5.
56 K. A. H. Murray, 'Agriculture', in K. Hancock (ed.), *History of the Second World War. United Kingdom Civil Series*, Vol. VI, London, HMSO, 1975, p. 275.
57 A. Calder, *The People's War. Britain 1939–45*, London, Jonathan Cape, 1969, p. 422.
58 Hansard, *Parliamentary Debates*, House of Commons, 5th ser., vol. 432, 27 January 1947, col. 625.
59 P. Self and H. J. Storing, *The State and the Farmer*, London, Allen & Unwin, 1962, p. 186.
60 'Impressions of the landowners' course', *Country Landowner*, June 1949, p. 71.
61 'Cirencester centenary', *The Field*, 18 May 1946, p. 553.
62 'Impressions of the landowners' course', *Country Landowner*, June 1949, p. 72.
63 ibid.
64 'Finance and fox-hunting', *The Field*, 1 November 1947, p. 499.
65 'Hunting Bill rejected by majority of 113', *The Times*, 26 February 1949, p. 4.
66 'The future of fox-hunting?', *The Field*, 7 April 1945, p. 344.
67 'The architect and current affairs', *Architects Journal*, 4 January 1951, pp. 10–13.
68 John, Duke of Bedford, *A Silver-plated Spoon*, London, Cassell, 1959, p. 190.

6 LIFE AFTER DEATH DUTIES, 1951–63

1 E. Waugh, *Brideshead Revisited*, London, Chapman and Hall, 1960, p. 10.
2 W. Mackworth Praed, 'Good-night to the season', in H. Gardner (ed.), *The New Oxford Book of English Verse 1250–1950*, Oxford, Clarendon, 1972, p. 626.
3 M. Bence-Jones and H. Montgomery-Massingberd, *The British Aristocracy*, London, Constable, 1979, p. 223.
4 R. Rhodes James (ed.), *Winston S. Churchill. His Complete Speeches 1897–1963*, Vol. VIII, *1950–1963*, London, Chelsea House Publishers, 1974, pp. 8,336, 8,464.
5 R. Rhodes James (ed.), *Chips. The Diaries of Sir Henry Channon*, London, Weidenfeld & Nicolson, 1967, p. 470.
6 'Notes in the Abbey', *Vogue*, July 1953, p. 27.
7 R. Buckle (ed.), *Self Portrait with Friends. The Selected Diaries of Cecil Beaton 1926–1974*, London, Weidenfeld & Nicolson, 1979, p. 251.

8 'Badminton', *Agriculture*, July 1958, pp. 179–81; 'Good estate management. The Bradford estate', *Journal of the Ministry of Agriculture*, June 1954, pp. 127–9.

9 'The property market in 1962', *Estates Gazette*, 5 January 1963, p. 25.

10 'More sales by auction', *Country Life*, 8 June 1961, p. 1,359.

11 'The property market in 1963', *Estates Gazette*, 4 January 1964, p. 25.

12 J. Pearson, *Stags and Serpents. The Story of the House of Cavendish and the Dukes of Devonshire*, London, Macmillan, 1983, p. 203.

13 ibid., pp. 204, 206.

14 Duchess of Devonshire, *The House. A Portrait of Chatsworth*, London, Macmillan, 1982, p. 77.

15 N. Fisher, *Harold Macmillan*, London, Weidenfeld & Nicolson, 1982, p. 180.

16 'The Leconfield estates', *Country Life*, 26 December 1952, p. 2,115.

17 'Three times sold in eighteen months', *Country Life*, 27 February 1953, p. 593.

18 'The Leconfield estates', op. cit., p. 2,115.

19 'Leconfield sales reach £555,000', *Country Life*, 1 August 1957, p. 229.

20 'Sussex and Cumberland estate sales', *Estates Gazette*, 16 February 1957, p. 195.

21 L. Field, *Bendor. The Golden Duke of Westminster*, London, Weidenfeld & Nicolson, 1983, p. 271.

22 ibid., p. 269.

23 R. Lacey, *Aristocrats*, London, Hutchinson and BBC, 1983, p. 187.

24 ibid., pp. 188–9.

25 'Estate duties', *The Field*, 25 February 1954, p. 297.

26 'Tavistock estates sale', *Country Life*, 2 February 1956, p. 221.

27 John, Duke of Bedford, *A Silver-plated Spoon*, London, Cassell, 1959, p. 229.

28 ibid., pp. 194, 198.

29 'A view of people's getaway places', *Queen*, 17 July 1963, p. 47.

30 R. Strong (ed.), *The Destruction of the Country House 1875–1975*, London, Thames & Hudson, 1974, p. 16.

31 ibid.

32 M. Secrest, *Kenneth Clark. A Biography*, London, Weidenfeld & Nicolson, 1984, pp. 15, 49.

33 'Henham Hall demolition sale', *Estates Gazette*, 9 May 1953, p. 512.

34 'English rooms in American museums', *Country Life*, 8 June 1961, p. 1,326.

35 J. M. Robinson, *The Latest Country Houses*, London, Bodley Head, 1984, pp. 197–234.

36 ibid., pp. 127–9.

37 ibid., p. 19.

38 'The English weekend', *Queen*, Christmas issue, 1963, pp. 60–1.

39 ibid.

40 'Débutantes in their ball backgrounds', *Vogue*, July 1954, p. 54.

41 'People are talking about . . .', *Vogue*, August 1955, p. 54.
42 ibid.
43 'Season scrapbook', *Vogue*, June 1956, p. 65.
44 N. Dempster, *H.R.H. The Princess Margaret. A Life Unfulfilled*, London, Quartet, 1981, pp. 26, 38.
45 'Season scrapbook', *Vogue*, June 1956, p. 62.
46 N. Mitford (ed.), *Noblesse Oblige. An Enquiry into the Identifiable Characteristics of the English Aristocracy*, London, Hamish Hamilton, 1956, p. 42.
47 ibid., pp. 28, 29, 31, 90.
48 'U-Syntax for beginners', *The Field*, 22 November 1956, p. 933.
49 Lord Home, *The Way the Wind Blows*, London, Collins, 1976, p. 191.
50 'The squire of Downing Street', *John Bull*, 4 January 1958, p. 35.
51 C. Hollis, 'The Conservative party in history', *Political Quarterly*, vol. 32, no. 3 (1961), p. 220.
52 C. Shirley Wilson and T. Lupton, 'The social background of "Top Decision Makers"', *Manchester School of Economic and Social Studies*, vol. 27, no. 1 (1959), p. 30.
53 A. Sampson, *Anatomy of Britain*, London, Hodder & Stoughton, 1962, between pp. 34 and 35.
54 'Lord Harlech', *The Times*, 28 January 1985, p. 14.
55 'Lord Harlech', *The Times*, 2 February 1985, p. 8.
56 H. Macmillan, *At the End of the Day 1961–1963*, London, Macmillan, 1973, p. 472.
57 ibid., p. 473.
58 Margaret, Duchess of Argyll, *Forget Not. The Autobiography of Margaret, Duchess of Argyll*, London, W. H. Allen, 1975, pp. 2–3.
59 R. Ingrams (ed.), *The Life and Times of Private Eye*, London, Allen Lane, 1971, p. 13.
60 Hansard, *Parliamentary Debates*, House of Lords, 5th ser., vol. 251, 4 July 1963, col. 1025.
61 'Labour would reject move to postpone MPs' return', *The Times*, 21 October 1963, p. 6.
62 Macmillan, op. cit., p. 475.

7 'LITTLE ELSE BUT A TITLE AND A DYING EMPIRE', 1964–79

1 'Labour would reject move to postpone MPs' return', *The Times*, 21 October 1963, p. 6.
2 A. Howard and R. West, *The Making of a Prime Minister*, London, Jonathan Cape, 1965, pp. 225, 235.
3 D. E. Butler and A. King, *The British General Election of 1964*, London, Macmillan, 1965, p. 147.
4 'The new prime minister', *Observer*, 20 October 1963, p. 11.
5 ibid.
6 Lord Home, *The Way the Wind Blows*, London, Collins, 1976, p. 217.
7 B. Levin, *The Pendulum Years. Britain and the Sixties*, London, Jonathan Cape, 1970, p. 406.

8 F. Rust, *Dance in Society. An Analysis of the Relationship between the Social Dance and Society in England from the Middle Ages to the Present Day*, London, Routledge & Kegan Paul, 1969, p. 113.

9 C. Booker, *The Neophiliacs. A Study of the Revolution in English Life in the Fifties and Sixties*, London, Collins, 1969, *passim*, pp. 19–31.

10 C. Hankinson, *My Forty Years with Debrett*, London, Robert Hale, 1963, p. 137.

11 N. Dempster, *H.R.H. The Princess Margaret. A Life Unfulfilled*, London, Quartet, 1981, pp. 60, 67.

12 'The Londonderrys', *Vogue*, 15 September 1966, p. 76; 'When a stately home is where you put your feet up', *Daily Mail*, 10 February 1970, p. 20.

13 'The swinging scene hits sacred Cowes', *Daily Mail*, 28 July 1967, p. 4.

14 R. Buckle (ed.), *Self Portrait with Friends. The Selected Diaries of Cecil Beaton 1926–1974*, London, Weidenfeld & Nicolson, 1979, p. 385.

15 Laura, Duchess of Marlborough, *Laughter from a Cloud*, London, Weidenfeld & Nicolson, 1980, pp. 185–6.

16 'Hippies at the top', *Newsweek*, 27 January 1969, p. 26.

17 'Newly-wed Lord Chris on drug charge', *Daily Mail*, 8 June 1968, p. 1.

18 'Hippies at the top', *Newsweek*, 27 January 1969, p. 26.

19 'Drummer peer marries', *Daily Mail*, 20 January 1970, p. 4.

20 *Daily Mail*, 29 October 1969, p. 4.

21 'Hippies at the top', *Newsweek*, 27 January 1969, p. 26.

22 D. Burnett, *Longleat. The Story of an English Country House*, London, Collins, 1978, p. 184.

23 'Lord Bath answers the pop critics', *Time and Tide*, 13–19 August 1964, p. 11; 'Pop peer', *Daily Mail*, 22 April 1970, p. 4; 'Vietnam's titled nurse is off again', *Daily Mail*, 12 January 1970, p. 4.

24 'Hippies at the top', *Newsweek*, 27 January 1969, p. 26.

25 'Balancing life', *Daily Mail*, 27 February 1969, p. 4.

26 'Lord Weymouth's costly whim', *Daily Mail*, 27 May 1969, p. 4.

27 'Hippies at the top', *Newsweek*, 27 January 1969, pp. 26–7.

28 'Jane's hippies walk out on a dream', *Daily Mail*, 9 February 1970, p. 4.

29 'Hippies at the top', *Newsweek*, 27 January 1969, p. 26; 'Search over', *Daily Mail*, 24 July 1970, p. 4.

30 'The property market in 1972', *Estates Gazette*, 30 December 1972, p. 1,975.

31 'The Bowood Estate', *Country Landowner*, June/July 1979, p. 42.

32 D. R. Denman, 'The Land Commission in profile and perspective', *National Provincial Bank Review*, no. 78 (1967), pp. 6–7.

33 ibid., p. 8.

34 'Lords of the land', *Observer Weekend Review*, 28 March 1965, p. 21.

35 'Red Letter Day', *Country Landowner*, October 1970, p. 21.

36 'The property market in 1972', op. cit., p. 1,975.

37 'The year of the great land rush', *Country Life*, 28 December 1972, p. 1,800.

38 'The Earl opens up glorious Goodwood', *Daily Mail*, 20 January 1970, p. 11.
39 'So what's happened to the Season?', *Sunday Times Magazine*, 17 October 1971, pp. 16–17.
40 D. Childs, *Britain since 1945. A Political History*, London, Benn, 1979, p. 237.
41 Hansard, *Parliamentary Debates*, House of Commons, 5th ser., vol. 871, 26 March 1974, col. 313.
42 ibid.
43 'Annual Report', *Country Landowner*, October/November 1977, p. 39.
44 'Annual Report', *Country Landowner*, October/November 1976, p. 39.
45 'The Duke's last stand', *Sunday Times Magazine*, 17 August 1975, pp. 14–15.
46 ibid.
47 J. Cornforth, *Country Houses in Britain: Can They Survive?*, London, Country Life, 1974, p. 80.
48 J. Butler, *The Economics of Historic Country Houses*, London, Policy Studies Institute, 1981, p. 88.
49 'Finding buyers for large houses', *Country Life*, 21 August 1975, p. 1,572.
50 Butler, op. cit., p. 89.
51 D. Barker, *One Man's Estate. The Preservation of an English Inheritance*, London, Deutsch, 1983, pp. 19–20.
52 Butler, op. cit., pp. 35, 37.
53 'Domus Britannicus. What future the country house?', *Architects' Journal*, 24 January 1979, p. 175.
54 ibid., p. 185.
55 'Mail Diary on Mustique', *Daily Mail*, 12 April 1976, p. 17.
56 ' "I may quit" shock from motor racing's Lord Hesketh', *Daily Mail*, 12 March 1975, p. 13.
57 'On view in the harbour, and yours, for only £200,000. . . . Pearson's super-yacht', *Daily Mail*, 9 May 1975, p. 15.
58 'The master of Warwick and the "misery" of his exile', *Daily Mail*, 27 April 1975, p. 15.
59 'New tax exile Lord Wimborne plans to spend April in Paris', *Daily Mail*, 29 September 1975, p. 15.
60 'Gentlemen v Players', *Harpers and Queen*, mid-April 1971, p. 76.
61 R. Perrott, *The Aristocrats. A Portrait of Britain's Nobility and Their Way of Life Today*, London, Weidenfeld & Nicolson, 1968, p. 182.
62 'The old rich: a survey of the landed classes', *Spectator*, 1 January 1977, p. 16.
63 'Wheeling the oils of Arabia', *Country Life*, 13 February 1975, p. 403.
64 ibid.
65 *Report of the Committee of Inquiry into the Acquisition and Occupancy of Agricultural Land*, 1979, Cmnd. 7599, pp. 60, 63.
66 'The landed view of land', *The Economist*, 14 July 1979, p. 71.
67 'The class of '65', *Queen*, 28 July 1965, p. 57.

8 EMBARRASSMENT OF RICHES

1 Calculated from House of Commons, *Register of Members' Interests on 5th June 1980*, London, HMSO, 1980.
2 R. Norton-Taylor, *Whose Land is it Anyway? Agriculture, Planning and Land Use in the British Countryside*, Wellingborough, Turnstone Press, 1982, p. 20.
3 *Register of Members' Interests*, p. 45.
4 J. Bruce-Gardyne, *Mrs Thatcher's First Administration*, London, Macmillan, 1984, p. 20.
5 'Two cheers down on the farm', *Sunday Times*, 25 March 1973, p. 12.
6 ibid.
7 R. Body, *Farming in the Clouds*, London, Temple Smith, 1984, p. 17.
8 'Where are we going?', *Country Landowner*, July 1986, p. 5.
9 M. Shoard, *The Theft of the Countryside*, London, Temple Smith, 1980, p. 24.
10 ibid., pp. 34, 49.
11 ibid., p. 51.
12 ibid., pp. 51–2.
13 R. Grove, *The Future for Forestry. The Urgent Need for a New Policy*, British Association of Nature Conservationists, 1983, p. 16. For a resumé of forestry and tax manipulation see pp. 16–17.
14 'As ye sow not, yet shall ye reap', *The Times*, 21 March 1984, p. 14.
15 ibid.
16 'Save this house', *Sunday Times Magazine*, 28 June 1981, p. 51.
17 M. Binney and K. Martin, *The Country House: To Be or Not to Be*, London, SAVE Britain's Heritage, 1982, p. 58.
18 Hansard, *Parliamentary Debates*, House of Lords, 5th ser., vol. 405, 12 February 1980, col. 60.
19 N. St John-Stevas, *The Two Cities*, London, Faber & Faber, 1984, p. 89.
20 ibid.
21 Hansard, *Parliamentary Debates*, House of Lords, 5th ser., vol. 405, 12 February 1980, col. 79.
22 B. Pimlott, *Hugh Dalton*, London, Jonathan Cape, 1985, pp. 455–6.
23 'Spending the heritage fund', *Connoisseur*, May 1981, p. 64.
24 ibid.
25 'The question-mark over Kedleston', *The Field*, 13 October 1984, p. 60.
26 'Chippendale collection of Nostell priory saved by heritage fund', *The Times*, 6 August 1986, p. 3.
27 ibid.
28 D. Lees and J. Coyne, 'Can we afford our national heritage?', *Lloyds Bank Review*, no. 131 (1979), p. 36.
29 'The high cost of keeping our heritage', *The Times*, 7 October 1980, p. 12.
30 St John-Stevas, op. cit., p. 92.

31 ibid.
32 'Gallery director', *Washington Post*, 7 November 1985, C2.
33 ibid.
34 'From the Director General. . .', *Historic House*, Winter 1985, p. 7.
35 'On loan from the landed', *Spectator*, 16 November 1985, p. 38.
36 ibid., pp. 38–9.
37 The Times, *Royal Wedding. In commemoration of the marriage of His Royal Highness the Prince of Wales to The Lady Diana Spencer*, 28 July 1981, p. 28.
38 T. Aronson, *Royal Family. Years of Transition*, London, Murray, 1983, p. 232.
39 ibid.
40 *The Times*, 30 July 1981, p. 1.
41 'Statement by princess', *The Times*, 1 November 1955, p. 8.
42 'Lady Di', *Sunday Times Magazine*, 5 July 1981, p. 27.
43 'Lady Di', *Sunday Times Magazine*, 12 July 1981, p. 40.
44 A. Stassinopoulos, *Maria. Beyond the Callas Legend*, London, Weidenfeld & Nicolson, 1980, p. 205.
45 'Drug slave marquis is freed', *Daily Mail*, 7 November 1986, p. 5.
46 Laura, Duchess of Marlborough, *Laughter from a Cloud*, London, Weidenfeld & Nicolson, 1980, p. 212.
47 ibid., pp. 213, 223, 231.
48 'A hurly-burly over Burghley', *Daily Mail*, 3 December 1982, p. 19.
49 'Hurly-Burghley', *Tatler*, June 1983, p. 103.
50 'Status', *Tatler*, December 1980, p. 70.
51 'Gallery director', op. cit., C2.
52 'Lionising at Longleat', *Tatler*, March 1981, p. 58.
53 ibid.
54 'Saturday night Belvoir', *Tatler*, September 1980, p. 46.
55 ibid.
56 A. Lees-Milne, *The Englishwoman's House*, London, Collins, 1984, p. 41.
57 ibid., pp. 42, 43.
58 ibid., pp. 45–6.
59 'A life in the day of Viscount Weymouth', *Sunday Times Magazine*, 6 April 1980, p. 110.
60 'Master', *Tatler*, June 1981, p. 57.
61 'Honour, manor and lordship', *Country Life*, 3 July 1980, p. 7.
62 'The rich in Britain', *New Society*, 22 August 1986, p. iv.
63 'Richest family in huge tax dodge', *Sunday Times*, 5 October 1980, p. 1.
64 ibid., pp. 13–14.
65 'Vestey: birth of an empire', *Sunday Times*, 12 October 1980, p. 54.
66 'Master', *Tatler*, June 1981, p. 57.
67 'Trust houses and family homes', *The Field*, 2 April 1980, p. 689.
68 ibid., p. 688.
69 'The fallacy of "open house" ', *The Field*, 17 February 1982, p. 253.

70 ibid.
71 *Minutes of the Thirteenth Annual General Meeting of the Historic Houses Association*, p. 3; *Historic House*, Winter 1986.
72 'New purpose for old farm buildings', *Country Landowner*, June 1986, p. 42.
73 'How Chatsworth tackles its Micawber problem', *The Field*, 6 October 1984, p. 50.
74 'The spirit of Elwes at Elsham Hall', *The Field*, 17 August 1985, p. 50.
75 'On location at Rainthorpe Hall', *The Field*, 20 October 1984, p. 52; 'The "Brideshead" castle', *Washington Post*, 30 October 1985, B2.
76 'The "Brideshead" castle', op. cit.
77 'Lord Howard of Henderskelfe', *The Times*, 28 November 1984, p. 14.
78 'Things go better with Eddie Coke', *Tatler*, December 1980, p. 65.
79 J. Wentworth Day, *Farming Adventure. A Thousand Miles through England on a Horse*, London, Harrap, 1943, p. 223.
80 'Farm woodlands to provide game income', *Country Landowner*, May 1986, p. 24.
81 'Secret of the duke's grouse moor', *The Field*, 18 January 1986, pp. 26–7.
82 'Young men of the Belvoir', *The Field*, 2 November 1985, p. 36.
83 'The death of the country house has been greatly exaggerated', *Daily Telegraph*, 24 May 1986, p. 14.
84 ibid.
85 'Surveying the future at Castletown', *The Field*, 12 January 1985, pp. 40–2; 'Mirehouse and the poets' view', *The Field*, 9 March 1985, pp. 46–8; 'Preston, medieval tower with a modern purpose', *The Field*, 18 May 1985, pp. 60–2; 'Unbroken links of Lancelyn', *The Field*, 21 September 1985, pp. 52–4; 'The Sheepshanks of Arthington', *The Field*, 11 January 1986, pp. 38–41; 'Statfold and the Wolferstan lines', *The Field*, 4 October 1986, pp. 44–5; 'The rejuvenation of Thorpe Hall', *The Field*, 2 August 1986, pp. 112–15.
86 'Gloucestershire manor and the Fust dynasty', *The Field*, 19 April 1986, pp. 50–3; 'The Bagge dynasty at Stradsett', *The Field*, 17 May 1986, pp. 60–3; 'Blake Hall and the Capel Cures', *The Field*, 24 May 1986, pp. 80–2.
87 'Orleton Hall below the Wrekin', *The Field*, 30 August 1986, p. 44.
88 'Sledmere House', *Interiors*, January 1982, p. 116.
89 ibid.
90 'Charles reveals his Mass appeal', *Daily Mail*, 23 September 1986, p. 17.

Bibliography

WORKS OF REFERENCE

J. Bateman, *The Great Landowners of Great Britain and Ireland*, Leicester and
    New York, Leicester University Press and Humanities Press, 1971.
Burke's Landed Gentry, London, Burke's Peerage.
Burke's Peerage, Baronetage and Knightage, London, Burke's Peerage.
D. Butler and G. Butler, *British Political Facts 1900–1985*, London,
    Macmillan, 1986.
G. E. Cokayne, *The Complete Peerage*, London, St Catherine Press.
Debrett's Peerage and Baronetage, London, Macmillan.
Dictionary of National Biography, Oxford, Oxford University Press.
Dod's Parliamentary Companion, Hurst Green, East Sussex, Dod's
    Parliamentary Companion.
Hansard, *Parliamentary Debates*.
I. Nairn and N. Pevsner, *The Buildings of England. Sussex*, London,
    Penguin, 1977.
Whitaker's Almanack, London, Whitaker.
Who's Who, London, A. & C. Black.
Who was Who, London, A. & C. Black.

PRIMARY SOURCES

Science Museum, London, Historical Archives of S. Pearson & Son Ltd.
West Sussex Record Office, Sales Particulars.

PARLIAMENTARY PAPERS

1895, XVI, Royal Commission on Agriculture.
1919, IX, Report by Investigators on Wages and Conditions of
    Employment in Agriculture.

189

1919, XI, Coal Industry Commission.

1941–2, IV, Report of the Committee on Land Utilisation in Rural Areas.

1979, Report of the Committee of Inquiry into the Acquisition and Occupancy of Agricultural Land, Cmnd. 7599.

H.M. Treasury, *Report of the Committee on Houses of Outstanding Historic and Architectural Interest*, London, HMSO, 1950.

House of Commons, *Register of Members' Interests on 5th June 1980*, London, HMSO, 1980.

BOOKS AND ARTICLES

Abshagen, K. H., *Kings, Lords and Gentlemen. Influence and Power of the English Upper Classes*, London, Heinemann, 1939.

Acton, H., *Memoirs of an Aesthete*, London, Methuen, 1948.

Amherst, J., *Wandering Abroad*, London, Secker & Warburg, 1976.

Amory, M., *The Letters of Evelyn Waugh*, London, Weidenfeld & Nicolson, 1980.

Argyll, Margaret, Duchess of, *Forget Not. The Autobiography of Margaret, Duchess of Argyll*, London, W. H. Allen, 1975.

Aronson, T., *Royal Family. Years of Transition*, London, Murray, 1983.

Baldwin, S., *On England and Other Addresses*, London, Philip Allan, 1933.

Balfour, P., *Society Racket. A Critical Survey of Modern Social Life*, London, John Long, 1933.

Barker, D., *One Man's Estate. The Preservation of an English Inheritance*, London, Deutsch, 1983.

Barrington, Charlotte, Viscountess, *Through Eighty Years (1855–1935)*, London, Murray, 1936.

Beard, M., 'The impact of the First World War on agricultural society in West Sussex', unpublished MLitt thesis, University of Cambridge, 1984.

Beaton, C., *The Years Between. Diaries 1939–1944*, London, Weidenfeld & Nicolson, 1965.

Beaufort, Duke of, *Fox-hunting*, Newton Abbot, David & Charles, 1980.

Bedford, Hastings, Duke of, *The Years of Transition*, London, Andrew Dukers, 1949.

Bedford, John, Duke of, *A Silver-plated Spoon*, London, Cassell, 1959.

Bell, A., *The Cherry Tree*, London, Bodley Head, 1932.

Belloc, H., *The County of Sussex*, London, Cassell, 1936.

Bence-Jones, M. and Montgomery-Massingberd, H., *The British Aristocracy*, London, Constable, 1979.

Binney, M. and Martin, K., *The Country House: To Be or Not To Be*, London, SAVE Britain's Heritage, 1982.

Birkenhead, Earl of, *Halifax. The Life of Lord Halifax*, London, Hamish Hamilton, 1965.

Blakiston, G., *Woburn and the Russells*, London, Constable, 1980.

Blewett, N., *The Peers, the Parties and the People*, London, Macmillan, 1972.

Body, R., *Farming in the Clouds*, London, Temple Smith, 1984.

Booker, C., *The Neophiliacs. A Study of the Revolution in English Life in the Fifties and Sixties*, London, Collins, 1969.

Borer, M. C., *Mayfair. The Years of Grandeur*, London, W. H. Allen, 1975.

Brandon, P., 'The diffusion of designed landscapes in south-east England', in H. S. A. Fox and R. A. Butlin (eds), *Change in the Countryside. Essays on Rural England, 1500–1900*, London, Institute of British Geographers, 1979.

Brodrick, A. H., *Near to Greatness; a Life of the Sixth Earl Winterton*, London, Hutchinson, 1965.

Bruce-Gardyne, J., *Mrs Thatcher's First Administration*, London, Macmillan, 1984.

Buckle, R. (ed.), *Self Portrait with Friends. The Selected Diaries of Cecil Beaton 1926–1974*, London, Weidenfeld & Nicolson, 1979.

Burnett, D., *Longleat. The Story of an English Country House*, London, Collins, 1978.

Butler, D. E. and King, A., *The British General Election of 1964*, London, Macmillan, 1965.

Butler, J., *The Economics of Country Houses*, London, Policy Studies Institute, 1981.

Butler, J. R. M., *Lord Lothian (Philip Kerr) 1882–1940*, London, Macmillan, 1960.

Cadogan, Hon. E., *Before the Deluge. Memories and Reflections 1880–1914*, London, Murray, 1961.

Calder, A., *The People's War. Britain 1939–45*, London, Jonathan Cape, 1969.

Cannadine, D., *Lords and Landlords: The Aristocracy and the Towns, 1774–1967*. Leicester, Leicester University Press, 1980.

Cecil, D., *The Cecils of Hatfield House*, London, Constable, 1973.

Chancellor, E. B., *The Private Palaces of London*, London, Kegan Paul, Trench, Trübner, 1908.

Childs, D., *Britain since 1945. A Political History*, London, Benn, 1979.

Christie, O. F., *The Transition to Democracy 1867–1914*, London, Routledge, 1934.

Churchill, Viscount, *All My Sins Remembered*, London, Heinemann, 1964.

Churchill, W. S., *Liberalism and the Social Problem*, London, Hodder & Stoughton, 1909.

Churchill, W. S., *My Early Life*, London, Thornton Butterworth, 1930.

Churchill, W. S., *The Second World War*, Vol. I, *The Gathering Storm*, London, Cassell, 1949.

Clemenson, H., 'Diminishing Derbyshire estates', *Geographical Magazine*, vol. 53, no. 2 (1980).

Clemenson, H., *English Country Houses and Landed Estates*, London and New York, Croom Helm and St Martin's Press, 1982.

Cloete, S., *A Victorian Son. An Autobiography 1897–1922*, London, Collins, 1972.

Colby, R., *Mayfair. A Town Within London*, London, Country Life, 1966.

Colville, J., *The Fringes of Power. Downing Street Diaries 1939–1955*, London, Hodder & Stoughton, 1985.

Cooper, D., *Old Men Forget*, London, Rupert Hart-Davis, 1960.

Cooper, D., *The Rainbow Comes and Goes*, London, Rupert Hart-Davis, 1958.

Cooper, D., *Trumpets from the Steep*, London, Rupert Hart-Davis, 1953.

Cornford, J. P., 'The parliamentary foundations of the Hotel Cecil', in R. Robson (ed.), *Ideas and Institutions of Victorian Britain*, London, Bell, 1967.

Cornforth, J., *Country Houses in Britain: Can They Survive?*, London, Country Life, 1974.

Cowper Powys, J., *Autobiography*, London, Bodley Head, 1934.

Cranworth, Lord, *Kenya Chronicles*, London, Macmillan, 1939.

Cross, C., *Philip Snowden*, London, Barrie & Rockliff, 1966.

Dangerfield, G., *The Strange Death of Liberal England*, London, MacGibbon & Kee, 1966.

A Dartington Anthology 1925–1975, Dartington, Dartington Press, 1975.

Davie, M. (ed.), *The Diaries of Evelyn Waugh*, London, Weidenfeld & Nicolson, 1976.

Dempster, N., *H.R.H. The Princess Margaret. A Life Unfulfilled*, London, Quartet, 1981.

Denman, D. R., 'The Land Commission in profile and perspective', *National Provincial Bank Review*, no. 78 (1967).

Denman, D. R., *Land in a Free Society*, London, Centre for Policy Studies, 1980.

Devonshire, Duchess of, *The House. A Portrait of Chatsworth*, London, Macmillan, 1982.

Donaldson, F., *Child of the Twenties*, London, Rupert Hart-Davis, 1959.

Eden, A., *Another World 1897–1917*, London, Allen Lane, 1976.

Fairfax-Blakeborough, J., *Country Life and Sport*, London, Philip Allan, 1926.

Falk, B., *The Bridgewater Millions. A Candid Family History*, London, Hutchinson, 1942.

Farrelly, R. J., 'The large landowners of England and Wales 1870–1939: an elite in transition', unpublished PhD thesis, University of Toronto, 1980.

Fedden, R., *The National Trust. Past and Present*, London, Jonathan Cape, 1968.

Field, L., *Bendor. The Golden Duke of Westminster*, London, Weidenfeld & Nicolson, 1983.

Fielding, D., *Mercury Presides*, London, Eyre & Spottiswoode, 1954.

Fisher, N., *Harold Macmillan*, London, Weidenfeld & Nicolson, 1982.

Fleming, L. and Gore, A., *The English Garden*, London, Michael Joseph, 1979.

Ford, F. M., *Parade's End*, London, Penguin, 1982.

Fussell, P., *The Great War and Modern Memory*, London and New York, Oxford University Press, 1975.

Gardiner, A. G., *The Life of Sir William Harcourt*, Vol. II, *1886–1904*, London, Constable, 1923.

Gibbs, P., *England Speaks*, London, Heinemann, 1935.

Gilbert, B. B., 'David Lloyd George: land, the budget and social reform', *American Historical Review*, vol. 81, no. 5 (1976).

Girouard, M., *The Victorian Country House*, London and New Haven, Yale University Press, 1979.

Glendinning, V., *Vita. The Life of Vita Sackville-West*, London, Weidenfeld & Nicolson, 1983.

Gore, J. (ed.), *Mary Maxse (1870–1944). A Record Compiled by her Family and Friends*, London, Rolls House Publishing Company, 1939.

Graves, R., *Goodbye To All That. An Autobiography*, London, Jonathan Cape, 1929.

Grove, R., *The Future for Forestry. The Urgent Need for a New Policy*, British Association of Nature Conservationists, 1983.

Guinness, J. and Guinness, C., *The House of Mitford*, London, Hutchinson, 1984.

Hall, C. (ed.), *The Twenties in Vogue*, London, Octopus, 1983.

Hamilton, Lord E., *Forty Years On*, London, Hodder & Stoughton, 1922.

Hamilton, Lord E., *The Halcyon Era. A Rambling Reverie of Now and Then*, London, Murray, 1933.

Hamilton, Lord F., *The Days Before Yesterday*, London, Hodder & Stoughton, 1920.

Hankinson, C., *My Forty Years With Debrett*, London, Robert Hale, 1963.

Harris, A., 'Agricultural change on a Yorkshire estate: Birdsall 1920–1940', *Journal of Regional and Local Studies*, vol. 3, no. 1 (1983).

Havinden, M. A., *Estate Villages*, London, Lund Humphries, 1966.

Heape, R. G., *Buxton under the Dukes of Devonshire*, London, Robert Hale, 1948.

Hollis, C., 'The Conservative party in history', *Political Quarterly*, vol. 32, no. 3 (1961).

Home, Lord, *The Way the Wind Blows*, London, Collins, 1976.

Horn, P., *Rural Life in England in the First World War*, Dublin and New York, Gill & Macmillan and St Martin's Press, 1984.

Howard, A. and West, R., *The Making of a Prime Minister*, London, Jonathan Cape, 1965.

Hunn, D., *Goodwood*, London, Davis Poynter, 1975.

Huxley, E., *White Man's Country. Lord Delamere and the Making of Kenya*, Vol. I, *1870–1914*, London, Chatto & Windus, 1953.

Ingrams, R. (ed.), *The Life and Times of Private Eye*, London, Allen Lane, 1971.

Jackson, S., *The Sassoons*, London, Heinemann, 1968.

Kaye-Smith, S., *Little England*, London, Cassell, 1918.

Kennedy, D. K., 'A tale of two colonies: the social origins and cultural consequences of white settlement in Kenya and Rhodesia, 1890–1939', unpublished PhD thesis, University of California, Berkeley, 1981.

Kilmuir, Earl of, *Political Adventure*, London, Weidenfeld & Nicolson, 1964.

Lacey, R., *Aristocrats*, London, Hutchinson and BBC, 1983.

Lambton, Hon. G., *Men and Horses I Have Known*, London, Thornton Butterworth, 1924.

193

Lees, D. and Coyne, J., 'Can we afford our national heritage?', *Lloyds Bank Review*, no. 131 (1979).

Lees-Milne, A., *The Englishwoman's House*, London, Collins, 1984.

Lees-Milne, J., *Ancestral Voices*, London, Chatto & Windus, 1975.

Lees-Milne, J., *Caves of Ice*, London, Chatto & Windus, 1983.

Lejeune, A., *The Gentlemen's Clubs*, London, Macdonald & Jane's, 1979.

Levin, B., *The Pendulum Years. Britain and the Sixties*, London, Jonathan Cape, 1970.

Londonderry, Marchioness of, *Henry Chaplin. A Memoir*, London, Macmillan, 1926.

Lyttleton, O., *The Memoirs of Lord Chandos*, London, Bodley Head, 1962.

McCallum, R. B. and Readman, A., *The British General Election of 1945*, London, Oxford University Press, 1947.

Mackworth Praed, W., 'Good-night to the season', in H. Gardner (ed.), *The New Oxford Book of English Verse 1250–1950*, Oxford, Clarendon, 1972.

Macmillan, H., *Winds of Change 1914–1939*, London, Macmillan, 1966.

Macmillan, H., *At the End of the Day 1961–1963*, London, Macmillan, 1973.

McTaggart, L., *Kathleen Kennedy. The Untold Story of Jack Kennedy's Favourite Sister*, London, Weidenfeld & Nicolson, 1983.

Magnus, P., *King Edward the Seventh*, London, Murray, 1964.

Marlborough, Laura, Duchess of, *Laughter from a Cloud*, London, Weidenfeld & Nicolson, 1980.

Marshall, F., *London West*, London and New York, The Studio, 1944.

Marwick, A., *Women at War 1914–1918*, London, Croom Helm, 1977.

Masters, B., *The Dukes. The Origins, Ennoblement and History of Twenty-Six Families*, London, Blond & Briggs, 1975.

Mersey, Viscount, *A Picture of Life 1872–1940*, London, Murray, 1941.

Middlemas, K., *The Master Builders*, London, Hutchinson, 1963.

Mitford, N. (ed.), *Noblesse Oblige. An Enquiry into the Identifiable Characteristics of the English Aristocracy*, London, Hamish Hamilton, 1956.

Moore, H. T. (ed.), *The Collected Letters of D. H. Lawrence*, Vol. I, London, Heinemann, 1962.

Morgan, K. O., *Consensus and Disunity. The Lloyd George Coalition Government 1918–1922*, Oxford, Clarendon, 1979.

Morgan, K. O., *Labour in Power 1945–1951*, Oxford, Clarendon, 1984.

Morris, J. *Pax Britannica. The Climax of an Empire*, London, Faber & Faber, 1968.

Morris, J. and Winchester, S., *Stones of Empire. The Buildings of the Raj*, Oxford, Oxford University Press, 1983.

Mosley, N., *Julian Grenfell. His Life and the Times of his Death 1888–1915*, London, Weidenfeld & Nicolson, 1976.

Mosley, Sir Oswald, *My Life*, London, Nelson, 1968.

Mowat, C. L., *Britain Between the Wars 1918–1940*, London, Methuen, 1955.

Murray, K. A. H., 'Agriculture', in K. Hancock (ed.), *History of the Second World War. United Kingdom Civil Series*, Vol. VI, London, HMSO, 1975.

Nicolson, N., (ed.), *Harold Nicolson. Diaries and Letters 1930–1939*, London, Collins, 1966.

Nicolson, N., *Portrait of a Marriage*, London, Weidenfeld & Nicolson, 1973.

Norton-Taylor, R., *Whose Land is it Anyway? Agriculture, Planning and Land Use in the British Countryside*, Wellingborough, Turnstone Press, 1982.

Olivier, E., *Without Knowing Mr Walkley. Personal Memories*, London, Faber & Faber, 1938.

Pearson, J., *Stags and Serpents. The Story of the House of Cavendish and the Dukes of Devonshire*, London, Macmillan, 1983.

Perren, R., 'The landlord and agricultural transformation', in P. J. Perry (ed.), *British Agriculture, 1875–1914*, London, Methuen, 1973.

Perrott, R., *The Aristocrats. A Portrait of Britain's Nobility and their Way of Life Today*, London, Weidenfeld & Nicolson, 1968.

Pimlott, B., *Hugh Dalton*, London, Jonathan Cape, 1985.

Prince, H., 'Parkland in the English landscape', *Amateur Historian*, vol. 3, no. 8 (1958).

Purser, P., *Where Is He Now? The Extraordinary Worlds of Edward James*, London, Quartet, 1978.

Ramsden, J., *The Age of Balfour and Baldwin 1902–1940*, London, Longman, 1978.

Raybould, T. J., *The Economic Emergence of the Black Country. A Study of the Dudley Estate*, Newton Abbot, David & Charles, 1973.

Rhodes James, R. (ed.), *Chips. The Diaries of Sir Henry Channon*, London, Weidenfeld & Nicolson, 1967.

Rhodes James, R. (ed.), *Winston S. Churchill. His Complete Speeches 1897–1963*, Vol. VIII, *1950–1963*, London, Chelsea House Publishers, 1974.

Ribblesdale, Lord, *Charles Lister. Letters and Recollections with a Memoir by His Father, Lord Ribblesdale*, London, T. Fisher Unwin, 1917.

Robinson, J. M., *The Latest Country Houses*, London, Bodley Head, 1984.

Rose, K., *Superior Person. A Portrait of Curzon and His Circle in Late Victorian England*, London, Weidenfeld & Nicolson, 1969.

Rubinstein, W. D., 'New men of wealth and the purchase of land in nineteenth-century Britain', *Past and Present*, no. 92 (1981).

Rubinstein, W. D., *Men of Property. The Very Wealthy in Britain since the Industrial Revolution*, London, Croom Helm, 1981.

Rust, F., *Dance in Society. An Analysis of the Relationship between the Social Dance and Society from the Middle Ages to the Present Day*, London, Routledge & Kegan Paul, 1969.

Sackville-West, V., *English Country Houses*, London, Collins, 1941.

Sampson, A., *The Anatomy of Britain*, London, Hodder & Stoughton, 1962.

Sassoon, S., *Memoirs of a Fox-hunting Man*, London, Faber & Gwyer, 1928.

Secrest, M., *Kenneth Clark. A Biography*, London, Weidenfeld & Nicolson, 1984.

Self, P. and Storing, H. J., *The State and the Farmer*, London, Allen & Unwin, 1962.

Sheppard, F. H. W. (ed.), *Survey of London. The Parish of St Paul Covent Garden*, London, Athlone, 1970.

Sheppard, F. H. W. (ed.), *Survey of London. The Grosvenor Estate in Mayfair Part I*, London, Athlone, 1977.

Shirley Wilson, C. and Lupton, T., 'The social background of "Top Decision Makers"', *Manchester School of Economic and Social Studies*, vol. 27, no. 1 (1959).

Shoard, M., *The Theft of the Countryside*, London, Temple Smith, 1980.

Simon, N. (ed.), *The Edward James Foundation*, London and Bradford, Lund Humphries, 1981.

Simpson, K., 'The officers', in I. F. W. Beckett and K. Simpson (eds), *A Nation in Arms. A Social Study of the British Army in the First World War*, Manchester, Manchester University Press, 1985.

Sitwell, O., *The Scarlet Tree*, London, Macmillan, 1946.

Sitwell, O., *Great Morning*, London, Macmillan, 1948.

Sitwell, O., *Queen Mary and Others*, London, Michael Joseph, 1974.

Spender, J. A., *Weetman Pearson, First Lord Cowdray, 1856–1927*, London, Cassell, 1930.

Stassinopoulos, A., *Maria. Beyond the Callas Legend*, London, Weidenfeld & Nicolson, 1980.

St John-Stevas, N., *The Two Cities*, London, Faber & Faber, 1984.

Stone, L. and Fawtier Stone, J. C., *An Open Elite? England 1540–1880*, Oxford, Clarendon, 1984.

Strong, R. (ed.), *The Destruction of the Country House 1875–1975*, London, Thames & Hudson, 1974.

Sturmey, S. G., 'Owner-farming in England and Wales 1900 to 1950', *Manchester School of Economic and Social Studies*, vol. 23, no. 3 (1955).

Sutherland, D., *The Yellow Earl. The Life of Hugh Lowther, 5th Earl of Lonsdale, K.G., G.C.V.O., 1857–1944*, London, Cassell, 1965.

Sutherland, Duke of, *Looking Back*, London, Odhams, 1957.

Sykes, C., *Evelyn Waugh. A Biography*, London, Collins, 1975.

Sykes, C. S., *Private Palaces. Life in the Great London Houses*, London, Chatto & Windus, 1985.

Tennyson, Lionel, Lord, *From Verse to Worse*, London, Cassell, 1933.

Terraine, J., *Impacts of War 1914 & 1918*, London, Hutchinson, 1970.

Thompson, F. M. L., *English Landed Society in the Nineteenth Century*, London, Routledge & Kegan Paul, 1963.

Thompson, F. M. L., 'Free trade and the land', in G. D. Mingay (ed.), *The Victorian Countryside*, Vol. I, London, Routledge & Kegan Paul, 1981.

Trzebinski, E., *Silence Will Speak. A Study of the Life of Denys Finch Hatton and his Relationship with Karen Blixen*, London, Heinemann, 1977.

Tuchman, B., *The Proud Tower. A Portrait of the World Before the War, 1890 to 1914*, London, Hamish Hamilton, 1966.

Vanderbilt Balsan, C., *The Glitter and the Gold*, London, Heinemann, 1953.

Wake, J., *The Brudenells of Deene*, London, Cassell, 1953.

Walker Watson, W., *Agricultural Death Duties. A Handbook for Landowners*, London, Country Gentlemen's Association, 1952.

Warwick, Frances, Countess of, *Afterthoughts*, London, Cassell, 1931.

Warwick and Brooke, Earl of, *Memories of Sixty Years*, London, Cassell, 1917.

Waterson, M., *The Servants' Hall. A Domestic History of Erdigg*, London, Routledge & Kegan Paul, 1980.

Waterson, M., *The Country House Remembered. Recollections of Life Between the Wars*, London, Routledge & Kegan Paul, 1985.

Waugh, E., *The Life of the Right Reverend Ronald Knox*, London, Chapman and Hall, 1959.

Waugh, E., *Brideshead Revisited*, London, Chapman and Hall, 1960.

Weber, E., *Peasants into Frenchmen. The Modernisation of Rural France 1870–1914*, Stanford, Stanford University Press, 1976.

Wentworth Day, J., *Farming Adventure. A Thousand Miles through England on a Horse*, London, Harrap, 1943.

Westminster, Loelia, Duchess of, *Grace and Favour*, London, Weidenfeld & Nicolson, 1961.

Whetham, E. H., 'The mechanisation of British farming 1910–1945', *Journal of Agricultural Economics*, vol. 21, no. 3 (1970).

Whetham, E. H., *The Agrarian History of England and Wales 1914–39*, Vol. VIII, Cambridge, Cambridge University Press, 1978.

Willoughby de Broke, Lord, *The Passing Years*, London, Constable, 1924.

Windsor, Duchess of, *The Heart Has Its Reasons*, London, Michael Joseph, 1956.

Winter, J. M., 'Some aspects of the demographic consequences of the First World War in Britain', *Population Studies*, vol. 30, no. 3 (1976).

Winter, J. M., 'Britain's "Lost Generation" of the First World War', *Population Studies*, vol. 31, no. 3 (1977).

Winterton, Earl, *Pre-War*, London, Macmillan, 1932.

Wright, P. E., *Portraits and Criticisms*, London, Eveleigh, Nash & Grayson, 1925.

Young, D., *Member for Mexico*, London, Cassell, 1965.

Young, M., *The Elmhirsts of Dartington. The Creation of an Utopian Community*, London, Routledge & Kegan Paul, 1982.

Ziegler, P., *Diana Cooper*, London, Hamish Hamilton, 1981.

INDEX